The Islington Crime Survey

The Islington Crime Survey

Crime, victimization and policing in
inner-city London

Trevor Jones, Brian MacLean
and Jock Young

Gower

Published by
Gower Publishing Company Limited,
Gower House, Croft Road,
Aldershot, Hants GU11 3HR,
England

and

Gower Publishing Company,
Old Post Road, Brookfield,
Vermont 05036,
U.S.A.

ISBN 0 566 05264 4

Young, Jock
    The Islington crime survey: crime, victimization and policing in inner-city London.
    1. Crime and criminals – England – London
    2. Islington (London, England)
    I. Title II. Jones, Trevor III. MacLean, Brian IV. Islington. Council
    364'.942143   HV6950.L7

Printed and bound in Great Britain by
Biddles Ltd, Guildford and King's Lynn

List of Contents

Acknowledgements

This project would not have been completed without the constructive support of colleagues at the Centre for Criminology. In particular, John Lea and Alan Phipps, who were involved in the planning and design of the project throughout. We would also like to thank the University of Saskatchewan for extending Brian MacLean's research leave and, in so doing, helping us to complete the project. The following colleagues all made valuable contributions to the project: Victoria Greenwood and Roger Matthews from the Centre for Criminology, Dave Cowell (Polytechnic of Central London), Paul Rock and David Downes from the LSE, Doug Wood (SCPR), Mike Maguire (ORU), Walter Easey (ALA Policing Adviser), Dr Paul Corrigan, Chris Smith MP and Richard Kinsey (Edinburgh).

The Bounds Green Data Centre (Middlesex Polytechnic) and the following Islington Council Departments put in long hours and/or offered patient cooperation: the Borough Secretary's Department, particularly Terry Bonomini and Sylvia Allen, and the Printing Section. Helen Downer in the typing pool, Data Prep and the Computing Division, the Town Hall cleaners and Attendants, Sue Green and the Press and Publicity Unit, Linda from the Graphics Section, the Planning Office, Tony from Security, the Transport Division and the Housing Department. A special thanks to the Council's Police Sub-Committee, particularly Councillor Derek Sawyer and Councillor Rosemary Nicholson, the Policy Committee, the Race Relations Committee, the Women's Committee, Eric Dear – the Chief Executive – and Officers from 'N' District, Metropolitan Police.

We also thank the Polytechnic of North London students who participated in the Pilot Study and for a great deal of help and constructive criticism from Dawn Currie of the University of Saskatchewan and Cathy Doran and Bonnie Miller of Hackney Social Services. Last, but not least, our gratitude to our interviewers, particularly Mick Miles, and the respondents for devoting their time.

The Centre for Criminology at Middlesex Polytechnic

The Centre was set up in order to foster research in the area of crime and criminal justice. It is a London-based organization which is interested in making links for comparative work both nationally and internationally (for example, in terms of the replication of the present victimization study). Communication should be addressed to the Head of the Centre: Dr J. Young, Middlesex Polytechnic, Queensway, Enfield, Middlesex, UK.

About the authors

Trevor Jones is Head of Islington Council's Police Committee Support Unit. He is also an Associate Research Fellow at The Centre For Criminology. He has contributed numerous reviews and articles, over the years, in the area of crime and policing to both UK and foreign publications and he was a co-editor of *Policing the Riots*.

Brian D MacLean, Brian MacLean was Temporary Research Officer for Islington Council during the period of the survey, and is currently an Associate Research Fellow at The Centre For Criminology and Professor of Criminology at the University of Saskatchewan, Canada. His recent publications include *The Political Economy of Crime: Readings for A Critical Criminology*.

Dr. Jock Young Is the Head of the Centre of Criminology and Reader in Sociology at Middlesex Polytechnic. His previous books include *The New Criminology, The Drugtakers, Critical Criminology*, and *What is to be done about Law and Order?*. His most recent book is *Losing the Fight Against Crime*. His research has concentrated on the areas of criminal victimization studies and on patterns of contemporary drug abuse.

List of Tables

LONDON, SHOWING ISLINGTON BOUNDARIES

Miles
0 1 2 3 4

ILEA Boroughs

Foreword

For anyone who is concerned about the issues of crime, policing and law and order in our country this book is essential reading. With authority, detail and original research it shows the impact of crime – and the fear of crime – on one community. A quarter of the residents of that community – one third of its women – said they never left their homes at night because of the fear of crime. It shows up the extent of crime hidden from the official statistics, because people thought it would do no good to report it.

In its own words this survey shows "a crisis of extraordinary proportions in the policing of the inner city" – one which the police cannot tackle on their own, for the book demonstrates convincingly that crime prevention needs the work of many agencies. It also reveals what the community wants from its police, and how it wants its say in policing policy, through local democratic control.

The facts in this book are about Islington. The lessons are for Britain.

Gerald Kaufman MP

Introduction

In 1985 the London Borough of Islington commissioned the Middlesex Polytechnic Centre for Criminology to undertake a crime survey of the Borough. The Islington Crime Survey (ICS) was the culmination of over a decade of British work in the field and a direct descendant of the pioneering National Crime Surveys begun in the United States during the Kennedy–Johnson administrations.

It is no accident that the notion of the mass victimization study as a guide to public policy was innovated in the 1960s by an American Democratic Party committed, at home if not abroad, to what Alan Phipps has rightly called "a vision, social democratic in all but name, of social justice as a necessary basis for social order" (1986, p101). It is perhaps no coincidence that such a technique, sharpened and refurbished, should be brought into play in the mid-1980s in an inner-city area of London by a council committed to a radical socialist programme. Indeed, when one reads Ramsey Clark, the Attorney-General of the period, lambasting against crime, one detects a sentiment in 1970 which pervades the work of the new radical, realist approach to crime today (see Lea and Young, 1984; Young, forthcoming)

> "While on the average a citizen may be the victim of violent crime only once in 400 years, there are indications that the poor black urban slum dweller faces odds five times greater – one in eighty. Since violent crimes are more frequently unreported in the slums, the chance of being a victim there may be substantially higher. If only one-fourth of the violent crime of the ghetto is reported, which is quite possible, the odds for those living there of being a crime victim within a year are one in twenty.
>
> The white middle class city dweller by contrast is likely to be the victim of violent crime at the rate of once every 2,000 years, while upper middle class income and rich suburbanites have one chance in 10,000 years." (R. Clark, 1970, p50).

If you add to the concern for blacks as victims a concern for the working class, for the poor, for the vulnerable and for women, you have an understanding of the realist approach to crime today.

Victimization studies on a national scale arose in the United States in the context of a criminology which was social democratic. It located the causes of crime in relative deprivation; it saw the role of the state as intervening in the cause of social justice; and it declared a war on poverty which also embraced a war on crime. Both offender and victim were located in the same structural context, i.e. the lack of opportunities in a society with extraordinarily high ideals of achievement yet very limited social mobility. And for a short while, interest in the causes of crime *and* victimization coexisted in the same theoretical and political framework (see J. Young, 1986a). But none of this was to last. The move to the right in American politics was accompanied by the rise of a new administrative criminology: a criminology no longer interested in causality but focussing almost solely on matters of social defence and control.

As is argued in *Realist Criminology* (J. Young, forthcoming), the reason victimization studies began to proliferate in the United States was qualitative as well as quantitative. The rapidly emerging paradigm of the new administrative criminology swept all before it. It absorbed victimization studies quite naturally: they provided a mapping of the problem areas which it was necessary to administer. The victim surveys were, on the one hand, just what was needed for the natural growth of administrative criminology but, on the other, they caused no anomalies: they assimilated easily into this new paradigm. To a criminology which was interested solely in the problem of where to administer and where to apply resources in the endless and never-to-be-won war against crime, they were indispensable yet uncontroversial. At no point did they raise the question of why the patterns of victimization were such – why the structures of society *caused* crime to appear in one place rather than another and what could be done to eliminate such patterns of injustice.

If the new administrative criminology moved into the ascendant in the 1970s – both in the United States and Britain – what of radical criminology, the competing paradigm of the period? David Friedrichs, in his survey of the relationship between a radical perspective and the emerging discipline of victimology, noted that it was remarkable that victimology and radical criminology emerged and flourished at exactly the same time, but: "the two developments . . . have proceeded quite independently of each other, with little if any reciprocal influence" (1983, p23). He is quite right, of course. There was not at first much immediate contact between the two sub-disciplines as they are conventionally constructed. Radical criminology, after all, was committed to locating the *causes* of crime within the wider social structure whereas victimology, as it had developed within the rubric of the new administrative criminology, was concerned merely with mapping the field for the purposes of prevention and control. The two paradigms were not talking the same language. But the influence of the victim was not absent in radical criminology, for very early in the period a radical victimology had emerged. Friedrichs' myopia regarding this is simply an inability to look in the direction from which it was coming. That direction was the women's movement. Studies of domestic violence, rape, and sexual harassment have been central to the feminist case since the mid-sixties. Feminist victimology was to create enormous theoretical problems for the radical paradigm in criminology, just as feminism as a whole generated very creative debates for socialist thought in general.

Radical criminology had tended to focus on crimes of the powerful and on the way in which vulnerable groups in society are criminalized. All very worthy stuff, but the traditional concern of criminology – crimes occurring within and between the working class – was a conceptual no-go area (see A. Phipps, 1981). This was part of a general tendency in radical thought to idealize their historical subject (in this case the working class) and to play down intra-group conflict, blemishes and social disorganization (see J. Young, 1986b). But the power of the feminist case resulted in a sort of cognitive schizophrenia amongst radicals: they accepted that there were grave problems for women – for example in the inner city – but remained reluctant to see other sorts of crime (eg burglary and assault) as being of great importance. Indeed, the tendency was to see working class crime as only a minor irritant in urban life when compared to the other myriad problems, and to view much of the fear of crime as a "moral panic" fanned by the mass media.

But once breached by the feminists, the walls of the radical paradigm became increasingly vulnerable to the abrasive intrusions arising from the conventional victimization studies. For if victimology created no anomalies for those theoreticians who sought to administer the system – merely providing them with better maps of the problem areas – it created enormous problems for those who worked to change it. In this fashion, both feminist and conventional victimization studies became a central problematic for radical criminology. Thus the results of the studies which chart the high victimization rates of women in terms of male violence raise immediately the problems of a patriarchial social criss-cross cutting problems of class. The insistent findings from conventional victimology of the intra-class and intra-racial nature of much crime pointed to a degree of disorganization, particularly within the working class, which creates self-inflicted wounds outside of those already generated by the corporations, the police and the courts. It was in this theoretical context that radical realism arose within criminology. At heart, this started from the premise of taking people's fear of crime seriously and arguing that these were more realistic than either radical or conventional criminologists made out (see Kinsey, Lea and Young, 1986). Further, criminology must embrace the totality of the criminal process: it must be true to its *reality*. And this reality must include the offender, the victim, informal social control and the state (eg policing). These are the four dimensions of criminology. Victimization studies fit into this paradigm to the extent that they indeed represent an audit of people's experiences, anxieties and problems of crime. Further, as victimization studies extended themselves from a study of the victims to that of the police, to public attitudes to penality etc., they began to provide the sort of empirical basis necessary for a realist criminology.

Let us turn now to the development of criminal victimization studies in Britain, noting that here, as in the United States, the predominant paradigm was administrative criminology.

The history of victimization studies in Britain is not a long one, but once started the process has proceeded fairly rapidly. The first major study was the pioneering work of Sparks, Genn and Dobb (1977), the main aim of which was to test methodology and technique. Then in 1982 the first large scale national survey was carried out in England and Wales, *The British Crime Survey* (BCS) (Hough and Mayhew, 1983), and in Scotland (Chambers and Tombs, 1984). The second sweep of the BCS occurred in 1984 (Hough and Mayhew, 1985). But a particular problem of national surveys – however useful – was their lack of detail and their inability to deal with the fundamental fact that crime is both geographically and socially focussed (see Lea and Young, 1984). This was recognized by the Home Office: "As the BCS is a national survey, it cannot provide detailed information about the extent and impact of crime in particular neighbourhoods or communities. However, crime tends to be geographically concentrated and its impact in those places is thus correspondingly more severe" (HORU, 1984, p5). For this reason the British Home Office encouraged local surveys and indeed helped finance two: a study of Nottinghamshire and adjacent counties (Farrington and Dowds, 1985) and Merseyside (Kinsey, 1984). The Nottinghamshire study deals brilliantly with the problem of the lack of relationship between crimes recorded by the police and the actual extent of crime in order to explain why a fairly peaceful county like Nottinghamshire tops the "league table" of crime with rates equal to Merseyside and London. The Merseyside Crime Survey (MCS), jointly funded by Merseyside County Council, was a local crime survey with the more conventional aim of mapping crime in Liverpool and the surrounding areas. This survey involved R. Kinsey from the Centre for Criminology, Edinburgh as director and two members of the Centre at Middlesex as consultants (see R. Kinsey, J. Lea and J. Young, 1986). The Islington Crime Survey followed the MCS a year later – the two questionnaires being developed together and overlapping to a high degree.* Of considerable influence on these questionnaires was the work of the Policy Studies Institute on Londoners' attitudes to and experience of the Metropolitan Police (see D. Smith, 1983a and 1983b).

The MCS and ICS questionnaires are hybrids constructed very largely out of the two British Crime Surveys on crime and the PSI study on policing. As second generation victimization studies, this construction emphasizes their movement away from a predominant interest in victimization to include actual responses to crime by the police and public evaluation and expectations of police performance. In addition they include, as did the BCS, questions of penality as a further enlargement of the scope of the victimization survey. Innovations in the ICS are questions on sub-legal harassment (eg being followed, stared at, shouted at in the street), a documentation of interracial incidents and questions on heroin use and on victimization and political affiliations. These two local studies are not only considerably more focussed than the national studies but embrace a much greater part of the whole process of criminalization – namely, the pattern of victimization, the impact of crime, the actual police response to both victim and offender, the public's requirements as to an ideal police response and the public's notions of appropriate penalties for various offences. If the aim of a realist criminology is to encompass the total scope of this process then these new-style surveys go a long way towards providing the necessary empirical base.

What is unique about ICS is that it is the only study (certainly in Britain and most probably in the US) *of this width* to focus solely on an inner-city area. The term "inner city" is, of course, frequently ill-used. Many inner-city areas – like Kensington and Chelsea in London – are far from deprived and include the most desirable residences of the entire city. But Islington is undoubtedly an impoverished area. Despite pockets of gentrification and enclaves of Georgian grandeur there is a high level of poverty. At least 18 per cent of the working population is unemployed and 67 per cent of *households* have annual incomes of less than £8,000 – compared to 60 per cent for the whole of Greater London. According to the Department of the Environment, Islington is the seventh most deprived area in England and the fifth worst area where housing is concerned. Between 3,000 and 4,000 households live in overcrowded conditions and approximately 6,000 households share a bath and toilet. There are 7,000 people on the council house waiting list and 9,000 people waiting for a transfer to better accommodation. Thirty people register as homeless every week and this figure excludes single people and childless couples who are not considered to be in "priority need". In terms of social care, Islington has a higher percentage of children in residential or foster homes than the whole of Greater London.

* The main differences between the MCS and ICS questionnaire are that the latter included questions on police malpractices (derived from the PSI study) and on interracial incidences, on heroin use and on political affiliation and victimization (the latter three areas being innovations) and knowledge of other people who had crimes committed against them (from the BCS). Less important items are that the ICS contained questions on frequency of leaving the home, security locks, and hypothetical response to overhearing people planning a break-in which were omitted in the MCS, whereas public estimation of graded police response to various crimes was not included in the ICS. The ICS and MCS surveys, therefore, overlap to a 90 per cent extent and both are comparable with much of the BCS and PSI databases.

The ICS is able to focus on such a deprived area, with its high crime rate and break down the incidence of victimization and police–public encounters by subgroup, based on age, gender, income and race.

We have described the theoretical perspective out of which a realist criminology emerged. Let us close this introduction by noting the political context in which a radical council ended up commissioning a crime survey. First of all, it had become increasingly obvious that there was an extraordinary hiatus in Labour Party policy over crime. Despite the fact that socialist administrations control virtually every inner-city high crime area in Britain (as is true, incidentally, of most of Europe), the Labour Party had come to regard law and order as the natural and exclusive realm of Conservatives. The question is how to develop policies which help protect women, ethnic minorities and the working class – those who suffer most from the impact of crime – who are the natural constituents of Labour, whilst refusing to accept the draconian policing policies and penal practice of the Tories. That is, how to develop policies which protect and give succour to the victims of crime, who are all the more affected because of their vulnerable position in the social structure, whilst controlling the urban offender who is himself often a product of the same oppressive circumstances. To do this demands humane policies which accurately reflect people's needs, which are guided by the facts and which can be monitored effectively. All of this is provided by the local crime survey. The second political circumstance was the need to have some objective assessment of police–public relations, a gauge of the efficacy of existing police methods and a measure of public demands as to the sort of service they would ideally want. And this endeavour to construct independently a public audit of police behaviour must be seen in the context of the current debate in Britain about the need for democratically accountable police authorities (see Lea and Young, 1984).

Thus the local survey fits into the upsurge in demand for the democratization of public institutions and the need to fit policy to public demand, particularly in the context of a decentralization of power. As such, the lessons to be learnt from such surveys both about crime and policing have a purchase outside of the context of a particular inner-city London Borough. They are essential in formulating and implementing policy in this vital area and the results can be applied to the urban heartlands of all Western industrial societies.

1 Public Attitudes Towards Crime

Any assessment of the public's attitude towards crime implicitly involves a number of fundamental questions. Is crime a problem in your area? How big a problem is it in the context of other neighbourhood problems? Do you worry about crime? Are the streets safe? Do you think crime has increased in your area in the past five years? Furthermore, people's attitudes to and perceptions of, these basic questions constitute a backdrop and pointer to an evaluation of the service provided by the police in any given area.

Neighbourhood problems

People in Islington perceive crime as a big problem, second only to unemployment and lack of youth facilities. They place it ahead of housing, education and transport.

Table 1.1   Viewing neighbourhood issues as a problem

	Big Problem	Bit of a Problem	Total % Problem
Unemployment	65.0	22.1	87.1
Poor housing	35.7	25.3	61.0
Heavy lorry noise	26.8	18.6	45.4
Crime	36.7	34.0	70.7
Poor schools	15.3	19.8	35.1
Poor public transport	10.5	16.0	26.5
Poor street lighting	11.8	23.0	34.8
Race relations	7.9	17.1	25.0
Vandalism	34.2	34.1	68.3
General unfriendliness	5.5	13.0	18.5
Not enough places for children to play	31.5	27.6	59.1
Not enough things for young people to do	38.2	28.2	66.4

Base: All respondents weighted data

Interestingly, a majority of people also see crime-related issues like vandalism and lack of child play facilities as a problem whereas only 25% see race relations as a problem, of which 7.9% think it is a "big problem". The latter indicates that most people in Islington have no difficulty in getting on with people of a different ethnicity from their own.

This raises the question of what kind of people perceive crime as a big problem in their area? Our findings indicate women rather than men and younger people rather than older. In fact, in terms of overall satisfaction with the neighbourhood, women were more likely to be dissatisfied than men.

Table 1.2 Satisfaction with neighbourhood (by gender)

	Men	Women
Low	21.4	27.7
Medium	77.7	70.2
High	0.9	2.1

Base: All respondents weighted data

Blacks are as likely as whites to view crime as a big problem, in contrast to Asians who see it as less of a problem. Amongst blacks, younger women are more likely than men to perceive crime as a big problem, especially those in the 25 to 44 age group.

Table 1.3 Viewing crime as a big problem (by age, race and gender)

	16–24		25–44		45+	
	Men	Women	Men	Women	Men	Women
White	31.0	37.8	40.6	46.4	38.6	27.8
Blacks	35.7	46.9	25.7	55.6	32.1	36.8
Asian	18.9	37.5	21.7	25.8	25.0	14.3

Base: All respondents weighted data

Given the level of victimization of younger women, in general, and the particular kinds of victimization inflicted upon younger black women, (mentioned in Chapters 2 and 4), these findings are not surprising.

Fear of crime

We also asked people if they worried about crime and found that a majority of people worry about being burgled and almost half worry about being a victim of street robbery.

Table 1.4   Worrying "quite a bit" or "a lot"

	"Quite a Bit"	*"A Lot"*	*Total*
Being burgled	29.8	26.6	56.4
Being 'mugged and robbed'	24.5	21.5	46.0
Being raped (Women only)	22.3	23.2	45.5
Being sexually molested (Women only)	22.6	21.9	44.5
Having your home or property damaged by vandals	26.9	18.7	45.6
Being attacked by strangers	23.2	15.5	38.7
Being insulted or bothered by strangers	16.0	10.2	26.2

Base: All respondents weighted data

Nearly half of all women in Islington worry about being raped, sexually molested or pestered. As we outline in Chapter 4, there are good reasons for this, particularly among younger women. Substantial minorities of people also worry about having their home or property damaged and about being attacked by strangers. In short, substantial numbers of Islington residents worry about the possibility of being a victim of crime.

We constructed composite tables, "Scale B" and "Scale C", to evaluate fear of crime and perception of the likelihood of victimization in the next year. Although the youngest and oldest age groups have the highest fear of crime, there is an inverse relationship with age in terms of likelihood of victimization.

Table 1.5   Scale scores (by age)

		16–24	*25–44*	*45+*
	Low	11.2	8.4	11.8
FEAR OF CRIME	Medium	55.6	62.7	55.5
	High	33.2	28.9	32.7
	Low	10.2	11.5	17.2
PROBABILITY OF CRIME	Medium	69.0	69.8	68.8
IN NEXT YEAR	High	20.8	18.7	14.0

Base: All respondents weighted data

Table 1.5 illustrates that although people worry about crime, they also have an informed notion of the likelihood of actually being a victim of crime. This is highlighted by the over 45 age group which, although they have a high fear of crime, also have lower notions of probability of victimization.

Safety in the streets

We asked three questions designed to find out whether people thought the streets were safe in their area. Towards the beginning of the interview, informants were asked:

"Do you think there are risks for women who go out on their own in this area after dark?

If Yes How likely is it that something might happen to them?

And, do you, yourself ever feel worried about going out on your own in this area after dark?"

The first two questions are about women, and the relevance of trying to evaluate perceptions of vulnerability at night-time is obvious. Although Chapter 4 deals with our findings on these questions in greater detail, it is worth noting at this stage, two important differences between Islington residents and the Policy Studies Institute's Survey of Londoners' (D. Smith, 1983) [henceforth PSI] findings. Firstly, a higher proportion of Islington residents than Londoners as a whole think there are risks for women and secondly, although there are only modest differences in perception of risks for self between the PSI and the Islington Crime Survey, blacks in Islington are more likely to fear for their own safety on the streets.

Table 1.6   Risks in going out after dark

	PSI		ICS	
Risks for Women	*Total*		*Total*	
Serious	41		60.1	Fairly likely
Slight	30		19.9	Not very likely
None	25		14.0	None
Don't know/Not stated	4		6.0	Don't know/Not stated
Risks for Self				
Yes	47		50.8	Yes
No	51		49.2	No
Don't know/Not stated	1		–	Don't know/Not stated Eliminated from 'ICS'

Table 1.7   Risks in going out after dark (by race) (% believe in risk)

	PSI			ICS		
	Whites	*West Indian*	*Asian*	*Whites*	*Blacks*	*Asian*
Yes	48	28	52	51.4	46.6	46.4
No	52	72	48	48.6	53.4	53.6

Base: All respondents weighted data

One would expect to find a higher perception of risk for women in inner city areas, and, as we outline in Chapters 2 and 4, this level of perception directly relates to the level of risk. Although direct comparison with the PSI Report is problematic, our findings cast doubt on the PSI's assertion that blacks may deny that a serious problem exists for them as a reflection of their being made scapegoats for street crime. In Islington, blacks are as likely to fear for their safety on the streets as Asians, and only modestly less than whites.

Belief about crime

Finally, we sought to evaluate whether people thought crime had increased in the past 5 years as any indication that a majority of people believed this to be the case would point to something being badly wrong.

Respondents were asked if various criminal offences and other problems in their area had become more common, less common, or remained the same in the last five years. Overall, 69.8% said they had become more common, 27.1% said they had remained the same and 3.29% said they were less common.

Specifically, respondents were asked about trends in burglary (residential), street robbery, "rowdiness by teenagers", "fights and disturbances in the street", vandalism, sexual assaults on women and "women being molested or pestered". The items about teenagers and "fights and disturbances in the street" were included to assess the notion floated by the British Crime Survey (Maxwell, 1984) [henceforth BCS] that the fears urban residents have about crime could be a product of anti-social behaviour and urban decay which then lead residents to believe there was more going on than there was in reality.

Overall, responses were as follows:

Table 1.8 Belief about crime (by offence)
(% believe increase in past 5 years)

	More Common	Less Common	Same
Robbery/Mugging	60.7	11.7	28.2
Burglary	67.6	9.8	22.6
Teenage rowdiness	44.3	18.4	37.3
Fights and disturbances in the street	31.0	25.4	43.6
Vandalism	53.0	16.4	30.6
Sexual assault on women	48.1	20.1	31.8
Women being molested or pestered	47.8	19.6	32.5

Our findings are at variance with the BCS in that Islington residents believe that burglary and vandalism are more prevalent, and street robbery
and teenage rowdiness less prevalent, than indicated by the BCS findings.

Table 1.9   Belief about crime: BCS and ICS
              (% believe increase in past 5 years)

	British Crime Survey Inner City Areas	Islington Crime Survey	% Difference (+ or −)
Burglary	53	67.6	+14.6
Robbery/Mugging	72	60.7	−11.3
Teenage rowdiness	60	44.3	−15.7
Vandalism	28	53.0	+25

Islington residents, in comparison, see teenage rowdiness as less of a problem and only 31% of them believe that "fights and disturbances in the
street" are more common. In fact the majority of respondents seem to see
these phenomena as something that historically has always been a by-
product of inner-city life (Pearson 1984).

Our findings are in line with those of the PSI in that there is a high level
of belief that certain criminal offences and anti-social acts had become
more prevalent over the last five years.

Table 1.10   Belief about crime: PSI and ICS (% believe increase)

	PSI Report	ICS	% Difference (+ or −)
Burglary	62.0	67.6	+4.4
Street robbery	57.0	60.7	+3.7
Fights and disturbances	37.0	31.0	−6.0
Vandalism	60.0	53.0	−7.0

Base: All respondents weighted data

The PSI point out that they conducted their fieldwork just after the 1981
Riots and that this could have influenced their findings on "fights and
disturbances in the street". They state ". . . informants who were particularly concerned about riots could and would have mentally included
them under the heading of fights and disturbances in the street".[1] This
factor partially negates comparison between the PSI and the Islington
Crime Survey [henceforth ICS], but our findings go some way towards

supporting their hypothesis. We also found higher levels of belief for burglary and lower levels for vandalism.

There is a higher level of belief that street robbery has increased in Islington than that found by the PSI in London, as a whole. But the PSI did find, in Wards with an Asian and black population of 11% to 15%, that 67% of respondents believed that street robbery had become more common over the past 5 years. This is a higher figure than for the ICS, but we are unable to draw any conclusions until we analyse our data on a Ward basis by their ethnic composition. The PSI attributed this to the role of the media in associating blacks with street robbery. While we would not deny the role the media plays in influencing public opinion, we would gravitate closer to the PSI's conclusion on the inner-city population's beliefs about crime:

"These findings again demonstrate that people's beliefs about crime do bear a close relation to the real facts about the areas in which they live".[2]

Our criticisms about making sweeping generalizations about the media in general, and the argument advocated by Stuart Hall and others in particular, is outlined in Chapter 2.

Age, race and gender

In line with the findings of the BCS, older Islington residents are less likely to feel these problems are more common, and there is a slight difference between men and women.

In terms of race, white people are more likely than blacks or Asians to perceive these problems as very common.

Table 1.11 Belief about crime (by age, race and gender)
(% believe increase in past 5 years)

AGE	*16–24*	*25–44*	*45+*
	70.1	75.5	66.0
GENDER	*Men*	*Women*	
	68.5	70.9	
RACE	*White*	*Black*	*Asian*
	70.9	62.9	58.3

Base: All respondents weighted data

Taking these problems as a whole, there is an inverse relationship between satisfaction with neighbourhood and belief that these problems are more common, and a direct relationship between both fear of crime and likelihood of victimization and belief that they are more common.

Table 1.12   **Belief about crime by scale scores**
                 (% believe increase in past 5 years)

	Low	*Medium*	*High*
Satisfaction with neighbourhood	85.0	66.0	10.3
Fear of crime	48.0	66.3	82.0
Probability of crime in the next year	60.4	67.7	85.0

Base: All respondents weighted data

There is also, on the one hand, a strong direct relationship between belief that these problems are more common and, on the other, contact with the police, rate of victimization and the number of times going out in the evening per week.

In terms of social activity in the evening, those who were out at least one evening per week are likely to believe that these problems are more common. Looking at it another way, 14.4% of those who believe the problems are more common never go out, 45.9% go out once or twice a week and 39.7% go out three or more times a week. It would seem that, the greater your exposure to the world outside your home, the more likely you will perceive crime as being more common.

Table 1.13   **Belief about crime, by contact with the police**
                 (% believe increase in past 5 years)

	0	*1*	*2+*
Contact with the police last 12 months	64.6	67.2	78.6
Criminal victimization last 12 months	62.8	67.8	79.5
Number of times 'out' in the evening per week	55.3	74.4	73.5

Base: All respondents weighted data

While people's beliefs about crime may or may not reflect reality, we would agree with the PSI that ". . . if a substantial majority of people think that the crime rate is going up, this cannot be good."[3]

Street robbery

60.7% of Islington residents think street robbery is more common than 5 years ago, 28.2% think it is about the same and 11.1% think it is less common. There is little overall difference in terms of age and gender, but there are differences when gender is broken down by age. The older men are, the more likely they are to believe there has been an increase in street robbery while for women the reverse is true.

Table 1.14   Belief about street robbery (by age and gender)
(% believe increase in past 5 years)

	Age 16–24	25–44	45+
Men and women	59.6	61.8	62.5
Men (all 61.5%)	54.3	60.3	64.3
Women (all 62.0%)	64.2	62.9	60.6

Base: All respondents weighted data

Race
There is a slight difference in belief between people of different ethnicity, with blacks being more likely to believe that street robbery is more common that it was 5 years ago. This belief is more pronounced in the younger and oldest age groups which could reflect differences in the family structure, in terms of child care and lifestyle of young blacks.

Table 1.15   Belief about street robbery (by age and race)
(% believe street robbery increase in past 5 years)

	Age All	16–24	25–44	45+
Whites	61.9	59.0	62.6	62.2
Blacks	65.0	64.1	56.3	72.4
Asians	50.8	50.2	52.2	50.1

Base: All respondents weighted data

This is further illustrated when one looks at differences between black men and women.

Table 1.16   Belief about street robbery (by age, race and gender)
(% believe street robbery increase in past 5 years)

	Age 16–24		25–44		45+	
	Males	Females	Males	Females	Males	Females
Whites	52.7	64.5	61.5	63.4	64.9	59.5
Blacks	63.2	64.8	44.4	65.0	65.4	83.3

Base: All respondents weighted data

Older black women have a high level of belief that street robbery has increased whereas black women in the middle age group have a low level of belief. Otherwise, there are few differences between white and black men or women in the other age groups, with the exception of young white men. Asians in all age groups possess a low level of belief in an increase in street robbery.

Tenure

Islington residents living in Council housing or the private rented sector are more likely than those who own their own accommodation to believe that street robbery is more common than 5 years ago – 62.2%, 65.4% and 56.4% respectively.

Fear of crime and belief in probability of crime in next year

There is a direct relationship between on the one hand, fear of crime and belief in likelihood of victimization and, on the other, belief that street robbery is more common than 5 years ago.

Table 1.17   Belief about street robbery (by scale scores)
(% believe street robbery increase in past 5 years)

	Fear of Crime	Probability of Crime in Next Year
Low	44.7	54.5
Medium	56.7	58.4
High	76.2	79.7

Base: All respondents weighted data

As we indicate in Chapter 2, the survey data strongly suggest that people's perceptions and fear of crime are not out of proportion to their experiences. This point is highlighted when we look at belief that street robbery is more common by the number of evenings out per week.

Table 1.18   Belief about street robbery (by evenings out)
(% believe street robbery increase in past 5 years)

None per week	56.7
1 or 2 per week	66.8
3+ per week	58.0

Base: All respondents weighted data

Those who stay in have the lowest belief that street robbery is more common and those who go out have the highest. The difference between those who go out one or two evenings and those who go out three or more evenings per week could be due to one or more of a number of factors: income, age, lifestyle and levels of street robbery in a particular area. Obviously, those going out are more vulnerable to street robbery and this is reflected in the section on "theft from person" in Chapter 2.

Knowledge of street robbery victims

At a later stage in the interview respondents were asked, "apart from your own household, do you personally know anyone who has been mugged and robbed in the last 12 months?" Just over one third answered in the affirmative, claiming knowledge of "street robbery" in their area by a margin of nearly two to one. 65.1% said no, 11.9% said yes (but out of their area) and 23% said yes (and in their area).

Whites are more likely than blacks to claim to know personally someone who is a victim of street robbery, but this might only reflect reticence by blacks to claim to know someone personally as opposed to a general belief that street robbery is more prevalent in their area. In the youngest and oldest age groups among blacks, women were more likely than men to claim personal knowledge of a victim of street robbery.

Table 1.19   Knowledge of street robbery victims (by age, race and gender)
           (% claiming knowledge)

	Age 16–24		25–44		45+	
	Male	Female	Male	Female	Male	Female
Whites	35.1	42.1	41.2	43.0	35.6	26.6
Blacks	22.6	29.6	29.7	25.9	15.6	23.8

Base: All respondents weighted data

Black reticence to claim personal knowledge of street robbery victims is highlighted when one looks at whether claimed knowledge of victims is "in the area" or "out of the area". Young black men and older black women are more likely to claim knowledge *outside* the area while all other sub-groups tend to claim knowledge *inside* the area.

Perhaps these differences reflect patterns of family life in that older women in the black family undertake a greater responsibility for childcare than their white counterparts. Certainly, the outlook of older black women is more in line with that of young black men than any other section of the black community. In contrast, older white women are out of step with the perceptions of the rest of the white community and are less likely to claim personal knowledge of a victim of street robbery than any other white sub-group.

Table 1.20   Knowledge of street robbery victims inside and outside the area (by age, race and gender) (% claiming knowledge)

	Age 16–24		25–44		45+	
	Male	*Female*	*Male*	*Female*	*Male*	*Female*
Whites (inside)	21.8	22.9	24.8	25.7	27.2	20.6
Whites (outside)	13.2	19.2	16.4	17.3	8.4	6.0
Blacks (inside)	10.9	21.1	18.9	17.2	12.5	4.8
Blacks (outside)	21.7	8.5	10.8	8.6	3.1	19.0

Base: All respondents weighted data

Satisfaction with neighbourhood

There is an inverse relationship between satisfaction with neighbourhood and claimed personal knowledge of street robbery, the lower the satisfaction the higher the claimed knowledge. This clearly illustrates the impact of perceived and/or actual crime upon a person's notion of the neighbourhood they live in. 43.5% of those with low satisfaction claimed personal knowledge of a victim of street robbery as opposed to 33.4% of those with medium satisfaction and 13.2% of those with high satisfaction.

Perceptions of street robbery victims

At a later stage in the Questionnaire, we asked respondents "What kinds of people do you hear about being mugged and robbed in this area. Is it mostly men, *or* mostly women *or* both equally?"

We supplemented this question by asking whether they are "mostly young *or* mostly old *or* does it happen to all ages equally?"

By and large, people believe that victims are either women or both genders equally and they are either old or of all ages. Women are more likely to say that they hear of victims of all ages and older people are more likely to claim they hear of elderly victims.

There is little difference between whites and blacks. 54.4% of blacks and 55.3% of whites say they hear about women. 53% of whites say they hear about old people and 51% of whites and 51% of blacks say they hear about old people. Almost identical proportions of whites and blacks say they hear about both genders equally – 41.4% and 42% – and all ages equally – 34.3% and 33.1%. Asians are more likely to say that they hear about male victims and young or in between age victims but 42.8% of them say they hear about women victims and 43.3% of them say they hear about elderly victims.

Table 1.21 **Local knowledge of street robbery victims**
(by age and gender)

| | Age | | | Gender | |
	16–24	25–44	45+	Males	Females
Mostly men	4.6	3.5	2.9	4.5	2.5
Mostly women	50.1	58.4	54.3	54.2	55.6
Both equally	45.3	38.1	42.8	41.3	41.9
Total	100	100	100	100	100
Mostly young	6.0	3.3	2.5	3.0	3.9
Mostly old	44.3	50.0	57.6	57.6	47.5
Mostly in between	9.5	10.2	9.6	8.9	10.6
All ages equally	40.2	36.5	30.3	30.5	38.0

Base: All respondents weighted data

On the face of it, responses seem to be orientated towards the media stereotype of the elderly women, "viciously", robbed on the street. But, how far is this shared "local knowledge" out of step with reality? Obviously, young men are completely invisible in terms of the "local grapevine", and, as we outline in Chapter 2, elderly people, *as a whole*, are less likely to be victims of street robbery. But, nearly 55% of all groups, except Asians, say they hear about women and our findings indicate that women are more likely to be street robbery victims than men. Perhaps it is not that local knowledge is out of step with reality, and/or a victim of media images and messages, but is in fact very much in line with reality in the sense that street robberies which become a talking point tend to be those which evoke comment based on a moral evaluation of the impact upon the victim. Perhaps people, on a common sense level, expect that kind of experience to happen to young men and understand that its impact, and the ability of young men to recover from that kind of experience, is qualitatively different from that of women in general, and older women in particular. We found high levels of victimizations among white and black women in the 16 to 44 age groups and among black women over 45. Most people realize that bodies can be broken and/or psyches can be bent, and, in that context, it is unsurprising that people are more likely to "hear of" street robberies involving victims who are more vulnerable than male adolescents.

Perhaps it is about time that the assumption of the myth of the equal victim is finally laid to rest. Clearly, local knowledge would seem to be neither a regurgitation of a media message nor a crude transparency of life, but, rather, an informed slice of reality.

Burglary

67.6% of Islington residents think burglary is more common than 5 years ago, 22.6% believe it is about the same and 9.8% think it is less common. On the face of it, there is a slight difference between men and women, and clear differences in terms of age and ethnicity. Whites and blacks are more likely than Asians to think burglary is more common, and the 25 to 44 year old age group believe it is more common than do the younger and older age groups.

Table 1.22   Belief about burglary (by age)
(% believe burglary increase in past 5 years)

16–24	66.8
25–44	73.8
45+	63.7

Base: All respondents weighted data

Table 1.23   Belief about burglary (by race)
(% believe burglary increase in past 5 years)

Whites	68.0
Blacks	65.6
Asians	56.1

Base: All respondents weighted data

Table 1.24   Belief about burglary (by gender)
(% believe burglary increase in past 5 years)

Men	68.4
Women	66.7

Base: All respondents weighted data

Sharper contrasts emerge when you contrast whites and blacks by age and gender.

Table 1.25   Belief about burglary (by age, race and gender)
(% believe burglary increase in past 5 years)

	Age 16–24		25–44		45+	
	Males	*Females*	*Males*	*Females*	*Males*	*Females*
Whites	66.7	67.8	74.5	75.8	68.4	59.3
Blacks	67.5	70.9	48.0	72.1	55.6	78.9

Base: All respondents weighted data

Older blacks have a high level of belief in increased burglary, as for street robbery, whereas black men in the middle age group have a low level of belief. Men and women in the other age groups have similar beliefs, with the exception of white men in the middle age group who possess a high belief in increased burglary, and older white women and older black men a moderately lower level of belief.

In contrast to the PSI report, we find higher levels of belief among the two younger age groups: 66.8% as opposed to 54% in the youngest group and 73.8% as opposed to 59% in the middle aged group. In contrast, we found a relatively lower level of belief in increase in the over 45 age group: 63.7% as opposed to 67% in the PSI survey. This, we believe, further illustrates that inner-city populations' beliefs about crime are more in tune with the reality of crime than are the beliefs of those who live in suburban and urban areas.

Tenure
There is a slight difference between those who own their homes and Council tenants, but a marked difference between both those groups and those in the private rented sector.

Table 1.26 Belief about burglary (by tenure)
(% believe burglary increase in past 5 years)

Owner-occupiers	67.8
Council tenants	65.4
Private rented	76.8

Base: All respondents weighted data

There are a number of reasons why one would expect these contrasts. In an inner-city area like Islington the private rented sector is more likely to incorporate those from the lowest socio-economic groups and those whose lifestyle, and the material condition of their "home", encourage them to go out rather than stay in, thus making them more vulnerable to burglary. This certainly appears the case if one examines the beliefs of those who go out one or more evenings per week.

Table 1.27 Belief about burglary (by number of evenings out)
(% believe burglary increase in past 5 years)

None per week	57.6
1 or 2 per week	70.0
3+ per week	70.2

Base: All respondents weighted data

Furthermore, given the crime prevention consciousness of Islington and other Local Authorities, one would expect their various crime prevention initiatives to have some level of impact and be reflected in the belief of its tenants. The slightly higher belief among owner-occupiers, as opposed to Council tenants, is in line with other studies including the 1983 Canadian Victims' Survey.

The Canadian Survey found that when inner-city areas are in a state of demographic flux, and there is a social interface in the same streets between different socio-economic groups, the better-off suffered disproportionately to their counterparts living in areas where there is clear geographical boundaries between different socio-economic groups (Federal/Provincial Task Force on Justice of Victims of Crime, Toronto, Canada, 1983, pp14-15).

It would appear that when the "normal" geographical separation of different socio-economic groups breaks down and a mixed socio-economic street is created as a result of different ownership of the properties (ie Council owned street properties, Housing Association owned properties, landlords letting houses to private sector tenants and owner-occupiers), a kind of socially-based "fear and loathing" emerges in that you break the habits of generations by burgling your new middle class neighbour instead of someone from the same socio-economic group. At least, you won't leave empty-handed whereas your working class neighbours' homes hold no such guarantee.

Knowledge of burglary victims
At a later state in the interview, we also asked respondents "apart from your own household, do you personally know anyone who had their home burgled or broken into?"

49.5% said no, 12.3% said yes (but *out* of the area) and 38.2% said yes (and *in* the area).

People in the 25–44 age group and women are far more likely to claim personal knowledge of a burglary victim than other sub-groups. But there is only a modest difference between whites and blacks, although there is a substantial difference between both these groups and Asians. All groups are more likely to claim personal knowledge of burglaries inside their area as opposed to outside their area.

Table 1.28   Knowledge of burglary victims (by age and gender)
              (% claiming knowledge)

	Age 16–24	25–44	45+	Males	Females
No	46.0	37.0	59.9	46.9	51.6
Outside area	16.4	19.4	5.4	13.7	11.0
Inside area	37.7	43.7	34.6	39.4	37.4

Base: All respondents weighted data

Table 1.29 Knowledge of burglary victims (by race)
(% claiming knowledge)

	White	Black	Asian
No	48.7	52.7	59.2
Outside area	11.5	17.2	16.0
Inside area	39.8	30.1	24.8

Base: All respondents weighted data

In contrast to street robbery, there is no evidence of reticence on the part of blacks to claim personal knowledge of burglary victims. Asians are less likely to claim personal knowledge – but just over 40% of them claim personally to know someone who has been burgled. It is unsurprising that people in the 25 to 44 year old age group are more likely to claim to know someone who has been burgled as they are the most mobile group amongst householders and, apart from young people living on their own, the group most at risk.

In short, burglary is a thorn in the side of *all* inner-city inhabitants and is likely to be a constant topic of conversation and a general irritant.

Perceptions of burglary offenders
At the same stage in the interview, we asked respondents "do you think burglaries in this area are committed by . . . people from the area, *or* people who live outside it?" and ". . . are (they) committed by children under 16, *or* people aged 16 to 20 *or* older people?"

Most people believe that burglaries are committed by 16 to 20 year olds, and by people from their area; although blacks and Asians are more likely than whites to say by people outside their areas.

Differences between whites, on one hand, and blacks and Asians on the other, could reflect a measure of defensiveness on the part of those communities and/or the specificity of burglary for these communities.

Table 1.30 Perception of burglary offenders (by age and gender)
(% believe)

	Age			Gender	
Offenders	16–24	25–44	45+	Males	Females
People from the area	79.6	81.6	76.4	78.0	79.6
People from outside the area	20.4	18.4	23.6	22.0	20.4
Total	100	100	100	100	100
Children under 16	3.9	6.5	9.6	5.1	9.6
People aged 16 to 20	78.0	80.7	79.1	80.9	78.0
Older people	18.1	12.9	11.3	13.9	12.5

Base: All respondents weighted data

Table 1.31   Perception of burglary offenders (by race)
(% believe)

Offenders	White	Black	Asian
People from the area	80.1	72.9	66.2
People from outside the area	19.9	27.1	33.8
Total	100	100	100
Children under 16	7.6	5.5	5.7
People aged 16–20	79.3	80.9	79.1
Older people	13.0	13.5	15.2

Base: All respondents weighted data

But the overwhelming majority of all inner-city inhabitants have a clear and realistic perception of who is committing burglaries in their area. They know it is not the "professional" burglar, but youth(s) who live within half a mile of them or even on the same street.

Security precautions
Given the high rate of inner-city burglary, as outlined in Chapter 2, and people's general concern about domestic burglary we tried to ascertain what security precautions Islington residents took, if any, and, if it transpired that certain groups did not take special precautions, to try to identify the reasons for not doing so.

Respondents were asked if they had any special locks or other security devices in their home as a precaution against crime. 52.7% said yes and 47.3% said no. Older people, whites and women were more likely than other groups to have taken security precautions in their homes.

Table 1.32   Taking security precautions (by age)
(% taking security precautions)

16–24	42.1
25–44	57.2
45+	64.7

Base: All respondents weighted data

Table 1.33   Taking security precautions (by race)
(% taking security precautions)

Whites	60.1
Blacks	42.7
Asians	44.6

Base: All respondents weighted data

Table 1.34   Taking security precautions (by gender)
(% taking security precautions)

Men	55.2
Women	60.2

Base: All respondents weighted data

There is also a sharp difference between owner-occupiers, Council tenants and the private rented sector.

Table 1.35   Taking security precautions (by tenure)
(% taking security precautions)

Owner-occupiers	70.5
Council tenants	56.9
Private rented	50.0

Base: All respondents weighted data

This probably reflects the difference between the Council as a landlord and private-sector landlords, the latter being less likely to provide basic security measures for their properties. This suggests that, apart from age, income is a major factor in determining whether or not you install security devices. In fact, we found a clear relationship not only by income but also by age differences within household income groups.

Table 1.36   Taking security precautions (by income and age)
(% taking security precautions)

Household Income	Age 16–24	25–44	45+
Under £3,000	33.0	50.9	55.7
£3,000–£7,999	38.7	50.0	68.0
£8,000–£11,999	50.6	57.6	67.2
£12,000+	48.0	73.0	78.1

Base: All respondents weighted data

The contrast by age is further highlighted when one looks at type of tenure divided into the three age groups.

Table 1.37   Taking security precautions (by tenure and age)
(% taking security precautions)

	Age 16–24	25–44	45+
Type of Tenure			
Owner-occupier	49.8	72.4	77.2
Council tenant	44.7	54.0	62.4
Private rented	34.5	49.9	65.0

Base: All respondents weighted data

The implication is that although middle aged and older people are more inclined to take security precautions in their homes, many of them cannot afford to do so. Women are also more likely than men to take security precautions in their homes, but we found some differences by ethnicity in that younger blacks and Asian men were less likely to do so than their white counterparts, and black women were less likely than white and older Asian women to take security precautions.

Table 1.38   Taking security precautions (by age, race and gender)
(% taking security precautions)

| | 16–24 | | 25–44 | | 45+ | |
	Males	Females	Males	Females	Males	Females
Whites	40.7	47.2	56.2	62.1	66.7	68.0
Blacks	28.3	40.8	32.4	45.6	53.1	47.6
Asians	31.8	36.1	38.3	55.9	52.0	53.3

Base: All respondents weighted data

Whether this is due to socio-economic or other factors has to remain a matter of conjecture at this point in time. But our findings do lend weight to the explanation posited but untested in the BCS, that property protection is more strongly related to income than to risk of burglary or concern about being burgled. People who have had contact with the police are no more or no less likely to take security precautions in their home.

Table 1.39   Taking security precautions (by contact with police)

| | Number of contacts in past year. | | |
	0	1	2+
% taking security precautions	57.6	58.6	57.7

It is difficult to ascertain whether this reflects socio-economic factors or public perception that crime prevention is the job of others or an inadequate level of police advice in this area. But, as we outline in Chapter 3, Islington residents attach a low degree of importance to this function in terms of the prioritization of police resources.

Rowdiness by teenagers
In contrast to the BCS, fewer Islington residents perceive teenage rowdiness as increasing in the past 5 years than burglary or vandalism. 44.3% think teenage rowdiness is more common, 37.3% think it is about the same and 18.4% think it is less common. There are few differences by age or race, or by the number of evenings one goes out per week. But considerable differences emerge by gender and age, and by fear of crime and belief in the likelihood of victimization.

Table 1.40   Belief about rowdiness by teenagers (by age)
(% believing teenage rowdiness increase in past 5 years)

16–24	25–44	45+
44.5	45.4	42.1

Base: All respondents weighted data

Table 1.41   Belief about rowdiness by teenagers (by number of evenings out per week)
(% believing teenage rowdiness increase in past 5 years)

0	1 or 2	3+
42.7	46.2	43.1

Base: All respondents weighted data

Table 1.42   Belief about rowdiness by teenagers (by race)
(% believing teenage rowdiness increase in past 5 years)

Whites	Blacks	Asian
43.3	45.5	42.5

Base: All respondents weighted data

Table 1.43   Belief about rowdiness by teenagers (by age and gender)
(% believing teenage rowdiness increase in past 5 years)

Men			Women		
16–24	25–44	45+	16–24	25–44	45+
36.7	39.2	47.4	51.4	50.4	37.0

Base: All respondents weighted data

Table 1.44   Belief about rowdiness by teenagers (by scale score 'B')
(% believing teenage rowdiness increase in past 5 years)

	Low	Medium	High
Fear of crime	25.1	40.2	55.8

Base: All respondents weighted data

Table 1.45   Belief about rowdiness by teenagers (by scale score 'C')
(% believing teenage rowdiness increase in past 5 years)

	Low	Medium	High
Probability of crime in next year	42.3	39.1	60.5

Base: All respondents weighted data

In line with the BCS findings, there is a direct relationship between those who are worried and fearful about crime, on one hand, and belief that teenage rowdiness has increased, on the other. But although there is a direct relationship with age among men, the reverse is true among women. This difference between men and women could be due to different perceptions of potential vulnerability, in that younger women are likely to view rowdiness in terms of sexual harassment and men as a potential assault, particularly as they became older and increasingly fragile in physical terms. The underlying common factor is that both men and women perceive this problem from the standpoint of their relative and respective vulnerability in the world.

Fights and disturbances in the street

31% of Islington residents think this problem is more common, 43.6% about the same and 25.4% think it is less common. Younger people think fights and disturbances are more common and Asians and blacks more so than whites.

Table 1.46   Belief about fights and disturbances amongst blacks and
Asians (by age)
(% believe fights and disturbances in the street increase in
past 5 years)

	16–24	25–44	45+
Blacks	46.9	30.1	24.0
Asians	30.3	34.2	39.0

Base: All respondents weighted data

Women are more likely to believe this problem is more common than
men although, as for teenage rowdiness, their perception appears to be
determined by their relative level of vulnerability. Young men see this
problem as more common than older men, but they are more likely than
older men to be the victims of fights in the streets.

Table 1.47 Belief about fights and disturbances (by age and gender)
(% believe fights and disturbances in the street increase in
past 5 years)

	16–24	*25–44*	*45+*
Men	29.1	26.4	27.5
Women	41.8	33.4	22.3

Base: All respondents weighted data

Table 1.48 Belief in fights and disturbances (by age)
(% believe fights and disturbances in the street increase in
past 5 years)

16–24	*25–44*	*45+*
35.9	30.2	25.0

Base: All respondents weighted data

Table 1.49 Belief in fights and disturbances (by race)
(% believe fights and disturbances in the street increase in
past 5 years)

Whites	*Blacks*	*Asians*
27.8	32.8	35.0

Base: All respondents weighted data

When we look at differences by age within different ethnic groups, clear
reflections of diversity in culture and lifestyle emerge. Young blacks and
young whites believe this problem is more common than their older counterparts, whereas older Asians believe it is more common than their
younger counterparts.

Table 1.50 Belief in fights and disturbances among whites (by age)
(% believe fights and disturbances in the street increase in
past 5 years)

16–24	*25–44*	*45+*
34.0	29.5	25.0

Base: All respondents weighted data

As for teenage rowdiness, there is a direct relationship between those who are worried and fearful about crime and belief that fights and disturbances in the street are more common. There are few differences by the number of evenings one goes out per week which suggests that belief in the problem being more common does not influence people's movements and lifestyle.

Table 1.51 Belief in fights and disturbances (by number of evenings out per week)
(% believe fights and disturbances in the street increase in past 5 years)

0	1 or 2	3+
27.4	28.9	29.7

Base: All respondents weighted data

Vandalism

53% of Islington residents think this problem is more common, 30.6% about the same and 16.4% think it is less common.

People in the middle age group are more likely to believe that this problem is more common than younger or older people.

Table 1.52 Belief in vandalism (by age)
(% believe vandalism increase in past 5 years)

16–24	25–44	45+
50.6	57.2	50.8

Base: All respondents weighted data

Whites and blacks have similar perceptions about vandalism, but Asians are more likely to believe that vandalism has not become more common in the last five years – 52.9% of whites, 52.6% of blacks and 42.9% of Asians believe this problem has become more common. People living in Council housing or the private rented sector are more likely to believe that this problem is more common than those who own their homes.

Table 1.53 Belief in vandalism (by tenure)
(% believe vandalism increase in past 5 years)

Owner-occupier	Council tenants	Private-rented
46.5	53.7	55.9

Base: All respondents weighted data

When tenure is split by age, people in the middle age group emerge as being most likely to believe that this problem is more common.

Table 1.54   Belief in vandalism (by tenure and age)
(% believe vandalism increase in past 5 years)

	16–24	*25–44*	*45+*
Owner-occupiers	39.4	51.3	44.2
Council	53.1	57.2	52.0
Private rented	51.8	63.3	50.9

Base: All respondents weighted data

People with a high fear of crime and belief in the likelihood of victimization are more likely to believe this problem is more common.

Table 1.55   Belief in vandalism (by scale scores)
(% believe vandalism increase in past 5 years)

	Low	*Medium*	*High*
Fear of crime	29.4	48.5	67.7
Probability of crime in next year	46.7	50.8	66.5

Base: All respondents weighted data

There also is a direct relationship between contact with the police and belief that vandalism is more common.

Table 1.56   Belief in vandalism (by contact with the police)
(number of contacts in the last year)

	0	*1*	*2+*
% believe vandalism increase in past 5 years	47.1	52.2	61.6

Base: All respondents weighted data

This suggests that the level of reportage to the police is determined by the motivation of those who experience or witness vandalism. Owner-occupiers are more likely to perceive vandalism in terms of damage to their personal property whereas Council tenants are likely to perceive it in terms of damage to public/common areas on their estate.

In relation to the PSI report, we found a lower level of belief amongst the youngest and oldest age groups: 50.6% compared with 57% in the younger age group and 50.8% compared with 64% for over 45s, and an almost identical level of belief among the middle age group, 57% compared with 57.2%. Given the high proportion of people over 45 in Council housing in Islington, this further illustrates the difference in perceptions between vandalism to public property and vandalism to private property. Unsurprisingly, although Council estate tenants are annoyed about vandalism to public areas on estates, people get far more annoyed when their own personal property is vandalized.

Sexual assaults on women

48.1% of Islington residents think sexual assault is more common, 31.8% believe it is about the same and 20.1% think it is less common.

People in the middle age group, blacks, women and victims of crime are more likely to think that sexual assaults are more common than other groups, and there is a direct relationship between fear of crime and belief in likelihood of victimization.

Table 1.57   Belief in sexual assault (by age)
             (% believe sexual assault increase in past 5 years)

16–24	*25–44*	*45+*
47.8	52.7	43.7

Base: All respondents weighted data

Table 1.58   Belief in sexual assault (by race)
             (% believe sexual assault increase in past 5 years)

Whites	*Blacks*	*Asians*
47.1	51.8	39.3

Base: All respondents weighted data

Table 1.59   Belief in sexual assault (by gender)
             (% believe sexual assault increase in past 5 years)

Men	*Women*
43.9	50.2

Base: All respondents weighted data

Table 1.60   Belief in sexual assault (by scale score)
(% believe sexual assault increase in past 5 years)

	Low	Medium	High
Fear of crime	32.7	42.4	61.0
Probability of crime in the next year	42.4	44.4	64.4

Base: All respondents weighted data

Table 1.61   Belief in sexual assault (by victimization)
(% believe sexual assault increase in past 5 years)

None	40.3
Once or twice	45.8
3+	57.7

Base: All respondents weighted data

When one examines differences within sub-population groups sharper contrasts in levels of belief emerge. Black women, as a whole, and younger white women have the highest level of belief in increased sexual assault.

Table 1.62   Belief in sexual assault (by age, race and gender)
(% believe sexual assault increase in past 5 years)

	16–24		25–44		45+	
	Males	Females	Males	Females	Males	Females
Whites	41.6	53.5	46.0	58.2	44.4	41.3
Blacks	33.3	62.0	32.0	63.9	50.0	60.0

Base: All respondents weighted data

Men, with the exception of blacks over 45, have a much lower level of belief in increased sexual assault. Younger blacks are particularly disbelieving that sexual assault has increased and older white women have a level of belief as low as that for young white men.

Women being molested or pestered
47.8% of Islington residents think sexual harassment is more common, 32.5% believe it is about the same and 19.6% think it is less common.

Similar patterns emerge for sexual harassment as for sexual assault. Younger people, blacks, women and victims of crime are more likely than other groups to believe sexual harassment has increased and there is a direct relationship with our "scale scores".

Table 1.63   Belief in sexual harassment (by age)
(% believe sexual harassment increase in past 5 years)

	16–24	*25–44*	*45+*
	50.5	50.3	43.4

Base: All respondents weighted data

Table 1.64   Belief in sexual harassment (by race)
(% believe sexual harassment increase in past 5 years)

	Whites	*Blacks*	*Asians*
	46.7	50.7	37.1

Base: All respondents weighted data

Table 1.65   Belief in sexual harassment (by gender)
(% believe sexual harassment increase in past 5 years)

Men	45.4
Women	48.1

Base: All respondents weighted data

Table 1.66   Belief in sexual harassment (by scale scores)
(% believe sexual harassment increase in past 5 years)

	Low	*Medium*	*High*
Fear of crime	34.2	42.1	58.9
Probability of crime in the next year	40.5	44.4	62.2

Base: All respondents weighted data

Table 1.67   Belief in sexual harassment (by victimization)
(% believe sexual harassment increase in past 5 years)

None	39.2
Once or twice	47.6
3+	56.7

Base: All respondents weighted data

Again, as for sexual assault, there are sharp contrasts in levels of belief within sub-populations. Black women, particularly younger women, and white women between 16 and 44, have the highest level of belief in increased sexual harassment and younger black men and older white women the lowest.

Table 1.68 Belief in sexual harassment (by age, race and gender)
(% believe sexual harassment increase in past 5 years)

	16–24		25–44		45+	
	Males	*Females*	*Males*	*Females*	*Males*	*Females*
Whites	45.2	54.7	46.7	53.8	45.9	40.4
Blacks	37.9	64.7	40.0	54.1	45.0	56.2

Base: All respondents weighted data

Although the overall patterns for sexual harassment are similar to those for sexual assault, there is a contrast in belief between the two for white and black women in the middle age group. 58.2% of white women between 25 and 44 believe sexual assault has increased in the past 5 years whereas 53.8% believe sexual harassment has increased, and 63.9% of black women between 25 and 44 believe sexual assault has decreased whereas 54.1% believe sexual harassment has increased.

By and large, as we outline in Chapters 2 and 4, these beliefs are not based on moral panic but on an underlying level of reality and realistic assessment of risk.

Summary and conclusions

Over 70% of Islington residents see crime as a "problem". In a list of potential neighbourhood problems, it is seen as second only to unemployment and (just) to lack of youth facilities. People's perceptions of crime are not based on moral panic and/or a regurgitation of media stereotypes, but bear a close relationship to the real facts about the areas in which they live. Their perception of risk is often related to their relative vulnerability; for example younger women are more likely than older women to believe that fights and disturbances in the street are more common in the past 5 years whereas older men are more likely than younger men to believe this phenomenon is more common. The former view this phenomenon in terms of potential sexual harassment while the latter see it in terms of potential assault.

There is little difference in terms of perception between people of different ethnicity, although young black men and older white women tend to hold views about crime which are out of step with the rest of their respective communities. Women are more likely than men to see crime as a problem, particularly younger women, but this, again, is in line with their potential risk and vulnerability.

The main findings of this section can be summarized as follows:
a) A substantial majority of Islington residents see crime-related issues such as vandalism and lack of child play facilities as a problem – 68.3% and 59.1% respectively.

b) Most people do not see race relations as a problem – only 7.9% think it is a "big problem".

c) Over half of Islington residents worry about being burgled and nearly half worry about being a victim of street robbery (56.2% and 46%).

d) Nearly half of all women worry about being raped or sexually molested.

e) Inner-city populations are more likely to think there are risks for women on the streets after dark.

f) People are more worried about crime than general public order.

g) 60.7% of people think street robbery has become more common in the past 5 years and 44.9% claim to know someone personally who has been "mugged and robbed" in the last 12 months.

h) People's views on victims of street robbery tend to be morally determined in that they "hear" more locally about women and older victims than young men, and are, for obvious reasons, more outraged by the former than the latter.

i) 67.6% of people think burglary has become more common in the past 5 years and 40.5% claim to know someone personally who has been burgled in the last 12 months.

j) People have an accurate picture of who carries out burglaries in their area.

k) Crime prevention precautions in the home are related to socio-economic factors. Many people who would like to take crime prevention precautions can't afford to do so.

l) 44.3% of people think teenage rowdiness has become more common in the last 5 years and 31% think "fights and disturbances in the street" have become more common. But people are more concerned about crime and vandalism and many see hooliganism as a feature of inner-city life.

m) 53% of people think vandalism has become more common in the past 5 years.

n) 48.1% of people think sexual assault of women has become more common in the past 5 years. 50.2% of all women, and 58.2% of white women and 63.9% of black women between the ages of 25 and 44, believe this to be the case.

o) 47.8% of people think sexual harassment of women has become more common in the past 5 years. 48.1% of all women, and 54.7% of white women and 64.7% of black women between the ages of 16 and 24, believe this to be the case.

Notes

1. Smith, D. *Policy Studies Institute's Survey of Londoners* (1983), p. 40.
2. *Ibid.*, p. 41.
3. *Ibid.*, p. 33.

2 Frequency and Distribution of Crime in Islington

Introduction

One of the major purposes of conducting the Islington Crime Survey was to measure the extent of unrecorded crime. Virtually every major victimization study revealed that a great deal of the crime that is reported to interviewers never gets recorded in the official statistics. There are a number of reasons why this occurs, and for purposes of illustration it is useful to trace what happens as crime gets either processed or ignored by the criminal justice apparatus.

Initially, not only must a crime occur, but it must be recognized as occurring and defined as a crime by someone before it can be brought to the attention of the police. Sometimes people are unaware of a criminal event, sometimes people do not consider an act to be a crime, sometimes people do not wish to report a crime when they have recognized it to occur, sometimes the police do not consider an act to be criminal within the legal definitions set out by the criminal code, and sometimes the police recognize the event to be criminal but can see no resolution to it.

In any event much crime goes both unrecorded and unreported. For purposes of the ICS, we shall define reported crime as that crime which comes to the attention of the police. Recorded crime on the other hand shall be defined in this report as that crime which comes to the attention of the police and is considered by them to be an event which is worth recording in the official crime statistics. The purpose in making this distinction is that not all crime gets reported to the police and not all crime which comes to the attention of the police gets recorded. When a crime is considered as such by an individual he or she must make the decision to report or not to report to the police or other agency. When the police receive notification that an alleged crime has occured, they must make a decision to record it or not to record it. If recorded, an investigation is begun, but even so it sometimes happens that the police consider after a preliminary investigation that a crime has not occurred and the original crime report is nullified. This process of nullification of crime reports after an investigation has been called *no-criming* for purposes of this report.

This simple overview of the discretionary levels of the system whereby events come to be recorded or not recorded in official criminal statistics, illustrates that *reported crime is largely a product of the willingness of the public to co-operate with the police, while the process of recording crime is largely a product of the police's willingness to co-operate with the public.*

Non-reporting of crime

The BCS found that there was a great discrepancy between what people reported to them as incidents of crime and what they reported to the police. In short, unreported crime was high. For example, in the 1984 survey they found the following percentages of unreported crime:

Offence	% Reported	Offence	% Reported
Vandalism	21	Assault	37
Theft from M.V.	43	Theft from person/	
Burglary of dwelling	68	robbery	33
M.V. theft	97	Sexual offences	8
Bicycle theft	68	Other personal	
Theft in dwelling	23	theft	31
Other h/h theft	19		

(Source: Hough and Mayhew, 1985, p61)

It can be seen from the above table that in England and Wales much of what the public defines as crime gets unreported. The recent Merseyside Crime Survey [henceforth MCS] conducted by the Centre of Criminology University of Edinburgh had similar findings. The following table drawn from the MCS illustrates that the BCS is not the only piece of research to uncover large frequencies of unreported crime:

Offence	% Reported	Offence	% Reported
Theft from person	25%	Theft from M.V.	44
Wounding	27%	Burglary in dwelling	73
Robbery	72%	M.V. theft	100
Vandalism	27%	Bicycle theft	53
		Theft from dwelling	16

(Source: MCS, 1984, p11)

Furthermore the PSI reports that only 52% of all crimes disclosed to the interviewers ever came to the attention of the police. It would seem from all the available evidence in England that unreported crime remains high and virtually every study illustrates this point. In fact, it is not just in England and Wales where there are high rates of unreported crime. In Canada, the United States, Holland, and Scandinavia studies have all come to similar findings.

There are many reasons why people do not report crimes to the police. The BCS found for example that the largest categories for not reporting crimes were:

1. 55% said there was no loss or it was too trivial
2. 16% said the police would be unable to do anything
3. 10% said it was not a matter for the police
4. 2% claimed it was too inconvenient
(Hough and Mayhew, 1985, 19)

Both the MCS and PSI cite similar reasons for non-reporting behaviour. Unfortunately, none of these studies provides a full account of the responses given for not reporting an incident of victimization to the police.

Table 2.1 below presents the response to the question "Why Not?" when respondents on the ICS answered that the police did not come to know about the incident:

Table 2.1 Reasons for not reporting an offence when a victim

Reason	% of Responses	% Respondents
Wouldn't do any good	37.8	44.9
Too trivial	26.2	31.1
Too much trouble	12.9	15.4
Fear of reprisal from offender	3.6	4.4
Felt sorry for offender	0.5	0.6
Because offender was too close a friend or relative	1.4	1.7
Fear or dislike of police	2.0	2.4
Not a matter for police	5.1	6.0
Someone else handled the matter	3.4	4.0
Don't know/other	7.1	8.4
	100%	118.7

Base: All victims weighted n= 3979

Unlike the other surveys carried out in England and Wales, the ICS has illustrated that, at least in Islington, the most frequent reason for not notifying the police of an incident of personal victimization is that the victim feels that it would do no good. Unfortunately no other studies in London have asked why the police were not notified and in studies outside of London the information is not wholly presented, leading one to question what the other categories of response are. *One thing is eminently clear from the ICS data: there is an alarming lack of confidence in the local police's ability to deal with crime.* In some cases where this response was given, it may be interpreted as either an insufficient or highly knowledgeable understanding of the mechanics of criminal justice functioning.

The following is a selection of short citations in which some respondents give their reasons for not reporting:

White female, 40	"I couldn't expect the police to find my purse . . . it was my fault . . ."
White male, 43	". . . Because it was the police who did it . . . It's not worth complaining, they are at it all the time . . ."
White female, 24	". . . I was frightened to tell them because of the police not believing me and know from the experience of others that the police are not very receptive in these matters . . ."
Irish female, 25	". . . I've been told that the police will not get involved in these matters (domestic violence) . . . Might have been partly my own fault showing my boyfriend my fear . . ."
W.Ind. female, 35	"I felt ashamed of what was going on . . . I did not want anyone to know about it . . ."
White male, 19	"I felt that there was nothing I could do about it . . . there's no way of giving proof . . . I felt that if they did they would pick me up on 'sus' or kick my head in . . . accidentally of course . . ."

The advantage gained by making qualitative, as well as quantitative measures, is demonstrated by the above citations. While in all fairness to the police we are only reiterating attitudes that may or may not be an indication of the reality of policing in the Borough, they certainly are real in their consequences in that it is precisely this kind of attitude which prevents nearly one half of all the victims of serious crime, who do not report their victimization to the police, from reporting it.

Non-recording of crime

Even when respondents do report their victimization to the police, the reports are not always recorded. Various surveys have attempted to relate their findings to the official criminal statistics and in almost all cases the estimates of reported crimes given by the research do not correspond to published records of recorded crimes known to the police. There are a number of reasons why this occurs, which also help to explain why the police records are consistently lower than the surveys' estimates.

Firstly, there is a certain level of sampling error, measurement error and errors of prediction which are inherent in all surveys of any kind. These are elaborated in Appendix 2. Unfortunately, some surveys such as the BCS and PSI do not report on the estimates of error. Although the BCS does discuss sampling error, they refuse to address the issues of prediction and measurement error.

These errors of measurement are also a problem for the police statisticians even if they do not acknowledge them publicly. There are, however, a number of other reasons why public reports of crime may not come to be recorded. For example, the Home Office Research and Planning Unit is worth quoting at length:

> "One likely reason for the shortfall is that the police do not accept victims' accounts of incidents; they may – quite rightly – think that a report of an incident is mistaken or disingenuous, or they may simply feel that there is simply insufficient evidence to say that a crime has been committed. Some incidents will have been recorded, of course, but in different crime categories – where for example it is indisputable that criminal damage has been committed, but less clear that a burglary has been attempted. Some incidents may have been regarded as too trivial to warrant police action – particularly if complainants indicated they wanted the matter dropped or were unlikely to give evidence, or if the incident had already been satisfactorily resolved." (1975, p13)

The extent of reported but unrecorded crime is difficult to establish, as are the reasons. One reason for the differences is that the victim could have easily reported the crime to a different district so that the report would not come under the jurisdiction of the local police. While this would not hold for the BCS, in that they did a national sample which was compared to national police statistics, this would certainly be a factor in the ICS. Another reason that we should expect a difference in an inner-city London borough is that, as Sir Kenneth Newman stated in his annual report, the Metropolitan Police are subject to competing and conflicting demands for limited resources. This would mean that the police, by admission, must use discretion in deciding when to record and investigate a crime which has been reported. While this is an admirable exercise in the efficient use of resources, our data will show that the selection of crimes to be recorded reveals a definite bias in police functioning.

Fragments of reputable research on the police have indicated that a number of police practices serve to reduce the number of reports of recorded crimes and that a great deal of attrition occurs at this level. McCabe and Sutcliffe in their research on the police forces in Salford and Oxford found that most reports of crime to the police were made either by personal visits to the police station or by telephone, indicating that the police are reliant on information from the public on crime related incidents. Nevertheless, on both of these forces less than one half of all reported crimes ended up on a crime report and, therefore, went unrecorded. In Salford 50% of all assaults, 70% of burglaries and only 11% of reports of domestic violence ever ended up as a crime record. By comparison, in Oxford only 29% of all assaults, 60% of burglaries, and only 2% of reports of domestic violence ended up being recorded by the police.

Once crimes have been recorded by the police, they do not always remain as such. Sometimes they are no-crimed. In one study of police work Bottomley and Coleman found that 17% of all assaults were no-crimed after they had been prepared. The now famous work of Sparks *et al.* in studying the local police of Hackney, Brixton, and Kensington found that 25% of all recorded crime was no-crimed in Hackney and Brixton, while the figure for Kensington remained at 17%.

The importance of these findings for this survey should be briefly elaborated. We should expect to find a much higher frequency of criminal victimization than the police records indicate. Since we did ask the respondents if the police came to know about the crime, we can calculate the rates of response. These will be an over-estimate, however, because police coming to know of the matter does not mean necessarily that it will be considered material for a crime report.

Since follow-up interviews were only sought with victims of burglary, vandalism, theft from person, assault and sexual assault we could not ascertain what the reporting behaviour was for other offences. For those with whom the follow-up interviews were completed in those categories we found that overall when asked: "Did the police come to know about this matter? (these matters)" respondents answered in the manner given by Table 2.2 below:

Table 2.2   Frequency of crimes reported to the police

Yes	50.1%
No	49.9%
	100%

Base: All victims weighted data n= 3979

It can be seen from Table 2.2 that only 50% of the crimes found by the survey came to the attention of the police. Overall this figure is in line with other studies. How the police came to be notified, however, was not always because the victim reported it. Table 2.3 illustrates how respondents on the ICS responded to the question: "How did the police come to know about it?"

Table 2.3   How police became aware of offence

Police told by respondent	66.5%
Police told by other person	28.6%
Police were there	3.8%
Police found out in another way	1.1%

Base: Victims whose crimes were reported, weighted n= 1939

This table illustrates that not only are the police primarily dependent upon the victims of crime for bringing crime to their attention, but also that the possibility is present for the police becoming aware of a crime without a crime report being processed.

Notes on data presentation

Before examining the data on the frequency and distribution of crime in Islington, it will be useful to spell out how the data have been prepared for presentation. Because some crimes happen to individuals and some crimes happen to households, it is difficult to compare frequencies of assaults, for example, with burglaries respectively. For this reason, except where it is useful to do otherwise, the rates of crime have been reported using the household rather than the individual as the unit of analysis. Where personal crimes such as assault, theft from person and sexual assault were investigated, it was decided that in order to capture enough cases of victimization for valid comparisons between subpopulations to be made, that the interviewers would ask about other members of the household. In this manner more cases of victimization could be generated for a cheaper cost and by taking a sum of the victimizations for any of these categories we would arrive at a measure of occurrences for a household rather than for individuals. The weighting procedure outlined in Appendix 2 was then followed to arrive at an accurate estimate for the Borough. This strategy allowed us to use the household as the unit of analysis so that accurate comparisons could be made across crime categories as rates per household. Furthermore for purposes of inferring actual estimates of the number of crimes during the year, we would use the number of households in the Borough rather than the number of individuals. In this way we would still arrive at the same numbers for estimates but the basis of comparison would be more valid and the actual sample of victims would be larger.

There were five major categories of crime for which we collected follow-up information. We felt that because, for example, auto theft has been shown by most research to be highly reported and recorded it would be redundant to illustrate it one more time. Because there was no way of partitioning out the various categories at phase one we did this at phase two after an assessment of the details of the crime could be made. Furthermore, we have included breakdown categories from the original five for two reasons. Firstly, even though respondents claimed that a particular offence had occurred, it was often the case that the offence was something else. For example, we isolated a number of cases reported to us as theft from person which turned out to be other forms of theft. For purposes of comparison to police statistics, it was necessary to partition out these offences. Secondly, we felt we should include instances of domestic assault, racist assault and police assault since these were of particular interest and not included in either the police statistics or other research studies. Also, it was felt that the broad category of sexual assault as used in the police statistics and other research is insufficient. Therefore, we broke this category down into the four categories of:

Rape or attempted rape
Multiple rape or attempted multiple rape
Other sexual assault
Multiple sexual assault

Because of the elaborate coding scheme which was necessary to produce these categories from the broader ones given by the questionnaire items, it was sometimes not possible to calculate standard errors, rates of reporting, police statistics, or projected estimates. Whenever the narrower categories are used in the report this lack of information will be noted as 'NA'. The final report should include these measures where they are available, after further computations and the merging of the two data files given by the project have been accomplished.

The strategy of presentation for the rest of this section will be to provide an overview of the narrower categories, estimates of the rates and numbers of crimes in each of these, and estimates of the reporting rates and recording rates and their inter-comparisons. This will help to illustrate the extent of crime for selected categories in the Borough.

Secondly, each of the five major categories, for which the reporting rates were obtained as well as the three categories of motor vehicle theft, motor vehicle vandalism, and bicycle theft for which reporting rates were not ascertained will be looked at individually and compared internally by ward, age, gender, race, and other control variables in order to estimate the distribution of crime as well as the frequency.

The extent and location of crime in Islington

As expected, the rates of crime in Islington are quite high because of its inner-city location. Table 2.4 (p.87) presents the overall rates of crime that were uncovered by the survey for the major headings of crime that were followed up. Crimes that were not followed up included most motor vehicle vandalism, all motor vehicle theft and all bicycle theft. Furthermore, it should be noted that because some of the categories provided in Table 2.4 could only be ascertained from the descriptions of the offences on the questionnaire, rates per 10,000 households were not calculated but have been expressed as the percentage of the wider category. Because the unit of analysis used is the household, these rates are not directly comparable to the BCS estimates on all categories, although for household crimes these comparisons can be made. The following illustrates the estimates provided by the 1984 BCS.

Offence	Rate per 10,000 Households
Vandalism	1597
Burglary	489
Motor vehicle theft	153
Bicycle theft	155

(Source: Hough and Mayhew, 1985, 84)

On each of these categories, the rates of crime are much higher in Islington than the national average as estimated by the BCS.

Table 2.5 (p.88) illustrates not only the actual number of offences estimated by the ICS, but also demonstrates the rates of reporting of these offences to the police, and the rates of recording these offences by the police. Again, because the survey did not follow up all categories of offence we cannot estimate in all cases the public's rate of reporting these offences. Furthermore, because we have broken down some offence categories into those which are not reported by the police statistics, it is impossible to estimate what the ratio of recorded offences might be. Because Table 2.5 reports on rates of reporting and recording, we can make direct comparisons on some categories with the BCS as illustrated.

Offence	% Reported	% Recorded	Recorded as % of Reported
Vandalism	21	8	37
Burglary	68	48	70
Bicycle theft	NA	50	NA
Assault	37	NA	NA
Theft from person/ Robbery	33	8	25
Sexual offences	8	11	133

(Source: Hough and Mayhew, 1985, 61)

In each of the categories above (except for sexual assaults and bicycle theft) it can be seen that the rates of reporting and rates recorded in the police statistics are higher than the national average. However, on all categories, the ratio of recorded offences to reported offences is less than the national average. A conclusion is that *although the rates of crime are higher, the reporting rates to the police are higher and the percentage of actual crimes committed recorded in the police statistics are higher, the police recording of reported offences is less than the national average.* Despite the problems of inner-city life and its relation to crime and policing, the Islington public look to their police for assistance on crime at a rate higher than the rest of the country.

However, the people of Islington would appear to be getting less of a service from their local police than the rest of the country. In all fairness to the police, however, more crimes are brought to their attention at a rate which is higher than the rest of the country, and it is to be expected that the rate of attrition of offences would be greater in Islington. When the reporting of offences to the police is seen as measure of public willingness to co-operate with the police we can see that in Islington the public is very divided in relation to the police and both these decisions are extreme. On the one hand as demonstrated earlier, almost half of the victims of crime have no confidence in the local police. On the other hand, the balance of victims look to their local police for assistance by reporting their crimes. A high willingness to co-operate with the police by one segment of the population is contrasted by a low estimate of police competence by another segment of the population. Furthermore, it is not unreasonable to expect that a portion of those reporting offences do so merely to register insurance claims without confidence in police efficacy.

This point will be further elaborated in Chapter 4. A lack of police confidence is problematic on its own, but it appears to be exacerbated by the fact that the Islington police may be less willing to co-operate with some segments of the population than their counterparts throughout the country. This would mean that despite good intentions, and a public relations programme aimed at increasing public co-operation with the police, the current police practice actually serves to alienate segments of the population even further. This would not be so likely to happen were the police able to reduce biases in recording practices and subsequent investigations. This point will be further elaborated later in this chapter.

Figure 2.1 is a graphic representation of the data presented in Table 2.5. It illustrates visually the comparative amounts of crime for each of the broader categories and their proportionate rates of reporting and recording. Each of these categories is broken down in the following sections and similar graphs present the comparisons of the sub-categories by offence.

Finally, Table 2.6 (p.89) presents the estimates per 1,000 households of the categories of offence by Ward from the previous two tables. Again under each of the following sections graphic representations will be provided for each offence by Ward indicating visually both the variation in the Borough of rates of offences, and which Wards inhere the least and the most risks for each category of offence.

Burglary

The ICS found that although respondents were given precise definitions on the questionnaire, sometimes they reported a case of Break and Enter and Theft or Damage when the offence did not involve breaking into the dwelling. Sometimes they left the door unlocked or in very few instances, they were conned at the door and allowed people into their flat or home under the misconception that the visit was official, only to find that the officials were really villains who subsequently removed items of value. For these cases, we have used the category "illegal" entry to separate out differences in reporting practices. For example, the victims might feel that it was their own fault and be more reluctant to report the offence to the police. The separation of these categories for analytical reasons allows us to make explicit any implicit offsetting trends. Figure 2.2 illustrates the comparative rates of burglary and the reporting and recording rates estimated by the survey. The survey found that 13% of the cases were actually illegal entry. Overall the rate of reporting to the police was 78%. This meant that comparison with the police statistics indicated recording rates of 52% of those reported to the police or 41% of the actual estimated number of burglaries.

As suspected, Figure 2.2 illustrates quite a difference in reporting rates between the two classifications. For burglaries involving break and entry 82% were reported to the police while of those not involving an actual break-in only 54% were brought to the attention of the police.

One strategy which the BCS followed was to classify the different areas of the country according to risk. Unfortunately, the report of the findings does not systematically compare the differential rates across the classifications. It does report on burglaries, however, that in the high risk areas (ie those most directly comparable to Islington as an inner-city location) the rate of burglary was 12%.

The rate of burglary uncovered by the ICS is very close to this figure at 12.25%.[1] However, what is interesting about our survey is that we are able to break down this rate of burglary which represents a Borough-wide average in order to measure the variation of rates of burglary, not only geographically by Ward but by various groups within the population as well. We found a striking range of rates of burglary in each of the separate Wards in the Borough. Mildmay, which incorporates a portion of Stoke Newington, was the highest rate of burglary (342 cases of burglary for every 1,000 households) while Holloway has the least number at 40 incidents of burglary for every 1000 households. In short, the area with the highest risk of burglary in Islington is eight and one half times as high as the area with the lowest rate of burglary.

Not only is this revelation obviously important for policing strategy, but it must also be borne in mind that a full 50% of the households in Islington were never touched by any of the crimes that we followed up in the survey. Holding the average constant for the entire Borough, we find that the estimated 342 burglaries in Mildmay really occurs for every five hundred houses that are hit by crime in any year. The conclusion to be drawn from this fact is that if a household in Mildmay has been burgled once this year, there is a higher probability that that household will be burgled again this year. It may seem odd that the best predictor of whether one's household will be burgled or not is whether or not it has been burgled already. In practice, however, contrary to popular opinion, it would seem that most burglary is neither professional nor opportunistic. *Rather the amateur burglars tend to break into the same places over and over again because they found that they were not caught there before, or that the household, by experience, was an easy target.*

When we break down the rates of burglary by sub-populations some very interesting patterns emerge. Table 2.7 illustrates the variation in rates of burglary by a number of selected variables.

Table 2.7 clearly illustrates that young people, black people and men are the most at risk for burglary, especially if they live in the Mildmay area. However, by breaking down the rates of burglary by the scales shown in Table 2.8 we can see that people's fear and satisfaction with the neighbourhood is directly related to their experience of burglary.

Table 2.8 clearly illustrates that the more people are burgled the more they expect to be burgled and the less they are satisfied with their neighbourhood.

Table 2.7   Burglary rates (by sub-population)

Group		Rate per 1000 Households
The entire Borough		122.5
Age	16–24	155
	25–44	139
	45 plus	100
Race	White	117
	Black	188
	Asian	112
	Other non-white	117
Gender	Male	140
	Female	108

Base: All households weighted n= 5939

Table 2.8   Breakdown of rates of burglary (by scale scores)

Scale		Rate per 1000 Households
Satisfaction with neighbourhood		
	high	000
	medium	80
	low	239
Fear of crime	high	122
	medium	132
	low	92
Probability of crime in next year		
	high	311
	medium	95
	low	52

Base: All households weighted n= 5939

Contrary to the findings of other surveys, people's fear of crime and conception of crime appears to be much more realistic than the analysis of the data from the first BCS suggests. The ICS, on the other hand, shows that those groups which have the highest rates of burglary are most likely to express a high fear of crime than those groups which have a lower rate of burglary.

Some other interesting findings are presented by breakdowns with other variables. People who go out in the evenings are putting their homes at great risk to burglary, so that we should expect a higher rate of burglary in those households where the occupants are more frequently out in the evenings. People who do not go out at all in the evening can expect 70 burglaries for each 1000 households while the rate is 152 per one thousand households where occupants are out more than twice per week. Also, contacts with the police in the last year are related to rates of burglary. For every 1000 households in which there has been no contact with the police we can expect 66 incidents of burglary while for every 1000 households in which more than one contact was made with the police we can expect 218 incidents of burglary. This is not to suggest that contact with the police causes burglary but rather the relationship between the public and the police as measured by contacts is directly related to the rate of burglary. In part this is due to people reporting their burglaries, and in part due to the police concentrating their efforts on a limited 'clientele' (Smith, 1983, p315).

In terms of socio-economic status it is not always the most financially well-off people who get victimized by burglary. Table 2.9 breaks down the rates of burglary by a number of socio-economic indicators:

Table 2.9   Burglary rates (by socio-economic status)

Indicator		*Rate per 1000 Households*
Income	under £3000	137
	3000–7999	79
	8000–11999	158
	12000 plus	156
Work status	unemployed	111
	employed	136
Tenure	owned	117
	public rental	119
	private rental	133
	squatters	275

Base: All households weighted n= 5939

Table 2.9 clearly demonstrates that people living in private rentals in Islington have a higher risk of burglary than people in public housing. Because Council housing is divided between street properties and housing estates it would be difficult to judge at this point which was more subject to risk. It seems that people in the 3000-7999 category are the only ones below the average, and people in the lowest income category have a higher than average rate of burglary indicating that a large proportion of burglary is aimed at persons in the lower socio-economic categories. A quick glance at the data in Table 2.9 shows that unlike other studies the rates of burglary in the inner city are not highest in the lowest income group.

The recent Canadian Urban Victimization Study found a similar pattern as the ICS and came to the following conclusion:

"Although professionals working in the field have long held the belief that break-and-entry offences occur more frequently among low income households, this is not so clearly the case in the seven urban centres studied. From these findings, families with incomes lower than (9,000 Dollars) per year or between (20,000 and 29,000 Dollars) had greater break and entry rates than households with incomes between (10,000 and 19,000 Dollars). The highest break and enter rates were for households with incomes over (40,000 Dollars). These complex relationships between income and risk may reflect changing demographic trends within our cities. The residential development of inner city areas may bring those with high and low incomes into closer proximity than has been the case since the first development of dormitory suburbs and communities, and this mix of income groups may well mean a wider distribution of risk across income groups."

(*Provincial Task Force on Justice for Victims of Crime*, 1983, pp14-15).

Because the ICS found identical patterns of burglary to those cited above within different income categories, we would agree with the conclusions of the Task Force. The high rate of burglary in Mildmay, therefore, is probably due more to its greater mixture of income groups than the relatively lower income areas characterized by high rates of burglary. Holloway, on the other hand, is probably characterized by a more homogeneous income group. If this conclusion is true, we should expect to find a similar pattern with vandalism.

From all of the data presented here on burglaries it would seem that there is indeed a wide degree of variation both by Ward and by other demographic characteristics. Table 2.10 breaks down burglary rates by the three variables, age, race, and gender in order to make explicit any offsetting trends.

Table 2.10   Burglary rates per 1000 households (by age, race and gender)

	White		Black		Asian		Other Non-Whites	
	Male	Female	Male	Female	Male	Female	Male	Female
16–24	153	149	125	194	319	16	207	139
25–44	135	140	209	144	10	193	103	152
45+	138	59	177	307	28	83	57	105

Base: All households weighted n= 5939

The table illustrates that while younger persons are more likely to have been victims of burglary, the most at risk are elderly black females and young Asian males. From the information presented in Table 2.10 it would seem that the most important predictor of burglary is race followed by gender, and then age.

Vandalism

A number of difficulties arise when developing indicators of vandalism. Firstly, of all crimes, criminal damage is the one which is most prevalent.

The 1985 N District *Divisional Plans* make the claim that one third of all crime is vehicle-related, and that the lion's share of these is criminal damage to vehicles as opposed to vehicle theft or theft from vehicle. It was obvious that a large number of criminal damage occurrences would be uncovered by the survey and to follow up each of these incidents with a phase II questionnaire would be very costly. As a result, it was decided that we would follow up only cases of vandalism to the home or property surrounding it. For this reason, we have two categories of vandalism: that followed up for which we are able to make estimates of reporting rates and that which was not followed up, *viz* criminal damage to vehicle, for which we could not make an estimate of reporting rates.

A second difficulty was that a number of the cases (23%) were discovered to be vandalism to vehicle when we actually followed them up. The difficulty here is that the police only report cases of criminal damage and do not distinguish between criminal damage to home or property and criminal damage to vehicle. By using a procedure whereby we developed a combination of both the followed-up categories and the one not followed up, we were able to arrive at estimates which allowed direct comparisons with the N District statistics. In order to accomplish this and present the findings in a consistent manner with the other categories of offence, it was necessary to make an estimate of the reporting rates of vandalism which was not followed up. This estimate was arrived at by calculating the reporting rate of vandalism to vehicles which was uncovered by followed-up cases of reported vandalism found to be against a vehicle rather than to the home.

Figure 2.4 is the graphic depiction of the relative rates of the different categories of vandalism, their respective reporting rates and the rates of recording as gleaned from a comparison of the survey data to the N District crime statistics. As can be seen from Figure 2.4, 77% of the vandalism which was disclosed on the survey actually turned out to be vandalism to the home, of which 38% of the occurrences were reported to the police. It can be seen that there is a much higher rate of reporting (45.6%) for vehicle-related vandalism than that done to the home. One probable reason for the difference is that insurance claims are more likely for vehicles than for home property. The overall rate of reporting vandalism as uncovered by the ICS is slightly higher than the national average of 21%, which explains why the percentage of actual vandalism recorded in the police statistics is also higher than the national average of 8%. However, as pointed out earlier, the ratio of recording to reported is lower in Islington than the national average of 37%.

Figure 2.5 represents the distribution of vandalism which was followed up on the survey by Ward. Canonbury West would appear to have the worst record for vandalism at 530 incidents for every 1000 households[2] while Highbury would appear to have the best record for rates of criminal damage at 13 cases per 1000 households in the Ward. As with burglary, the striking variation in rates from Ward to Ward cannot go unnoticed. Again, when we consider that 50% of the households were not even touched by any of the crimes followed up on the survey, the high rate of vandalism approximately doubles if we only consider the households which were affected by crime. This again indicates that vandalism as well as burglary is more often directed at the same targets over and over again. The implications for crime prevention initiatives, therefore, would be similar to those of burglary.

Table 2.11 breaks down the rates of vandalism across age, race and gender in order to examine what variations occur in these subpopulations.

Table 2.11   Vandalism rates (by age, race and gender)

Group		Rate per 1000 Households
The entire Borough		202
Age	16–24	247
	25–44	224
	45 plus	172
Race	White	192
	Black	324
	Asian	213
	Other non-white	121
Gender	Male	228
	Female	181

Base: All households weighted n= 5939

Table 2.11 shows that an inverse relationship exists between age and vandalism in that as age increases the number of reported occurrences of vandalism goes down. This does not mean to say that the older respondents are, therefore, unaffected by vandalism or that vandalism is less of a problem for this group. When we consider that the largest group by age is the older age group then it becomes obvious that in terms of absolute numbers the amount of vandalism directed towards this group is high. Nevertheless, it is the younger person who is most at risk of being victimized by an occurrence of criminal damage.

Black people are the ones who are the most likely to disclose occurrences of vandalism on the survey while the other ethnic groups seem to be very similar. Men have a higher risk than women of being victimized by criminal damage, although the difference does not seem to be great enough to consider in any detail. Victimization in the form of vandalism appears also to be related to the scale scores on satisfaction with the neighbourhood and fear of crime as illustrated in Table 2.12.

Table 2.12 indicates that there is a direct relationshp between fear of crime, probability of crime in the next year and rates of vandalism. An inverse relationship exists between vandalism and satisfaction with the neighbourhood. It would seem that these scales would be good predictors for the variations in rates of vandalism. More importantly, however, these data would once again indicate that people's fear of crime is directly related to their experiences of vandalism. Those people who experience the highest rates of vandalism are most likely to demonstrate a fear of crime and least likely to be satisfied with the neighbourhood, and this finding corroborates our findings on burglary.

Table 2.12   Vandalism rates (by scale scores)

Scale		Rate per 1000 Households
Satisfaction with neighbourhood		
	high	18
	medium	171
	low	318
Fear of crime	high	223
	medium	216
	low	83
Probability of crime in next year		
	high	400
	medium	183
	low	61

Base: All households weighted n= 5939

As with burglary, a relationship appears to exist between rates of vandalism and both contacts with the police and evenings per week absent from the home. For every 1000 households in which no contacts with the police were measured, the rate of vandalism was 91 as compared to 343 cases of vandalism for every 1000 households in which more than one contact with the police was measured. As with burglary this is most likely due to the reasons that police are more likely to be contacted by victims and police are more likely to concentrate their efforts on specific groups of people.

For every 1000 households in which no outings per week were measured, the rate of criminal damage occurrences was 113, as compared to 222 for every 1000 households in which more than two outings per week were measured. People going out in the evening are putting their property at more risk to vandalism than those who do not, but a careful look at the rates for other variables such as age and race would seem to indicate that outings per week is not as important a predictor as it is for burglary.

Since the findings of the variations of rates of vandalism so closely parallel those for burglary, we should expect to find similar findings for the socio-economic indicators and vandalism. Table 2.13 presents this breakdown:

Table 2.13   Vandalism rates (by socio-economic indicators)

Indicator		Rate per 1000 Households
Income	under £3000	174
	3000–7999	169
	8000–11999	242
	12000 plus	313
Work status	unemployed	220
	employed	170
Tenure	owned	345
	public rental	203
	private rental	95
	squatters	274

Base: All households weighted n= 5939

As with the findings on burglary, it would appear that most at risk of vandalism are those within the higher socio-economic categories since high income and ownership of housing are both associated with higher rates of vandalism. There are two reasons for this. Firstly, those people living on housing estates are most likely to experience vandalism vicariously. That is to say that while they are not directly the victims of a great deal of vandalism, most vandalism occurs to the public areas and these people would be less likely to report themselves as being the victim. Secondly, because of the smaller numbers of people in owned accommodation, the absolute occurrence of vandalism is probably much lower but because it is felt personally, criminal damage to personal property is more likely to be reported. *In any event the survey offers little doubt that the majority of vandalism occurs to public property and is most prevalent in an absolute sense on housing estates.* We would speculate once more that the diversity of income groups in a particular area is related in a similar way to rates of vandalism as it is to rates of burglary.

The variations of rates of vandalism is extreme in Islington, whether by Ward or by sub-population. Table 2.14 presents the breakdown by age, race and gender in order to make explicit any offsetting trends:

Table 2.14   Vandalism rates per 1000 households (by age, race and gender)

	White		Black		Asian		Other Non-Whites	
	Male	Female	Male	Female	Male	Female	Male	Female
16–24	232	207	178	553	99	418	000	346
25–44	230	211	173	422	73	84	112	101
45+	248	105	132	395	393	432	000	158

Base: All households weighted n= 5939

The data presented in Table 2.14 are staggering. *There can be no doubt that the infinitely highest category of risk of criminal damage is all black women.* Furthermore, it would seem that a very common target for criminal damage is elderly Asian people. Elderly Asian men are three times as likely as elderly black men to be victimized by vandalism. Because the figures for whites as opposed to all other groups are relatively similar across age and across gender, one might be led to conclude that a great deal of vandalism is both racially and sexually motivated.

In conclusion, there is a great deal of vandalism in Islington generally and the actual rates of vandalism vary from group to group and Ward to Ward. There appears to be both a racial and sexual bias towards victims of vandalism and the highest rates appear to be in the youngest category except for Asian people whose highest category of risk is the oldest age group. There can be little doubt that vandalism is directed most against those who are least able to prevent or defend it.

Theft

As with vandalism, the category of theft from person proved to be problematic. The first difficulty is that unlike burglary or vandalism, theft from person can occur anywhere away from home. This means that Islington residents are likely to experience victimization as theft from person outside the Borough and even if reported they would not necessarily end up on N District police statistics. Similarly, non-Islington residents could easily fall prey to this type of crime while visiting Islington and if reported, these incidents may end up on Islington N District police statistics. Secondly, the ICS was only interested in theft from person which could mean anything from being pickpocketed in the street or public place to actual armed robbery where violence is used. For purposes of the survey we were interested in only the categories which would be equated with the police statistics on theft from person which they break down into the two categories of snatches and pickpocketing, and robbery which the police report in the two categories of street robbery of personal property and other robbery.

In practice, however, this ideal was impossible to achieve. As with other categories of crime which the survey investigated, it turned out in the follow-up interviews that some of the cases reported as theft from person were some other kind of theft. Sometimes, for example, a respondent might report as an incident of theft from person an occurrence in which someone rifled their desk at the office while they were out to lunch or some similar type of event. These we classified as "other theft". The problem in doing so, however, is that there are a number of categories of theft which are reported in the police statistics, so that their residual category of "other" is very different from our residual category of "other". Comparisons of these categories, therefore, should not be taken as seriously as the others. When we calculated the total number of crimes of theft recorded by the police we did so for the following categories only: robbery, theft from person, other theft. Not included was the category of theft from motor vehicle. The consequence of these difficulties was that we showed a higher rate of recording than reporting on the category of other theft, although because of the definitional problems and the fact that we did not really enquire about other forms of theft from our respondents this difference was to be expected. Figure 2.6 provides a graphic depiction of the proportions of theft uncovered by the survey, and the accompanying rates of reporting and recording.

Figure 2.6 shows that, of all the occurrences uncovered and followed up by the survey, 63% turned out to be theft from person while 16% turned out to be robbery defined as a theft from the person where a weapon, threat of a weapon or physical violence was used to carry out the theft. There is a much higher recording rate for robbery than there is for either theft from person or other theft, indicating that there is a high police priority on this type of offence. The figure of 468% recorded other thefts or actual other thefts is meaningless because as indicated this category for police recording is defined quite differently for purposes of the survey. While theft from person and robbery have identical reporting rates, and while many more theft from person incidents happen than robberies, more robberies end up in the police statistics than do theft from person incidents. This finding illustrates that a police bias in recording robberies at the expense of thefts produces the conception that robberies are more prevalent than theft from person which is not the case. The work of Stuart Hall *et al.* (1978) is somewhat supported by our data, although it would seem that Hall makes the error of attributing the cause of public misconception about robbery to biased media reporting. *The ICS data, however, illustrate that the misrepresentation of rates of robbery in relation to other forms of theft is probably more due to biased policing practice as it pertains to the recording of crime than it is to biased media reporting.* The implications of this finding will be further elaborated in the section on bicycle theft. For now suffice it to say that a theory of police statistics would have to take into account the biases in the police recording and subsequent investigation of crime.

Figure 2.7 breaks down the category of all theft from person followed up by the survey into its distribution by Ward. This figure illustrates that the greatest risk of theft from person occurs for residents of St. Peter's, while the least risk of theft from person would be associated with residents of Holloway, the rates being 219 and 68 incidents per 1000 households respectively. The worst Ward in the Borough for risk of theft from person is 3.2 times as risky as the best indicating once more a wide degree of variation on this category of crime. Nevertheless, it would appear that there is less variation in theft than vandalism or burglary indicating that personal vulnerability is not as related to geographic location as are the household offences. While conducting the fieldwork, one of our interviewers was robbed of his briefcase in Hillrise. One white youth and one black youth approached him in the street during broad daylight, one of them spraying a chemical in his eyes with a water pistol. The point of the anecdote is that theft from person or robbery can occur anywhere and at anytime and although there is variation across the Borough in terms of rates of occurrence, simply staying away from areas where the rates are higher is no guarantee that one will not encounter this type of crime.

In order to illustrate who is the most likely target or victim of theft from person Table 2.15 presents the rates of theft by age, race and gender:

Table 2.15   Theft from person (by age, race and gender)

Group		Rate per 1000 Households
The entire Borough		139
Age	16–24	245
	25–44	188
	45 plus	71
Race	White	132
	Black	216
	Asian	156
	Other non-white	169
Gender	Male	120
	Female	155

Base: All households weighted n= 5939

Table 2.15 demonstrates that the risk of theft or robbery decreases with age. Younger persons are much more likely than older persons to be victimized by this type of crime. Similarly, black persons, generally, are more likely to be preyed upon by this type of victimization than their white counterparts. While men generally experience a rate of victimization below the average for the Borough, women generally have a higher rate of risk than the average for the Borough. The information from Table 2.15 illustrates that it is the less powerful who are most often preyed upon by this type of crime.

As with the categories of crime investigated above, the relationship of theft to the public's perception of satisfaction with the neighbourhood and fear of crime is a strong one, as illustrated in Table 2.16.

From Table 2.16 it is apparent that satisfaction with the neighbourhood has an inverse relationship with the risk of theft from person. Those households which have experienced higher rates of theft are more likely to be dissatisfied with their area than those experiencing low rates of theft from person. The converse occurs for the other two scales.

Table 2.16   Theft from person (by scales)

Scale		Rate per 1000 Households
Satisfaction with neighbourhood		
	high	37
	medium	128
	low	224
Fear of crime	high	179
	medium	129
	low	92
Probability of crime in next year		
	high	184
	medium	138
	low	93

Base: All households weighted n= 5939

Those persons from households where higher rates of theft occur are more likely to express both a fear of crime generally and the perception that they are more likely to experience crime in the next year than are their counterparts in areas where there are lower rates of theft from person. Once more the survey data strongly suggest that people's perceptions and fear of crime are not out of proportion to their experiences.

Contacts with the police and the number of evenings away from the home are strongly related to the victimization rates for theft. If once more we conceptualize the police as concentrating their efforts in specific sub-populations on the one hand and consider that the more times spent out in public increases the probability of risk, then we can predict that a positive relationship should exist between both of these variables and victimization rates for theft. Table 2.17 illustrates this relationship:

Table 2.17   Theft from person (by police contacts and outings)

Group		Rate per 1000 Households
Contacts with police	none	67
	one	183
	two plus	231
Outings per week	none	98
	one-two	134
	three plus	167

Base: All households weighted n= 5939

Table 2.17 clearly demonstrates that *those people who have had the most contacts with the police are also those most likely to be victims of theft from person.* In part, this relationship is due to reporting crimes to the police but, as the first category in the table illustrates, much of the crime does not even get reported. This finding does provide some support for the notion that the police concentrate their efforts on specific groups. As predicted, the risk of theft from person increases directly with the number of evenings out per week. Since going out in the evening generally involves some expense we should be able to predict that people in the middle income categories, those persons working for wage, should be the most vulnerable to theft. Table 2.18 provides a breakdown of the rates of theft from person by various socio-economic indicators:

Table 2.18 Theft from person (by socio-economic categories)

Indicator		Rate per 1000 Households
Income	under £3000	99
	3000–7999	168
	8000–11999	145
	12000 plus	215
Work status	unemployed	117
	employed	162
Tenure	owned	121
	public rental	125
	private rental	195
	squatters	325

Base: All households weighted n= 5939

Table 2.18 shows that socio-economic indicators are not necessarily directly related with theft from person. It would seem that people living in Council housing are in a better position than those living in private rentals, although squats are the most vulnerable to this type of crime. While people in the highest income brackets are the most vulnerable to crime, those living in owned accommodation are the least vulnerable. Due to the relative rarity of high income households in Islington, it would appear once more as if the bulk of the theft is aimed at working class persons in the low to middle income categories. This indicates that most of the thefts occur in the low to middle income categories, as people who own their homes are in a better position financially to protect themselves from thefts in the street. The concept of diverse income groups living in close geographic proximity is probably related to the distribution of theft.

Table 2.19 breaks down the rates for theft from person to illustrate any offsetting trends which may be implicit in the relationship among age, race, and gender. Once more the breakdown provided by Table 2.19 illustrates that not only are women at a much higher point on the risk curve, but black women in particular are the most vulnerable. Again because of the smaller populations of the various components of the black community, the majority of theft from person occurs outside this com-

munity. Nevertheless, the differential of risk rates between the white and
the black community are so striking that the vulnerable position in which
these people find themselves cannot and should not be ignored. A similar
situation can be conceptualized for women. There can be little doubt
whatever that most of the actual number of thefts from person occur to
female victims, and the risks for women are much higher than for men. It
would appear that the pattern of theft from person is similar to vandalism
in that, by the variables covered in Table 2.19, the most probable target of
theft from person is the least likely to have either much in the way of
valuables or ability to protect themselves, indicating the extreme pred-
atory nature of this type of crime. It may be fair to conclude that offenders
under this classification are more concerned with being successful in
carrying out the offence than they are about the financial rewards.

Table 2.19   Theft from person (by age, race and gender)

| | White | | Black | | Asian | | Other Non-Whites | |
	Male	Female	Male	Female	Male	Female	Male	Female
16–24	188	293	174	276	38	503	69	254
25–44	152	200	137	361	123	251	160	329
45+	85	54	66	233	000	223	000	105

Base: All households weighted n= 5939

Assault

Measurement of the frequency of assault proves to be a very limited exercise, especially if the purpose is for comparison to the official criminal
statistics. The police reporting of assault is limited to the category "violence against the person", leaving a very broad category for the numerous
types of assault which may occur. On the less serious side, many assaults
proved to be simple pushing, or sometimes a punch-up outside a pub after
closing time where no one is actually injured and the participants are
willingly partaking in the activity. On the more serious side some assaults
are very vicious attacks which leave the victim seriously injured or hos-
pitalized. Furthermore, there are many assaults which occur between
people who know each other, and there are those which happen to victims
who have no idea about the identity of the assailant. One of the more
frequent forms of assault in which the victim and offender know each
other is *domestic violence*. This category was included in the ICS,
although it is not reported in the N District crime statistics. The reason for
not reporting this form of assault is not because the police do not maintain
this information. McCabe and Sutcliffe (1978) report a number of occurrences of domestic violence which were known to be such by the police

but were either not recorded, claiming that it was not their responsibility, or were recorded but under a different classification:

"A woman asked for police assistance because her son had arrived home, attacked his sister, and was knocking the place to pieces. A patrol car was sent at once and the youth arrested. The charge in this case was not assault, but criminal damage . . . ." (page 50)

or on page 78:

". . . a police officer on patrol saw a man assaulting a woman in the street. On enquiry he found that the assaulter and victim were husband and wife. The man was very drunk and abusive. The police officer told both parties to behave themselves and go home. The wife began to walk towards home and her husband followed her, but, when he caught up with her, he knocked her to the ground and renewed his assault. The police officer intervened and tried to reason with the man, but he continued his abuse and refused to be quiet. He was arrested and taken to the station where he was charged with being drunk and disorderly."

and further on page 79:

"A man was arrested in the street when he was trying to kick in the door of the woman with whom he was living. He resisted all attempts to quiet him and assaulted the officer who was trying to restrain him. He too was brought to the station and charged with drunken and disorderly behaviour."

McCabe and Sutcliffe (1978:78) conclude: "There were several other 'domestic' incidents of this kind which were dealt with, in Salford at least, by charges of drunkenness." It is clear from this study that the police are often aware of domestic disputes and violence but they do not report them as a separate category. For purposes of the ICS, it was felt that the category of domestic violence is one which requires specific attention, both because of its significance as a social problem as well as its potential seriousness to the victims which are usually women and younger children.

Another category of assault which is of significant importance but is not recorded in the police statistics is *racial assault*. Again due to the absence of this category, estimates of the frequency of this type of assault remain speculative at best. For this reason, the category was included in the ICS in order to allow an estimate of the frequency of this type of assault which would be more scientific than current estimates.

A final category which was included in the survey, but which no other survey or publication of police statistics includes, is *police assault*. Once again, estimates of this type of assault are not readily available due to the lack of measurements. Both the Commander of N District and the Commissioner stand on public record as not tolerating this type of behaviour by their officers. In the recent case in Islington in which the victim lost one eye and was left almost blinded by a police assault, the officer responsible received a prison term while other officers were disciplined. This type of incident reinforces both the fact that this kind of assault occurs, and secondly that if detected can be subject to serious penalties in that senior officers will not tolerate this kind of behaviour. For this reason, we felt that it would be both important and simple to separate out those instances where a clear case of police assault had occurred. In all three cases, ie domestic violence, racist assault, police assault, the coders were instructed to read carefully the description of the offence given by the respondent and recorded by the interviewer and to code only those categories. All other assaults were recorded as "other assault". The following citations from the questionnaires give an example of each of the three categories of assault:

A. Domestic assault – white female, 20 years old:
"I was regularly beaten up by my boyfriend. The last time we just had an argument over something and it ended with him beating me up. I was nine months pregnant at the time and was taken into hospital for fear of harming the pregnancy."

B. Racist assault – West Indian male, 34 years old:
"I was jogging home from Christmas party at 2:00 A.M. My aunt and niece were driving the car with equipment in it – no place for me. Four youths shouted: 'Hey Paki we're going to beat you up.' They assaulted me. My aunt and niece drove up in the car and they assaulted them with road lamps. A passerby had called the police who came and arrested them. In my opinion the police tried to hush up the matter by having a summary trial. The Judge said he could not impose adequate punishment for the crime because it did not come up before the crown court."

C. Police Assault – West Indian male, 20 year old:
"I was walking down Blackstock Road. I was stopped by a policeman – uniformed officer I'd had trouble with before but he was off duty in plain clothes. He took me down a quiet side street and said; 'I've got you this time you fucking dirty nigger' and started to punch and kick me. I went down and he kicked me in the ribs and head before walking off whistling to himself."

While each of the above cases illustrates that sometimes the classifications are clear, sometimes the relationships are different in the domestic and racist assaults. Sometimes police assault is related to a situation which is interpreted as unusual by the police, as the following citations illustrate:

A. Domestic assault – West Indian female, 42 years old:
"My son-in-law kicked the door in (my daughter was staying) one morning and he just started hitting me and kicking me."

B. Racist assault – West Indian female, 23 years old:
"I was crossing the road when a woman attacked me from behind. She hit me with her bags and called me a black bastard."

C. Police assault – West Indian male, 18 years old:
"Coming home late one night with a group of friends and attacked by a group from the Irish club. Police arrived on scene before things got heavy and picked out respondent and one member of the rival group and made them fight in the back of the van. When respondent won, he was bashed on the head by a policeman and taken to court the next day."

All of the above examples show that it is often not too difficult to place certain events within the categories of assault which we recorded in the survey.

Figure 2.8 presents in graphic detail the numbers of assaults for all of Islington, the proportion which are reported, the proportions which are recorded and the relative proportions for each of the sub-categories of assault estimated by the survey. In following up all cases of assault reported, we discovered that an alarming proportion of assault – 22% – is domestic in nature. It can also be seen that of all the categories of assault, domestic assault is the least likely to be reported to the police. The survey estimates that 2500 incidents of domestic violence were aimed at residents of Islington in the last year, and this figure is probably an underestimate since we are fairly certain that at different times in the interview schedule it may have been difficult for the respondent to report a case of domestic violence, or that the respondent felt too ashamed to admit it to the interviewer.[3]

The survey estimates that 7% of all assaults which were aimed at Islington residents last year were racist in nature. Again this figure is probably an underestimate for two reasons. Firstly, not all of the descriptions provided by the respondents give sufficient enough detail to classify their assault as racist, if in fact it was. Secondly, there was a number of instances in which the respondent tended to ignore minor racist assault. During the supervision of an interview with a Bengali male, it became quite apparent to the field supervisor that the level of racial abuse to which the respondent's family had been exposed was quite high, although from the respondent's point of view it was no particular difficulty. It was only at the end of the interview and with a great deal of probing that the respondent remembered that he had been slapped in the head one day by two "skinheads". When asked why he did not relate this incident earlier in the interview he replied that "it was nothing". *It would seem from this example that some segments of the population are so over-exposed to this kind of behaviour that it becomes part of their everyday reality and escapes their memory in the interview situation, indicating that our estimate is probably low.* For this type of assault, the reporting rate to the police is the second lowest. While there is no special category for racist assault in the N District crime statistics, the Islington police do keep records on racial assault. At a meeting of the Islington Police Consultative Group June 11, 1985, statements regarding racial assault were presented orally to the Committee by the Community Liaison Officer and are worth citing here:

"Supt. Hill informed the Consultative Group that a total of 40 cases of racial harassment had been reported, which represented an increase over the last year. This did not indicate that there was any necessary increase in racial harassment within the Borough but rather that there were more cases being reported to the Police either by the Council or by the Community." (*Minute 32, Item 9 of the minutes*).

The above minute illustrates that the police do keep records and that they are certainly aware of the difficulties associated with interpreting their own statistics. In relation to the forty cases which the Community Liaison Officer mentioned, it can be seen that as with other offence categories, police statistics on racial assault grossly under-estimate the frequency. By contrast, the ICS estimates that at least 870 cases of racial assault occurred last year in Islington and that this estimate is conservative. Were we to consider Superintendent Hill's report as official, we could then calculate that the recording rate for racial assault in Islington is approximately 4.5%, which is by far the lowest of all categories for which we can make comparisons.

While only 3.5% of all assaults aimed at Islington residents last year were police assaults, this equates to an estimate of approximately 400 cases. Naturally, not all of these assaults would have occurred in Islington but some would have happened within other Districts of the MPD. Nevertheless, this category has the highest reporting rate of all assaults at 46%, and we should expect that approximately 180 police assaults would have been brought to the attention of the police. It may well be that a number of these occurred outside Islington or that a number of these may be unsubstantiated after more in-depth investigation. In either case, it would seem that because these figures are not published by the police an assessment of this nature cannot be made. Finally, it should be pointed out that just because an offence of alleged police assault is reported to them does not mean that a formal complaint has been lodged. Statistics are made available on the number of official complaints by the police.

Assault is one category of offence where the attrition rate through the system is highest. As the earlier citations from McCabe and Sutcliffe illustrate, often assaults brought to the attention of the police are defined as offences such as criminal damage. In all, only about 6% of all assaults make it into the criminal statistics in Islington. Unfortunately, neither the BCS nor the MCS provide sufficient information to make comparisons on recording of assault. BCS estimates that 473 incidents of assault occur for every 10,000 households on the average nationally. By comparison the rate in Islington is almost four times as high at 1,856.

As with the other categories of offence looked at this far, the distribution of assault demonstrates a considerable variation from Ward to Ward in Islington. Figure 2.9 illustrates the rates of assault per 1000 households by Ward. Rates range from a low of 41 in St George's to a high of 594 in Thornhill.

There is also a considerable variation in assault rates within various segments of the population. Table 2.20 illustrates the rates of assaults by age, race and gender.

Table 2.20   Assault rates (by age, race and gender)

Group		Rate per 1000 Households
The entire Borough		186
Age	16–24	486
	25–44	256
	45 plus	38
Race	White	176
	Black	297
	Asian	157
	Other non-white	185
Gender	Male	152
	Female	213

Base: All households weighted n= 5939

Clearly, the information in Table 2.20 illustrates a definite negative correlation with age. Younger people on average are nearly thirteen times as likely to be assaulted as people in the over 45 years of age category. Black people on average are almost twice as likely as other people to be victims of assault, and women half as likely again as men to be assaulted. Because only 6% of all assault ever gets recorded in the criminal statistics, it is very unlikely that the risks of assault can be established from these figures. When one recognizes the differentials in reporting by the sub-groups of the population, and the recording biases of the police, it becomes clear that the relative risks are probably very different from what we have been led to believe from the crime statistics. As the previous citations demonstrate, women are at risk of domestic assault and these incidents rarely get recorded as assault. In terms of the safety of women, it is clear that incidents of domestic violence should be recorded by the police and reported to the public, in order that recording biases can be identified and informed crime prevention initiatives aimed at the safety of women be developed.[4]

Table 2.21 presents the breakdown of rates of assault and the scale values for satisfaction with the neighbourhood and fear of crime. The table demonstrates that there is an inverse relationship between satisfaction with the neighbourhood and rates of assault. Households in which people express the highest satisfaction are twelve times less likely to experience an incident of assault than households with people expressing low satisfaction. Conversely, households from which the respondents expressed a high fear of crime are three times more likely to experience assault than households from which respondents expressed a low fear of crime. And this relationship is nearly identical with the perceived risk of assault occuring during the next year. Since the evidence in Table 2.21 is correlational only, it would be dangerous to speculate on a causal relationship between violence and satisfaction with the neighbourhood. It may be that due to the violence in some neighbourhoods people do not like living there, or it may be that the frustration of living there contributes to violent behaviour, or it may be both. Furthermore, it may well be that there is another variable or variables which contribute to both. Further analysis of the data should help to clarify the nature of this relationship.

As with the other offences examined in-depth by the survey, there are direct relationships between rates of assault and contacts with the police and number of evening absences from the home as illustrated by Table 2.22.

Table 2.21   Assault rates (by scale scores)

Scale		Rate per 1000 Households
Satisfaction with neighbourhood		
	high	29
	medium	142
	low	342
Fear of crime	high	244
	medium	169
	low	80
Probability of crime in next year		
	high	312
	medium	173
	low	120

Base: All households weighted n= 5939

Table 2.22   Assault rates (by contacts with police and absences from home)

Group		Rate per 1000 Households
Contact with the police	none	87
	one	165
	two plus	353
Evenings per week absent	none	91
	one-two	177
	three plus	243

Base: All households weighted n= 5939

Table 2.22 illustrates that people are much more likely to experience assault if they go out during the evenings, and people who have been victims of assault are much more likely to have had contact with the police in the last year. Again this is in part due to reporting (an overall rate of

38%) and in part due to the police concentrating their efforts on specific populations. Because going out in the evening to high risk areas such as pubs, night clubs and so forth involves expense, we should be able to predict that people in the middle categories of income would be at a higher risk. This is because, unlike those from the highest income category, these people are less likely to have vehicles and must make use of the street and public transport. Table 2.23 provides the breakdown of assault rates by various socio-economic indicators:

Table 2.23   Assault rates (by socio-economic status)

Indicator		*Rate per 1000 Households*
Income	under £3000	191
	3000–7999	179
	8000–11999	224
	12000 plus	152
Work status	unemployed	187
	employed	187
Tenure	owned	82
	public rental	285
	private rental	192
	squatters	203

Base: All households weighted n= 5939

Table 2.23, as predicted, demonstrates that those most likely to be victims of assault are those in the 8000-11999 category as are people living in public rentals. There does not seem to be any relationship between work and risk of assault. When one closely examines the tables on assault, it becomes clear that since some people never go out, and since some people never have contact with the police, that there are high levels of assault between people who know each other, probably domestic, and much that does not get reported to the police.

In order to examine the rates of assault in greater depth, Table 2.24 breaks them down by age, by race, by gender:

Table 2.24   Assault rates (by age, race and gender)

Category		*Rates per 1000 Households*		
			Age	
		16–24	*25–44*	*45+*
White	males	401	174	50
	females	588	311	20
Black	males	438	228	124
	females	414	492	44
Asian	males	143	206	112
	females	87	150	250

It is quite clear from Table 2.24 that in the younger two age categories white women are much more likely to experience assault than their male counterparts.

To an extent this may reflect differences in sensitivity to physical violence between men and women. If so, this difference is an indication that women register greater disquiet to physical violence than men, probably because women are more likely to be assaulted by men rather than women. These differences can only be interpreted as clear evidence for high rates of domestic violence in the younger age categories for white women. While black males from the youngest age category are more likely than their white counterparts to experience assault, the reverse is the case for females in this age category. Young white women are much more likely than their black counterparts to experience violence which is probably most often domestic. In the 25-44 category, however, the relationship reverses. Black men are still more likely than their white counterparts to experience assault, but black females are more likely than their white counterparts in this age category to experience assault. It would seem that the risk of domestic violence for black females reaches its mode in the 25-44 age range and is higher than whites at this period while the highest risk for whites is in the younger age category. In all cases, however, domestic violence appears to be quite high in the under 45 age group. The odd case from the table is Asian women whose risk of assault appears to increase with age rather than to decrease, as is the case with all other categories.

In summary, the data on assault presented in the categories covered by the survey illustrate that the frequency and distribution of assault in Islington is quite different than common conception or police statistics would lead us to believe. It is quite clear that when domestic violence is taken into consideration as a form of criminal assault, the people exposed to the greater risk are definitely women, and especially younger women.

Sexual assault

The measurement of sexual assault has traditionally proven to be the most difficult of all crimes. As Chambers and Millar note in their work *Investigating Sexual Assault*:

> "No studies in Britain have specifically sought to find out about how sexual assault victims themselves feel about police, prosecutors, courts and 'the law' after having made a report, nor about the difficulties they experience in making a complaint. One reason for the lack of research has undoubtedly been the methodological difficulties associated with carrying out research within victims of sexual assault, not the least of which is the problem of obtaining a sample of cases." (1983, p7)

It is precisely the methodological difficulties referred to in the above citation which had to be addressed by the ICS in its attempt to measure the frequency of sexual assault. Victimization studies have consistently been criticized, particularly by feminist academics, for grossly under-estimating the extent of this form of victimization. Because sexual assault generally, and particularly the more serious occurrence such as rape, has the potential of creating harmful effects on the victims and their families and because there is often a stigma attached to victims, it is very difficult to ask women in the interview situation to relive their experience. As most crime surveys illustrate, sexual assault is both largely unreported and unrecorded, so that the development of a set of contingencies in the research environment which encourage high rates of disclosure and also offer support to the victim, is ethically and technically necessary.

In one American study, Russel (1982) developed a set of methodologi-cal innovations for interviewing respondents in the crime survey situation aimed at encouraging high rates of disclosure for sexual assault. These included:

1. an interview schedule designed to encourage good rapport with the respondent
2. selection of interviewers based on interviewing skills and sensitivity to sexual assault
3. extensive training of interviewers which included education about rape and sexual abuse and desensitization of sexual words
4. matching interviewers with respondents on ethnic background
5. paying respondents 10 dollars for participation.

Russel found that her survey, carried out at the same location and time as the National Crime Survey in the United States, produced a rate of sexual assault which was seven times higher than the National Crime Survey es-timate. The ICS incorporated a number of Russel's innovations as well as some others. These included:

1. an interview schedule designed to encourage good rapport
2. selection of interviewers based on interviewing skills
3. extensive training of interviewers in relation to sexual assault and its investigation in the field
4. a carefully controlled experimental design which would allow com-parisons of interviewing situations
5. matching of black respondents from the booster samples with female interviewers of the same ethnic background
6. utilization of an indirect questioning procedure which would help to reduce embarrassment or difficulty of relating the incident directly to the interviewer.

Recent studies of sexual assault in England have criticized the BCS for not producing higher rates of disclosure and therefore under-estimating the frequency of sexual assault. In the first sweep of the BCS only one case of attempted rape and a total of 17 sexual assaults were uncovered while the second sweep generated 19 sexual assaults including only one attempted rape – both times with a sample of nearly 11,000 respondents.

By way of comparison Stanko (1983) in her Bradford University study in Leeds found that in a sample of 129 females, 3 rapes and one attempted rape were discovered (*Guardian*, Sept. 5, 1983). Furthermore, Stanko reports that two thirds of her sample reported some experience with violence (*Guardian*, Sept 5, 1983).

In another study carried out by Radford and Laffy (1983) in Balham it was found that, within a sample of 60 women, 118 incidents of violence were measured which ranged in severity from one attempted rape to many instances of verbal abuse (*Guardian*, Sept. 13, 1985).

In yet another study carried out in London, Hall (1985) found that in a sample of 1,236 women the following occurrences were measured:

Type of Assault	Number of Women	Percentage
Rape	214	17
Sexually assaulted	379	31
Raped or sexually assaulted	448	36
Attempted rape	243	20
Rape by more than one assailant	11	1

(Hall, 1985, p33)

The problems with Hall's study have been touched upon elsewhere (Maclean, 1985a) but the methodology of all of these studies is frought with difficulty. Partially due to the lack of sufficient funding which characterizes research in this important area, and partially because the researchers may be over-zealous in trying to illustrate the scope of the problem, these studies over-estimate the frequency of sexual assault and they do not lend themselves to a proper comparison of the BCS findings. For example, the Hall study asks its sample about their lifetime experiences whereas the BCS only asks about the past twelve months. Furthermore, as Hall illustrates, the greatest risk of sexual assault occurs below the age of 16 whereas the BCS only concerns itself with adults over the age of 16. In her criticisms of the BCS, Hall notes that some of the interviewers were men, under the bold assumption that victims of sexual assault will not disclose to male interviewers. It is precisely these kinds of unwarranted assumptions which need to be investigated, and the ICS makes the attempt to do this by making use of the methods described here.

A further difficulty is that the reporting categories found in the police statistics are not sufficient to allow an interpretation of the range of severity of all sexual assaults. The ICS reports in the four categories of:
1. Sexual assault
2. Sexual assault with more than one assailant
3. Rape or attempted rape
4. Rape or attempted rape with more than one assailant.
In order for an assault to be recorded as sexual assault there had to be an

indecent assault in which physical contact was made. The following citations illustrate the range of severity which the survey uncovered.

1. White female, 29 years old:
"My car broke down outside (a pub). Three or four men offered to fix it. After they had got it going again they said 'right, what are you going to do for us?' and one of them said 'it's rape time'. One of them put his arm around me and grabbed me. I handled the affair as well as I could. One of them said 'Alright, just as long as we can have a flash of your knickers' and he actually got down on his hands and knees and peered up my skirt. I said 'you are just like dogs you are' got into my car and drove away."

2. White male:
"A fellow who lives in my girlfriend's block of flats got hold of my daughter who is seven, took his penis out, took her track suit trousers down and started rubbing himself against her. Some children saw this and shouted and he ran off."

3. White female, 23 years old:
"Respondent was hitch-hiking . . . she got a lift in a van. The driver started chatting her up, then pulled off the road, grabbed a hold of her, and threatened to strangle her if she didn't have sex with him – which she did in sheer terror."

The first case was coded as a multiple sexual assault and the third was coded as a single rape. Unfortunately, the second case could not be coded as the child was below the age of our target population. The survey also uncovered a case of homosexual assault against an 11-year-old boy doing his paper round. These types of incidents were not recorded in the survey.

From the literature, and the criticisms which have been discussed, we should expect that Hall's work is an over-estimate in relation to annual occurrences of sexual assault when she claims that one in six women have been raped. On the other side of the coin, the BCS grossly underestimates sexual assault in both of its sweeps. The criticism that male interviewers will not uncover sexual assault is proved to be a fallacy by the ICS. All of the interviewers were well-briefed and trained for this part of the questionnaire, and the male interviewers were found to actually uncover more cases of sexual assault and rape than did the female interviewers. When a case was uncovered by a male interviewer he asked the respondent if she would rather have the follow-up interview conducted by a female interviewer. In most cases the option was not taken up. Of all the sexual assaults that were uncovered by the survey, 52% of those identified as rape and 70% of those that were identified as sexual assault were disclosed to male interviewers, indicating that with proper precautions being taken in preparation for fieldwork, men are just as likely as women to uncover cases of sexual assault. It may well be, of course, that some victims would not talk to men and for this reason the estimates given by the ICS are probably conservative.

Figure 2.10 is the graphic depiction of the proportions of the different categories of sexual assault, that portion which is recorded in the statistics and that portion which is reported to the police. The survey estimates about 1200 cases of sexual assault took place with Islington residents in the past year. Of these only 21% get reported and only about 9% of all sexual assault ever gets recorded in the criminal statistics.

By comparison, the BCS estimates that only 8% get reported and that of these 133% get recorded in the criminal statistics. Clearly, the problems of comparison are even further obfuscated by the fact that both the police and the BCS report all sexual assaults together under one category.

When sexual assault is broken down into the categories which we have established, however, a different pattern emerges. 50% of all rapes and 4% of all multiple rapes get reported to the police, presumably due to the severity of this offence as compared to sexual assault and multiple sexual assault which have reporting rates of 13% and 7% respectively. Of interest is that the victim is less likely to report incidents when there is more than one assailant in each of these two categories. 23% of all sexual assaults turn out to be rape or attempted rape and of these 32% involve more than one assailant. It would seem from these data that the frequency of sexual assault on Islington women is much higher than the BCS suggests and somewhat lower than Hall's data suggest. More importantly, however, is the relative proportions of rape and sexual assault. While Hall estimates that 36% of all sexual assault is rape, we estimate that 23% of all sexual assault is rape or attempted. The second sweep of the BCS estimates only 20% of all sexual assault is either rape or attempted. In either event, the proportion of rape to sexual assault is very high in Islington and probably even higher in some other inner-city locations. Unfortunately, the lack of data does not allow these kinds of comparisons. Farrington and Dowds (1983) Study, carried out in Nottinghamshire, Leicestershire, and Staffordshire found only 2 cases of sexual assault in a total sample of nearly 3000 respondents.

Figure 2.11 presents the variations of sexual assault by Ward. It can be seen from the graph that the Ward in which the most sexual assaults were uncovered was Sussex at an estimated occurrence of 108 incidents of sexual assault for every 1000 households. It should be pointed out, however, that because of the rarity of sexual assault in relation to other crimes as measured by the survey, the size of the sampling errors for Wards is much higher, and the range for any given Ward of the predicted levels is much higher than on other categories. Nevertheless, the mean values reported here are still the best estimates, regardless of the size of the standard error. The observed variation across segments of the population is just as pronounced. Table 2.25 is the breakdown by age and race of the victims of sexual assault:

Table 2.25 Sexual assault (by age and race)

Group		Rate per 1000 Households
Age	16–24	53
	25–44	26
	45 plus	3
Race	White	19
	Black	14
	Asian	12
	Other non-white	13

Base: All households weighted n= 5939

Table 2.25 illustrates that there is a negative relationship with age. The older the respondents the less likely they are to be victimized by sexual assault, the younger age group being approximately eighteen times as likely to experience sexual assault than older women. The table also demonstrates that white women are more likely than their black counterparts to be victimized by sexual assault, indicating that white women are more likely to disclose than black women despite the fact that matching was carried out for black respondents.

As with the other crimes investigated in this chapter of the report, there is a strong relationship between the observed values for the scales measuring satisfaction with the neighbourhood and fear of crime as illustrated by Table 2.26:

Table 2.26 Sexual assault (by scale scores)

Scale		Rate per 1000 Households
Satisfaction with neighbourhood		
	high	000
	medium	8
	low	27
Fear of crime	high	39
	medium	10
	low	00
Probability of crime in next year		
	high	77
	medium	9
	low	6

Base: All households weighted n= 5939

Table 2.26 clearly shows that women who have been sexually assaulted are least likely to be satisfied with the neighbourhood and most likely to express a fear of crime or the probability of being a victim of crime in the next year. As with the other categories of crime investigated by our survey, victimization in the form of sexual assault is strongly related to people's perceptions, indicating that they are not necessarily out of proportion with their experiences. Rather, being a victim of sexual assault has a definite impact on how the respondent tends to conceptualize her reality, and most likely has the further effect of restricting her activity. This relationship will be further explored in Chapter 4.

Contacts with the police and the number of evenings out per week bear the same relationship to sexual assault victimization as they do with other forms of criminal offence as illustrated by Table 2.27:

Table 2.27   Sexual assault (by contact with the police and evening absences)

Group		Rate per 1000 Households
Contact with police	none	4
	one	7
	two plus	48
Outings per week	none	5
	one–two	17
	three plus	29

Base: All households weighted n= 5939

These figures indicate that women who have had contact with the police more often are more likely to be victims of sexual assault. Again this is due in part to their reporting (even if the reporting rates are low) and in part due to the police concentrating their efforts on victims of crime as much as offenders. Clearly, women who do go out in the evening more often are putting themselves at risk more often than those who do not, the difference being women who go out in the evening are six times as likely than those who do not to be victims of sexual assault. As with assault, we can predict that those women who are most likely to be at risk by going out are those who can afford to go out in the evenings to public places and also those who must make use of the street and public transport. In short, we should expect that women in the middle income categories are more likely than others to be victims of sexual assault. Table 2.28 breaks down the rates of sexual assault by various socio-economic indicators.

Clearly, women who are employed and who are in the second highest income category are most at risk of sexual assault. Private rentals are also much more at risk than either Council housing or private ownership. It would appear from the data in Table 2.28 that the more women become economically independent, the more at risk they become to sexual violence, although women in the highest socio-economic group are more in a position to take certain precautions and are less at risk than their lower income counterparts.

Table 2.28   Sexual assault (by socio-economic indicators)

Indicator		Rate per 1000 Households
Income	under £3000	14
	3000–7999	13
	8000–11999	49
	12000 plus	12
Work status	unemployed	14
	employed	24
Tenure	owned	5
	public rental	15
	private rental	39
	squatters	26

Base: All households weighted n= 5939

Table 2.29   Sexual assault (by age and race)

Age	Race			
	White	Black	Asian	Other Non-white
16–24	63	7	0	10
25–44	26	33	0	0
45 plus	2	0	40	31

Base: All households weighted n= 5939

Table 2.29 reveals a similar pattern to that of assault. The greatest risk for white women occurs in the lower age category while the middle age category is the greatest risk for black women. While the survey did not pick up any occurrences of sexual assault in the two youngest age categories for Asian women, it did pick up cases in the older age group indicating that this is the age of greatest risk for these women. The results were similar for assault. These results must be interpreted with caution, however, since the numbers are so small that the degree of sampling error is higher for this offence than others covered by the survey.

In summary, although sexual assault is the most difficult of all offences to measure, the Islington Crime Survey incorporated a number of methodological innovations aimed at improving the accuracy of measurement for this category of offence. Younger women are the most likely to fall victim to sexual assault, and overall white women are more at risk than black women, although in the middle age category this relationship reverses. There can be little doubt from the data offered by the survey that the frequency of sexual assault is much higher than the British Crime Survey estimates in Islington, and lower than the estimates offered by Hall (1985). The implications of these findings for the public safety of women will be looked at more closely in Chapter 4.

Vehicle theft, vehicle vandalism and bicycle theft: a comparison with sexual assault

Both the BCS and the MCS reported high rates of reporting for motor vehicle theft at 100% while the figures for bicycle theft reporting were 60% and 53% respectively. By way of comparison, our survey shows that only 54% of car thefts made it into the criminal statistics (Figure 2.12). This relatively low figure is due to two reasons. Firstly, residents of Islington may have easily had their vehicles stolen outside of N District jurisdiction and reported the thefts elsewhere. Secondly, we have not included the category of "unauthorised taking of motor vehicle" reported in the N District statistics for purposes of comparison. If we consider the 1,556 occurrences of this offence recorded in the N District statistics for 1984, then we would actually end up with more cases of vehicle theft recorded in the statistics than estimated by the survey. While this is quite possible, given the degree of sampling error at a level greater than 186, it is more likely that the difference is due to the difference between jurisdiction of the offence and jurisdiction of residence as well as the definitional variations.

Bicycle theft proves to present an anomaly for the ICS. If we accept the rate of reporting for this offence as the national average, estimated by the latest sweep of BCS (we were unable to estimate this figure for our survey data) at 68%, we can estimate that approximately 1019 bicycle thefts were reported to Islington police last year, 700 of which were recorded (a recording rate of 69% of reported and 47% of actual compared to British Crime Survey estimates of 73% and 50% respectively). The anomaly is that by comparing these figures to those of sexual assault, we obtain the results illustrated in Table 2.30:

Table 2.30   Comparison of sexual assault and bicycle theft

	Bicycle Theft	*Sexual Assault*
Estimated actual	1498	1190
Estimated number reported	1019	255
% reported	68	21
Number recorded	700	110
% recorded of reported	69	43
% recorded of actual	47	9

Base: All households weighted n= 5939

Table 2.30 illustrates one of the most important limitations of the criminal statistics generally. Despite the fact that a similar number of sexual assaults and bicycle thefts occurred, and due to the differences between the two offences in terms of recording practices on the part of the police, and reporting behaviours on the part of the public, nearly seven times as many bicycle thefts end up being recorded than sexual assaults. The difference in the recording rates by the police helps to illustrate that from the public's perspective, they are more likely to have a report of bicycle theft recorded than sexual assault. The difference in recording practices of the police has a definite impact on reporting behaviour of the public as illustrated by the differences in reporting rates by the public, which favour bicycle theft. Bicycle thefts are more likely to be reported than sexual assault, they are more likely to be recorded than sexual assaults, and they appear in the statistics at a rate relative to sexual assault of 5 times what they should, taking the recording rate for sexual assault as constant.

Given the obvious reporting and recording biases which the example of bicycle theft and sexual assault illustrates, it can easily be seen that if the official statistics are used as measures of the frequency of a crime, one ends up with the misconception that bicycle theft is seven times more of a problem than sexual assault when in reality there are a similar number of occurrences of both.

Total crime followed up

As a conclusion to this section a short discussion on total crimes is warranted. The strategy was to take a sum of all the crimes which the survey followed up for each household, in order to provide a composite measure for these classifications of crime in the Borough. Figure 2.16 provides a graphic depiction of the results of this procedure. The graph shows that the overall worst rate of risk is in Sussex followed closely by Mildmay at 1007 and 995 incidents per 1000 households respectively, while the lowest overall rate is Holloway at 357 criminal incidents per 1000 households. When one considers that on the average 69% of the households in Islington were not touched by any of the crimes represented by this composite measure,[5] then one has a crude appreciation for the degree of multiple victimization uncovered by the survey both within each crime classification as well as between them.

Table 2.31 breaks down the rates for overall crimes followed up by age, and race, and gender, and illustrates that the rates of crime overall are quite high, particularly in the younger age groups. Both black and Asian people in the older age categories are much more at risk than their white counterparts. These data help to reinforce the fact that it is women who are at the greatest risk overall, and that as age increases the differences between blacks and whites overall become greater at the expense of the black persons. Were we to restrict ourselves to the criminal statistics only, we would not only have an incorrect picture of the frequency and types of crime, but we would also probably develop a very distorted picture of the distribution of crime as measured by the comparative frequency of victimization investigated by the survey.

Total crimes followed up (by age, race and gender)[1]

	Race							
	White		*Black*		*Asian*		*Other Non-Whites*	
	Male	*Female*	*Male*	*Female*	*Male*	*Female*	*Male*	*Female*
16–24	887	1220	889	1227	599	1024	1535	1323
25–44	710	821	748	1074	418	678	376	785
45+	482	233	500	890	589	987	175	421

For entire population: 620
1. Rates expressed per 1000 households
Base: All households weighted n= 5939

Because the Islington Crime Survey is the first survey in this country to carry out an in depth local survey with the ability to distinguish the experiences of different social groups in the population, the contribution it makes to a more complete understanding of counting crime, and the effect of official statistics on public conception is worth noting and is the subject of the next section.

Towards a theory of crime statistics

One process which has not been discussed previously is that of recording offences differently from one occasion to another. For instance, a crime report is recorded by the police but it may be recorded as something which is more or less serious than it really is. When police record a report of domestic violence as a charge of drunken disorderly behaviour, that is an instance of recording something as less serious than it is and has been called *down-criming*. When the police record something less serious as an offence which is more serious (a case of criminal damage being recorded as attempted burglary), the term used for this process has been *up-criming*. It can be seen that if the police regularly engage in the processes of up-criming and down-criming, even unwittingly, the potential for the statistics to misrepresent the crime trends is readily grasped, particularly if there is a pattern to their decisions. It appears that the Home Office counting rules for offences are a set of managerial instructions for the recording of offences, and that as such, any bias which they may possess, if followed to the letter by the police rank and file, would be included in the statistics. On the other hand, if individual rank and file are engaged in the decision making process in the field and are unknowingly emphasizing their personal views in that process, it is up to the management to correct this problem, possibly through better training procedures, and more importantly from unbiased estimates of crime frequency statistics, which are offered by crime surveys.

There can be little doubt that all of these processes produce statistics which misrepresent the actuality of crime trends and evidence to support

this comes from many sources other than crime surveys. We have already discussed McCabe and Sutcliffe (1978), Bottomley and Coleman (1981), as well as other research which demonstrates the problems associated with the under-reporting, under-recording and no-criming of offences. In relation to up-criming and down-criming, evidence comes to us from several studies carried out in the United Kingdom. Blom-Cooper and Drabble (1982) carried out a rigorous analysis of the crime statistics in Lambeth, focussing on Brixton, in an attempt to uncover why the rates of robbery there were so much higher, according to the police statistics, than any other district in the MPD. These authors suggest that the police case for operation SWAMP, in which heavy saturation techniques and the excessive use of stop and search powers were adopted, was presented to Lord Scarman as a consequence of Brixton having a much higher incidence of robbery and other violent theft than other Districts in the MPD. The authors go on to argue that, in fact, the police statistics did indicate this was the case but the statistics also showed that the incidences of other theft and handling in Brixton were much lower than other areas. After combining the two categories of:
a) Robbery and other violent theft
b) Other theft and handling
the authors demonstrated that the total for Brixton was no different from the totals for other areas. The authors conclude that this process of up-criming in Brixton became the basis for, firstly, the misconception that robbery was a serious problem there, and, secondly, the final justification submitted to Lord Scarman for policing practice prior to the riots.

The ICS data have shown that similar recording trends occur in N District. The figures for robbery and theft from person illustrate that although four times as many theft from person incidents occur than robberies, and although the reporting rate to the police for both categories of offence are identical, more robberies end up in the statistics. By taking the police statistics as reliable indicators we would end up with the misconception that robbery in Islington is more frequent than theft from person. In this case we may discover that more public demand is expressed towards the police to make the streets safer from robbers. If the police were then to respond to this public pressure by mounting a public relations programme aimed at convincing the public that the problem was being given police priority, the public may then be pleased to know that the police have done something positive towards resolving the problem. In reality, however, the processes of non-recording and up-criming reflect an existing police priority in the sense that their activity already places an emphasis on robbery over theft from person, as indicated by their statistics. What the public is demanding, therefore, is what the public already has from the police, that is an emphasis on robbery over theft from person.

The same process happens with bicycle theft and sexual assault in the ICS data. A police emphasis on bicycle theft over sexual assault as indicated by their statistics might produce in the public mind the possible conception that bicycle theft is more frequent than sexual assault. In reality, however, approximately the same number of incidents for each category of offence occurs despite the fact that there are nearly seven times as many bicycle thefts recorded in the police statistics. What the public may not realize is that because the police have placed a greater emphasis on bicycle theft at the expense of sexual assault, it appears more often in the statistics and produces the conception that it is more frequent than sexual assault.

It may well be that up-criming occurs when there is a clear case of a suspect and possible conviction, and down-criming occurs when the apprehension of a culprit seems unlikely. This may help to explain how the different emphases associated with the examples above become generated. It may also be that the police find cases of armed robbery more exciting to investigate than cases of theft from person where it is unlikely that a suspect will be apprehended. It is our contention that the nature of explanation at that level does not really matter. Rather, of crucial importance is that by acting in specific ways in both recording and subsequently investigating reports of crime, the police betray an emphasis on certain priorities, and these come to be accepted by the public in the form of public demand for more of the same.

When the police statistics are seen for what they really are – the product of an organization of individuals' labour – then one can also see that the media and the public see them for something else, namely, indicators of crime not law enforcement practice. The consequence of that activity has been reversed and seen as the cause. For the media and the public the crime statistics are the beginning of the process, the point of knowledge from which certain law enforcement activities are demanded. In reality, however, the statistics are the end product of a particular set of law enforcement activities. To the extent that these statistics generate public demands, the police in responding, therefore, only continue what has been their previous practice. In this manner, law enforcement practice which appears to be responding to public demand, but is really at divergence with public demand, is not only reproduced, but is accepted by the public willingly, all other things being equal. In practice, however, all other things are not equal. Public demands based on crime statistics are only representative of a minority of the population. This will be illustrated in Chapter 3.

For this reason, many researchers have concluded that the statistics given by the police are next to useless. because the statistics are the product of a set of police activities, they are much better measures of the activities of law enforcement agencies than they are of the frequency and distribution of crime (Maclean, 1985b, 1986).

In analysing the type of moral panic campaigns which are sometimes mounted by media and public response to published police statistics, Stuart Hall has argued that:

"The paradox is that the selectivity of police reaction to selected crimes almost certainly serves to increase their number (what is called a 'deviancy
spiral'). It will also tend to produce a cluster, or 'crime wave'. When the
'crime wave' is then invoked to justify a 'control campaign', it has become a
self-fulfilling prophecy. Of course, public concern about particular crimes can
also be the cause of a focussed police response. But public concern is itself
strongly shaped by the criminal statistics (which the police produce and inter-
pret for the media) and the impression that there is 'wave after wave' of new
kinds of crime. Of course, the contribution of criminals to 'crime waves' is
only too visible, whereas the contribution the police themselves made to the
construction of crime waves is virtually invisible." (1978, p38)

While Hall's work has been inspirational to some and certainly on the
right track, it would seem from the ICS data that he is only partially correct. Firstly, his analysis strongly suggests a conspiracy by the police to
"dupe" both the unsuspecting police and media, as if both of these did not
have any touch with reality or ability to think critically. In this sense he
does not differ from the BCS when in relation to the fear of crime they
suggest that one of the reasons for the disproportionate fear of crime
which they measured in the first sweep of the survey was due to the
media:

"In part the mass media simply reproduce the information provided by official
sources. Press releases from the Home Office or police forces are 'news' and
when these institutions tell the press, for example, that serious recorded
crimes have increased, inevitably this information is reproduced: 'Crime up
by X%'. In addition, newspapers have to sell, and television programmes
have to maintain an audience: the media face heavy pressure to enliven their
presentation of crime ('Crime soars by a massive X%'). And stories of extraordinary brutality dominate the headlines precisely because they are extraordinary. On top of this, people are increasingly exposed to crime prevention
publicity campaigns and advertising for crime prevention hardware, and this
material emphasises the most distressing aspects of victimisation in order to
jolt people into action – heavy financial losses, wanton damage to cherished
property and brutal attacks at the hand of sadistic thugs." (Hough and
Mayhew, 1983, p26)

We disagree with this argument for the most part since as the data in this
chapter show, people's fear of crime is directly related to their victimization; as was shown in the last chapter it is also related to their knowledge
of crime; and as will be shown in the next chapter, their expectations of
the police are based upon a more accurate knowledge of what is occurring
in their neighbourhoods than either Hall or the Home Office is prepared
to admit.

We are arguing that the evidence from the survey data suggests that
because of the recording and definitional biases structured into the activity of the policing institution, those people most directly affected by
crime will differ in their response from these people least affected by

crime. In the former case citizens may come to see law enforcement as not fulfilling their needs, while in the latter case citizens may be quite happy with current practices. This notion of a divided or fragmented community, as it pertains to satisfaction of the police, has been touched upon in this chapter in relation to the reporting behaviour of victims.

We are arguing that Hall's conception of the relationship between "focussed police response" and the justification of "control strategies" reverses the real relationship. The police statistics are the result of focussed police response not the cause of it. An emphasis on a particular form of crime, as indicated by official statistics, is already implicitly in place well before the statistics are produced. The statistics may well then become the starting point for media and public campaigns, but in reality these campaigns are already implicitly in operation in the form of police recording and investigation of certain types of crimes at the expense of others. This bias in combination with those of up-criming and down-criming is structural rather than individual in nature, and the misrepresentation produced must sooner or later contradict public experience in relation to crime. It is at this point that a crisis in policing emerges.

There are a number of ways in which this crisis might manifest itself with different segments of the community. Firstly, those who feel that the police are no longer receptive to their needs as citizens will stop turning to the police for assistance when victimized, such as one half of all the victims interviewed by the survey. This results in a loss of information about crime trends by the police. Secondly, some people will lobby for police reform, such as those now demanding an independent police authority for London. Thirdly, some people will increasingly look to the police for protection due to the misconception of the actual crime trends produced by the statistics, and the police will increasingly look towards these people for further support of their existing law enforcement practices and more information about crime, despite the fact that these people are least able to provide it. These are the people who have the least contact with crime and it is this response to which Hall (1978) actually refers. We see the current drive of Neighbourhood Watch Schemes as being but one example of this variation. Finally, some people, specifically those who are the recipients of the negative side of focussed law enforcement, may find themselves in open confrontation with this style of policing and more occurrences of the Brixton, Toxteth, Birmingham and Tottenham type are inevitable. Ironically, the result of these variations of public response to the crisis of policing is an even further fragmented community in which crime proliferates and which is increasingly more difficult to police.

Biased law enforcement as measured by biased crime recording and reactive policing practice are not conspiratorial as Hall suggests, but are organizationally produced in two ways. The first is the manner in which the policing institution is structured, and the second is the way in which

that institution is managed. Any management of any organization requires an informational base for two important reasons. Firstly, the organization requires a description of that which its activities are aimed towards. In the case of policing, this description is given by the crime statistics as measures for the frequency and distribution of the policing target –
crime. The statistics do not provide the police management with accurate
information and this fact has been illustrated by the ICS and every other
survey like it, regardless of who was responsible for conducting them. For
this reason, biases of police intervention are structured. Secondly, management requires a flow of information from the rank and file in order that
they may monitor their own performance. The crime statistics do not
allow for an accurate appraisal of structural bias to be made. Therefore,
those practices which propel the policing institution into crises cannot be
identified by a management whose purpose is essentially to prevent those
crises from occurring in the first place.

Unfortunately, a simple replacement of police management cannot re-
solve this problem nor can a simple restructuring of the institution itself.
Clearly, both of these changes are required but can only be effective if a
proper system of information gathering and dispersion as it pertains to
the frequency and distribution of crime is instituted. This does not mean
more surveillance of the public, and it does not mean more campaigns
encouraging members of the community to inform on one another.
Rather this means a structured form of community consultation which is
informed by unbiased estimates of the frequency and distribution of
crime. It is only in this way that fair policing can be achieved which sat-
isfies the needs of the community in relation to crime control, and it is
only in this manner that accountability of the policing institution to the
public they serve can be effected.

Summary and conclusions
An in-depth examination of the data provided by the Islington Crime
Survey has illustrated that a considerable variation in specific crime rates
occurs within the Borough. The observed variation in crime rates occurs
not only geographically, but it also occurs within various sub-
populations. By contrast, national surveys, such as the BCS, tend to mask
within group variation and for this reason are of little value to a Local
Authority.

It was found that not only are there a high number of criminal occurrences in Islington, but these tend to be concentrated within specific
households rather than being evenly distributed throughout the Borough. A full 50% of the households in Islington had a direct experience
with victimization when all crimes investigated by the survey are taken
into consideration. If only those crimes for which follow-up interviews
were sought are considered, the figure is reduced to 31% of all house-

holds being affected. This fact, combined with the high level of criminal occurrence uncovered by the survey, indicates that considerable levels of multiple victimization are in existence. The same people continue to be victimized. Table 2.32 summarizes the number of incidents for each of the five categories of crime followed up in the survey and compares this to the number of households which actually experienced at least one criminal incident. In this way, the level of multiple victimization per offence can be illustrated:

Table 2.32   Level of multiple victimization

Offence	Number of Incidents per 1000 Households	% of Households Affected	% of Households with Multiple Victimization
Burglary	123	9	24
Vandalism	202	11	37
Theft from person	139	11	17
Assault	186	10	38
Sexual assault	105	19	15
All crimes followed	619	31	47

As Table 2.32 shows, households which fall victim to crime are much lower than the number of incidents, demonstrating that the same households tend to be repeatedly victimized. Overall, this means that 619 incidents of the type investigated by the survey happen in only 31% of the households in Islington and of those households affected directly by these types of crime nearly one half were repeatedly victimized.

The survey found that there are high levels of both unreported and unrecorded crime in Islington, and that the rates of both categories vary from offence to offence. When compared to the national averages, the levels of crime are higher in Islington, but the level of reported crime is also higher, indicating that Islington residents look towards the police more often for crime control purposes. Conversely, it was found that the recording level of those crimes reported to the police is lower than the national average. This means that the police are less responsive to public demands in Islington than the national average, indicating the public in Islington are not receiving the services they are requesting. This idea will be further explored in the next chapter.

Women appear to be at greater risk of crime than men generally. Overall more women are assaulted and fall prey to theft from person than men. While assaults on women are higher, probably due to domestic violence, it would seem the more vulnerable people are victimized by personal crime.

Ethnic minorities experience higher levels of victimization than whites, the only exception being young white women who are more at risk of sexual assault than their black counterparts.

The data show that people's attitude to crime is probably much in line with their experiences of crime, with the exception of older white people who are the least likely of all groups to experience crime of any sort. How this finding relates to attitudes towards the police, and experiences with the police, will also be explored in Chapter 4.

A comparison of the ICS data to the police statistics revealed a number of organizational and managerial biases with law enforcement in Islington, and statistics produced by police do not provide sufficient information to correct these biases. When the statistics generated by the police are seen as indicators of police activities and policing priorities, it can be concluded that at some point the map of crime generated from police statistics has to conflict with that developed from people's direct experiences of crime. One example of the consequences is offered by the finding that nearly one half of the 50% of victims who did not report the crime to the police cited as the reason a lack of confidence in the ability of the police to do anything.

This chapter did not concern itself with public conception of the police in any detail, but dealt with people's direct experiences with crime. It was asserted that when policing practice does not conform to the demands being made by the community, a number of variations in people's perceptions of the police may occur. Furthermore, people's direct experiences with the police will have an impact on the way in which the community views law enforcement. The nature of the relationship between public experience, public perception and public attitude towards the police is the subject of the next chapter to which we now turn.

Notes

1. Actually this figure means that 1225 incidents of burglary were uncovered for every 10,000 households. Since some respondents had their homes burgled more than once, the rate of households affected by burglary is lower.
2. The probable reason for the high rate in Canonbury West is due to a portion of the Marquess Housing Estate coming into the sample. Marquess Estate is well known for its high rates of criminal damage.
3. The method incorporated by the survey to help overcome this difficulty has not been used elsewhere and probably encourages higher rates of disclosure by female respondents for incidents of domestic violence and sexual assault. Very simply, the questions pertaining to assault and sexual assault were reproduced identically on a separate sheet of paper. Interviewers were instructed to use the sheet in cases where husbands were at home, and in approximately 50% of all cases that involved a female respondent. This strategy not only allowed for some protection of those respondents who would be victims of domestic violence, but it

also reduced somewhat the anxiety, if any, of disclosing cases of domestic assault and sexual assault to the interviewer directly. The experimental design, therefore, for this procedure involved two situations: direct questions and indirect questions. Also, because there is considerable disagreement in the literature as to whether or not the sex of the interviewer is an important criterion for the variation in rates of disclosure, the sex of the interviewer was also included as an experimental contingency. In total, therefore, four experimental conditions were established: male to female direct, male to female indirect, female to female direct and female to female indirect. While this procedure undoubtedly contributed to improved rates of disclosure, the results of the comparisons for each of the experimental conditions have not been tabulated for purposes of this report.

4. The survey actually identified a few cases of domestic assault against males. Given the data, we estimate that 4 cases of this kind of domestic assault occur for every 1000 households in Islington.

5. This figure is higher at 69% than the earlier figure of 50% because the earlier figure includes all crimes touched upon by the survey while this figure only includes those crimes which were followed up.

Table 2.4 **Rates of selected crimes per 10,000 households with mutually inclusive categories of offence**

Offence	Rate per 10,000 Households	% of Inclusive Category
ALL BURGLARY	1225 ± 62	N.A.
Burglary	N.A.	87
Illegal entry	N.A.	13
ALL VANDALISM (Followed up)	2019 ± 92.3	N.A.
Vehicle vandalism	N.A.	23.06
To home	N.A.	76.94
To vehicle (not followed up)	2744 ± 106	N.A.
Total vand.	N.A.	N.A.
THEFT	1394 ± 60	N.A.
From person	N.A.	62.9
Robbery	N.A.	16
Other	N.A.	21.1
ALL ASSAULT	1856 ± 93	N.A.
Domestic assault	N.A.	21.63
Racist assault	N.A.	7.32
Police assault	N.A.	3.36
Other assault	N.A.	67.69
ALL SEXUAL ASSAULTS	186 ± 29	N.A.
Multiple rape or attempted	N.A.	7.5
Rape or attempted	N.A.	15.83
Multiple sexual assault	N.A.	17.5
Sexual assault	N.A.	59.17
Vehicle theft	374 ± 29	N.A.
Bicycle theft	234 ± 22	N.A.
Total crime followed up	6199 ± 157	N.A.

Base: All respondents weighted n = 5939

Table 2.5   Estimates of selected crimes with recording rates of police and reporting rates of respondents[1]

Offence	Estimated Actual		Number Reported	% of Actual	Number Recorded	% of Reported	% of Actual
ALL BURGLARY	7840 ±	397	6115	78	3205	52	41
Burglary	6821		5595	82	N.A.	N.A.	N.A.
Illegal entry	1019		540	54	N.A.	N.A.	N.A.
ALL VANDALISM	12921 ±	590	4988	38.6	N.A.	N.A.	N.A.
(Followed up)							
To home	9941		3628	36.5	N.A.	N.A.	N.A.
To vehicle	2980		1359	45.6	N.A.	N.A.	N.A.
To vehicle	17562 ±	678	8008	45.6	N.A.	N.A.	N.A.
(Not followed up)							
TOTAL							
VANDALISM	30483		12996	42.6	3153	24	10
THEFT	8921 ±	384	4559	51	4893	107	54.8
From person	5611		2951	52.6	365	12.36	6.5
Robbery	1427		751	52.6	572	76	41
Other	1883		845	44.9	3956	468	210
ALL ASSAULT	11878 ±	595	4561	38.4	762	16.7	6.4
Domestic assault	2569		694	27	N.A.	N.A.	N.A.
Racist assault	870		327	37.6	N.A.	N.A.	N.A.
Police assault	399		183	45.9	N.A.	N.A.	N.A.
Other assault	8040		3345	41.1	N.A.	N.A.	N.A.
ALL SEXUAL							
ASSAULTS	1190 ±	166	255	21.9	110	43	9.2
Multiple rape							
or attempted	89		37	41.3	N.A.	N.A.	N.A.
Rape							
or attempted	188		95	50.3	N.A.	N.A.	N.A.
Multiple sexual							
assault	208		14	6.5	N.A.	N.A.	N.A.
Sexual assault	705		94	13.4	N.A.	N.A.	N.A.
Vehicle theft	2393 ±	186	N.A.	N.A.	1227	N.A.	54
Bicycle theft	1498 ±	141	N.A.	N.A.	700	N.A.	47
Total crime							
Followed up	39673 ±	1004	19956	50	12123	61	31

1. Estimates are of actual numbers committed in Islington
Base: All respondents weighted n = 5939

Table 2.6 Selected crime rates (by ward)[1]

Ward	Burglary	Vandalism	Theft	Assault	Sexual Assault	Motor Vehicle Theft	Motor Vehicle Vandalism	Bicycle Theft	Total Crimes Followed Up
Barnsbury	58	99	125	227	22	17	274	22	516
Bunhill	182	165	94	197	20	53	293	24	643
Canonbury East	169	420	171	280	32	50	242	41	794
Canonbury West	196	530	76	106	1	65	419	22	878
Clerkenwell	64	168	160	243	17	31	199	6	603
Gillespie	48	248	149	246	13	20	311	28	663
Highbury	90	13	164	142	13	36	125	14	421
Highview	158	145	215	197	25	70	491	11	682
Hillmarton	115	76	148	83	1	48	207	4	418
Hillrise	96	271	207	176	19	52	374	49	724
Holloway	40	93	68	159	7	22	215	9	357
Junction	43	141	112	112	1	19	233	24	409
Mildmay	342	241	161	327	58	56	332	54	995
Quadrant	126	338	130	215	1	14	266	12	784
St. George's	230	314	174	41	6	22	265	21	609
St. Mary's	66	139	138	109	31	34	258	30	448
St. Peter's	77	158	219	111	1	22	194	19	560
Sussex	226	417	151	222	108	73	526	51	1007
Thornhill	165	75	130	594	49	39	171	25	961
Tollington	78	145	114	165	9	60	224	30	481
Entire Borough Average	123 ± 6	202 ± 9	139 ± 6	186 ± 9	19 ± 3	37 ± 3	274 ± 11	23 ± 2	620 ± 16

1. Expressed as rates per 1000 households
Base: All respondents weighted n = 5939

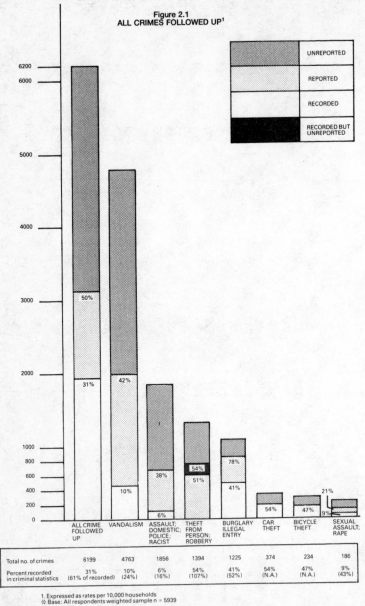

Figure 2.1
ALL CRIMES FOLLOWED UP[1]

	ALL CRIME FOLLOWED UP	VANDALISM	ASSAULT; DOMESTIC; POLICE; RACIST	THEFT FROM PERSON; ROBBERY	BURGLARY ILLEGAL ENTRY	CAR THEFT	BICYCLE THEFT	SEXUAL ASSAULT; RAPE
Total no. of crimes	6199	4763	1856	1394	1225	374	234	186
Percent recorded in criminal statistics	31% (61% of recorded)	10% (24%)	6% (16%)	54% (107%)	41% (52%)	54% (N.A.)	47% (N.A.)	9% (43%)

1. Expressed as rates per 10,000 households
※ Base: All respondents weighted sample n = 5939

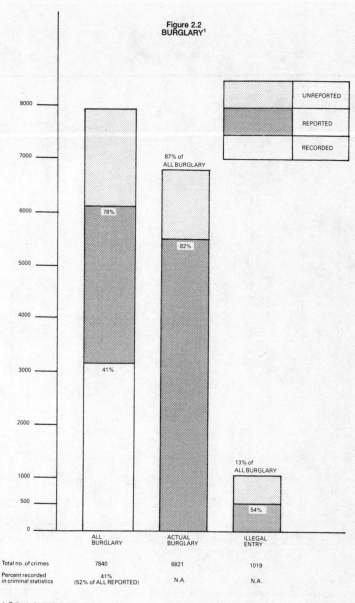

Figure 2.2
BURGLARY[1]

	UNREPORTED
	REPORTED
	RECORDED

8000

7000

87% of
ALL BURGLARY

6000   78%

5000   82%

4000

3000   41%

2000

1000   13% of
                              ALL BURGLARY

500   54%

0
        ALL   ACTUAL   ILLEGAL
        BURGLARY   BURGLARY   ENTRY

	ALL BURGLARY	ACTUAL BURGLARY	ILLEGAL ENTRY
Total no. of crimes	7840	6821	1019
Percent recorded in criminal statistics	41% (52% of ALL REPORTED)	N.A.	N.A.

1. Estimated actual occurrences
* Base: All respondents weighted n = 5939

Figure 2.3

BURGLARY BY WARD[1]

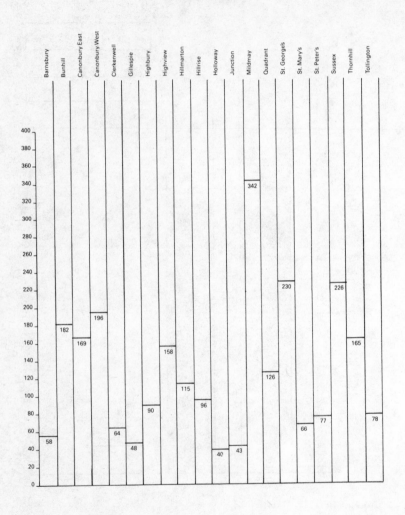

1. Expressed as rates per 1000 households
 ✻ Mean values only – standard errors not included
 ✻ Base: weighted sample all respondents n – 5939

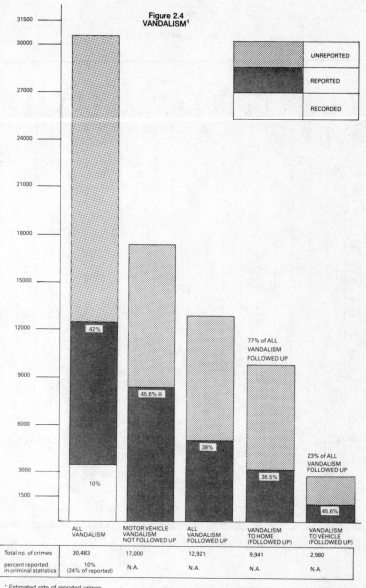

**Figure 2.4
VANDALISM[1]**

	UNREPORTED
	REPORTED
	RECORDED

	ALL VANDALISM	MOTOR VEHICLE VANDALISM NOT FOLLOWED UP	ALL VANDALISM FOLLOWED UP	VANDALISM TO HOME (FOLLOWED UP)	VANDALISM TO VEHICLE (FOLLOWED UP)
Total no. of crimes	30,483	17,000	12,921	9,941	2,980
percent reported in criminal statistics	10% (24% of reported)	N.A.	N.A.	N.A.	N.A.

* Estimated rate of reported crimes
1. Estimated actual occurrences
** Base: All respondents weighted n = 5939

Figure 2.5

VANDALISM BY WARD[1]

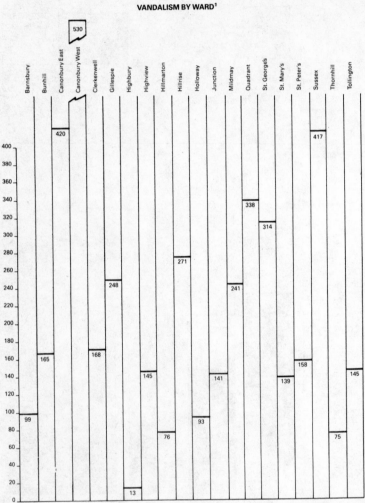

1. Expressed as rates per 1000 households
※ Mean values only – standard errors not included
※ Base: weighted sample all respondents n = 5939

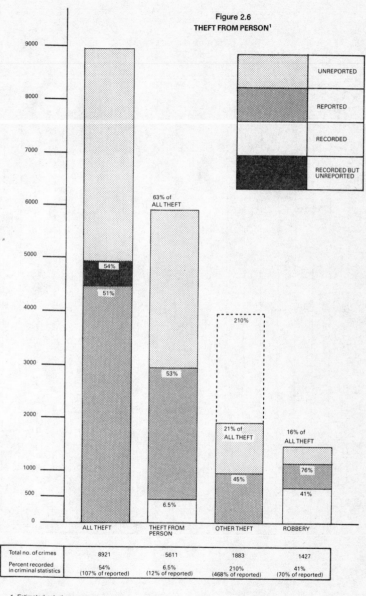

Figure 2.6
THEFT FROM PERSON[1]

	UNREPORTED
	REPORTED
	RECORDED
	RECORDED BUT UNREPORTED

	ALL THEFT	THEFT FROM PERSON	OTHER THEFT	ROBBERY
Total no. of crimes	8921	5611	1883	1427
Percent recorded in criminal statistics	54% (107% of reported)	6.5% (12% of reported)	210% (468% of reported)	41% (70% of reported)

1. Estimated actual occurrences
* Base: All respondents weighted n = 5935

Figure 2.7

THEFT FROM PERSON BY WARD[1]

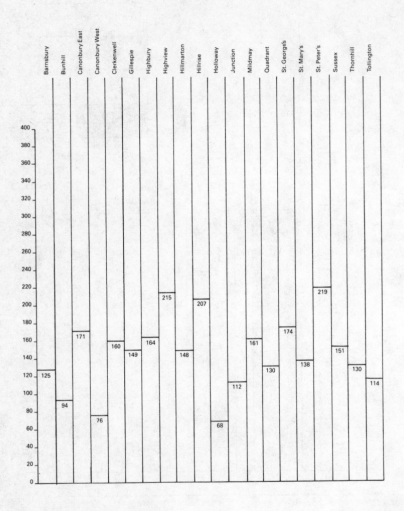

1. Expressed as rates per 1000 households
※ Mean values only – standard errors not included
※ Base: weighted sample all respondents n = 5939

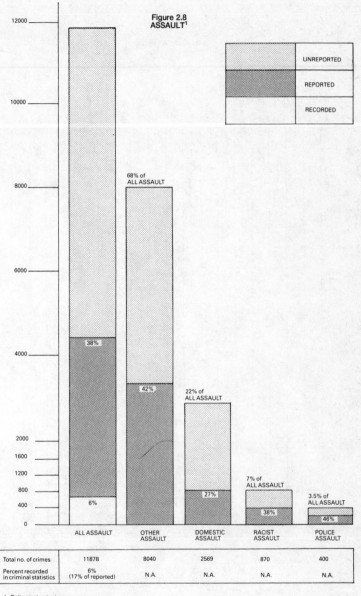

Figure 2.8 ASSAULT[1]

	UNREPORTED
	REPORTED
	RECORDED

68% of ALL ASSAULT

22% of ALL ASSAULT

7% of ALL ASSAULT

3.5% of ALL ASSAULT

38%

42%

27%

38%

46%

6%

	ALL ASSAULT	OTHER ASSAULT	DOMESTIC ASSAULT	RACIST ASSAULT	POLICE ASSAULT
Total no. of crimes	11878	8040	2569	870	400
Percent recorded in criminal statistics	6% (17% of reported)	N.A.	N.A.	N.A.	N.A.

1. Estimated actual occurrences
* Base: All respondents weighted n = 5939

Figure 2.9

ASSAULT BY WARD[1]

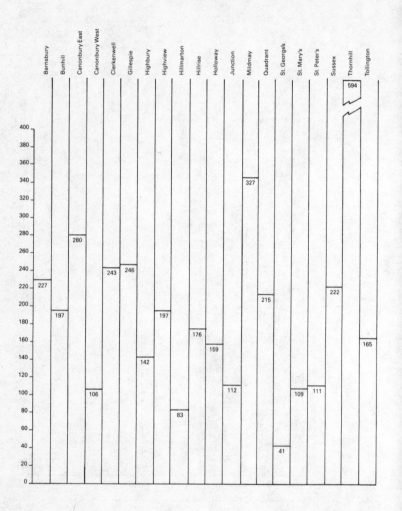

1. Expressed as rates per 1000 households
※ Mean values only – standard errors not included
※ Base: weighted sample all respondents n = 5939

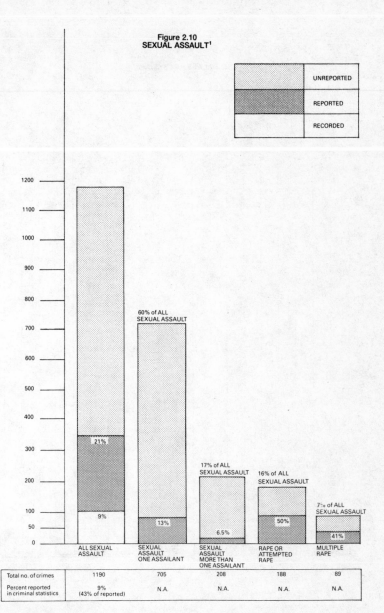

Figure 2.10
SEXUAL ASSAULT[1]

	UNREPORTED
	REPORTED
	RECORDED

	ALL SEXUAL ASSAULT	SEXUAL ASSAULT ONE ASSAILANT	SEXUAL ASSAULT MORE THAN ONE ASSAILANT	RAPE OR ATTEMPTED RAPE	MULTIPLE RAPE
Total no. of crimes	1190	705	208	188	89
Percent reported in criminal statistics	9% (43% of reported)	N.A.	N.A.	N.A.	N.A.

1. Estimated actual occurrences
* Base: All respondents weighted n = 5939

Figure 2.11

SEXUAL ASSAULT BY WARD[1]

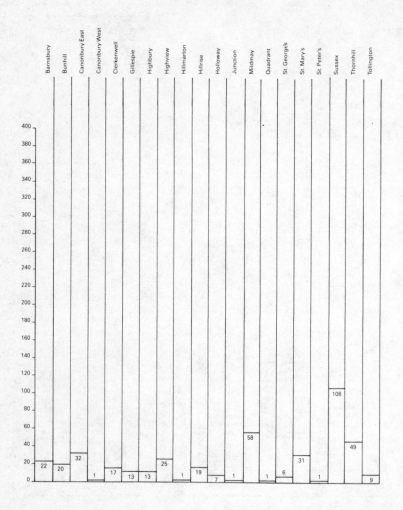

1. Expressed as rates per 1000 households
✻ Mean values only – standard errors not included
✻ Base: weighted sample all respondents n ~ 5939

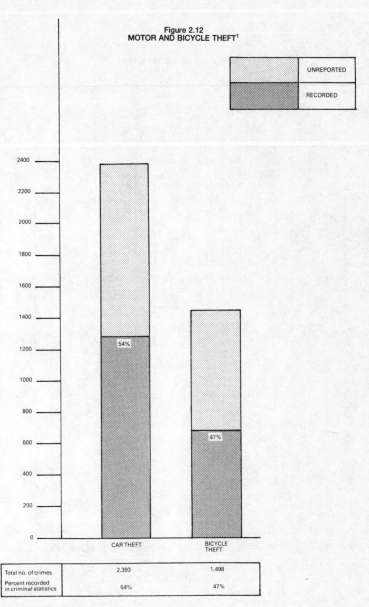

Figure 2.12
MOTOR AND BICYCLE THEFT[1]

	UNREPORTED
	RECORDED

	CAR THEFT	BICYCLE THEFT
Total no. of crimes	2,393	1,498
Percent recorded in criminal statistics	54%	47%

1. Estimated actual occurrences
* Base: All respondents weighted n = 5939

Figure 2.13

MOTOR VEHICLE THEFT BY WARD[1]

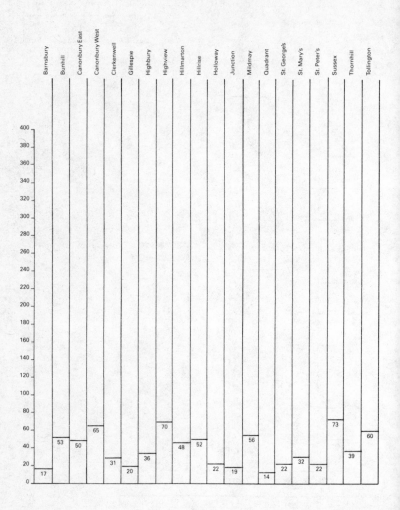

1. Expressed as rates per 1000 households
☆ Mean values only – standard errors not included
☆ Base: weighted sample all respondents n = 5939

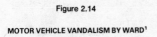

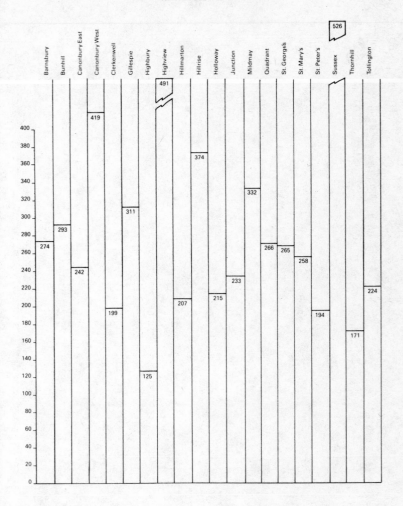

Figure 2.14

MOTOR VEHICLE VANDALISM BY WARD[1]

1. Expressed as rates per 1000 households
   ∴ Mean values only – standard errors not included
   ∴ Base: weighted sample all respondents n   5939

Figure 2.15

BICYCLE THEFT BY WARD[1]

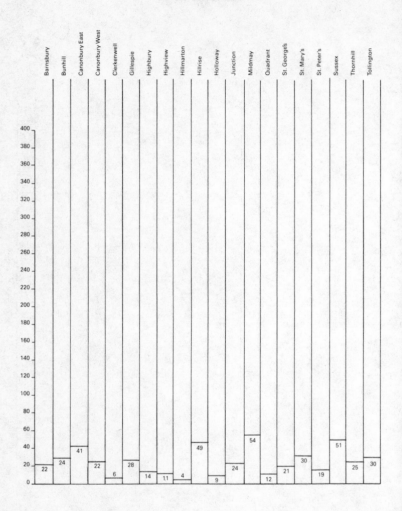

1. Expressed as rates per 1000 households
* Mean values only – standard errors not included
* Base: weighted sample all respondents n = 5939

Figure 2.16

TOTAL CRIME FOLLOWED UP BY WARD[1]

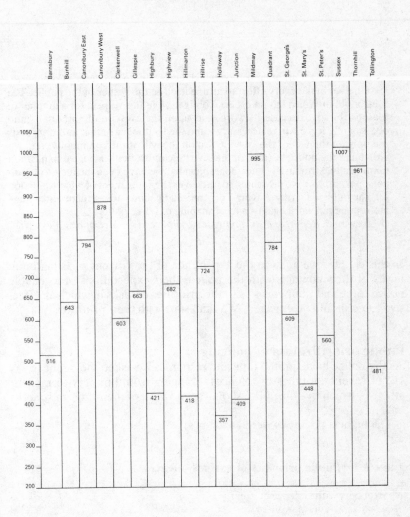

1. Expressed as rates per 1000 households
❖ Mean values only – standard errors not included
❖ Base: weighted sample all respondents n = 5939

3 Public Perception and Contact with Police

"It is essential for an organization which lays claim to the description of 'professional' to make every effort to attune itself to the wishes of the public. The Metropolitan Police has an especial obligation in this respect for a number of reasons. Firstly, because its work rests upon the exercise of authority – and occasionally force where necessary – and the legitimacy of that authority rests not only on the fact of the law but also on the will of the community; remove either and the police become oppressive. Secondly, being a huge organization numerically, structurally and geographically, we have been inclined to be impersonal and to have arrogated to ourselves the judgement of what was 'good for' the public. Thirdly, having a centralised headquarters structure in a huge metropolis can work against a local shaping of Force policy."
(K. Newman, *Report of the Commission of Police of the Metropolis*, 1984, p7).

In this chapter we analyze the experience of the citizens of Islington in terms of their contacts with the police, their expectations of a reliable police force and their views as to the priorities of tasks in which an effective force should be engaged. We shall start with their priorities.

Public prioritization of policing
As the police have limited time and resources we asked the public to say out of seventeen types of offences – ranging from burglary to racialist attacks – which *five* the police should spend *most* of their time and energy on.

The highest priorities were as follows:

Table 3.1 Public priorities of various offences

1.	Robbery with violence in street	70.7%
2.	Sexual assaults on women	69.3%
3.	Use of heroin or hard drugs	59.1%
4.	Burglary of people's houses	58.1%
5.	Drunken driving	43.5%
6.	Racist attacks	39.2%
7.	Vandalism	26.8%

8.	Bag snatching	25.2%
9.	Glue sniffing	22.8%
10.	Unruly behaviour at football matches	21.8%
11.	Use of cannabis	12.8%
12.	Rowdyism in the streets	9.8%
13.	Theft of motor cars	9.1%
14.	Burglary of shops/offices	8.3%
15.	Prostitution	7.5%
16.	Company fraud and embezzlement	6.0%
17.	Shoplifting	3.1%

We have included the full list of the public's five choices of offences on which the police should spend most of their time and energy in order to illustrate the high public consensus over the top five offences and the very low priorities given to many other offences. This is confirmed for the lowest priority offences, when we asked what are *four* offences that the police should spend *least* time on. These were prostitution (53.3%), shoplifting (43.0%), company fraud (37.3%) and rowdyism in the streets (27.7%). Perhaps, more to the point, when we asked which offences the police "spend more time on than is necessary" we found once again prostitution, shoplifting and company fraud but also that 24.3% of the public believed that undue attention was given to cannabis.

Table 3.2   Offences on which the public believe the police spend more time than necessary

		%
1.	Prostitution	32.7
2.	Cannabis	24.3
3.	Shoplifting	19.0
4.	Company fraud	15.4
5.	Unruly behaviour at football matches	12.8
6.	Rowdyism in the streets	10.8

That a third of the population of Islington think too much time is spent on prostitution and a quarter that undue attention is given to cannabis is a direct indication of public desire to direct resources to more important areas. It also shows in the case of cannabis that the public distinguish quite clearly between soft drugs and hard drugs such as heroin – the latter of which is the third *highest* policing priority. In the aftermath of the 1985 Handsworth riot *The Guardian* editorial noted "It is (genuinely it is) hard to draw the line between a resolute refusal to allow 'merchants of powdered death' – black or white – to ply their trade unhindered and the systematic harassment of youths who hang around the local pub smoking the odd joint. After all, if drug dealing is the menace it has been portrayed as being this year, then it would be intolerable to ignore it in ghetto areas. On the other hand, to legitimise heavy policing of the ghetto areas on the ground that drugs are involved, is to invite violent unrest. There is a fine and desperately difficult line here" (September 11, 1985). Our survey shows that for the people of Islington such a line is not at all desperate or difficult.

Such a listing of priorities provides us overall with very clear guidelines as to the public will, obedience to which Commissioner Newman rightly acknowledges to be in line with police legitimacy and professionalism. And the five priorities are also precisely the same as those found in the PSI Report covering London in general (D. Smith, 1983a) and the Merseyside Crime Survey (R. Kinsey, 1984).

Table 3.3   Comparison between priorities in Islington, London as a whole and Merseyside (percentages) (rank order in brackets)

	ICS	PSI	MCS
Robbery with violence in street	(1)71	(2)73	(1)75
Sexual assault on women	(2)69	(1)79	(2)73
Use of heroin	(3)59	(5)40	(4)55
Burglary	(4)58	(3)44	(3)68
Drunken driving	(5)44	(6)28	(5)57
Racialist attacks	(6)39	(4)40	–

Thus a remarkable consensus occurs with regard to seriousness of crimes. Violence whether against women or in street robbery is clearly the utmost public priority and burglary is viewed with a uniform concern. The public evidently displays a sophisticated discrimination between the dangers of different sorts of drugs, both legal and illegal. Thus the effects of one of the most dangerous legal drugs – alcohol – are clearly recognized, as are the dangers of illicit heroin use.

Important to note here is the extent to which racialist attacks are taken seriously by the Islington public – as they are in London as a whole. Thus at sixth place, they are seen as more serious an offence than, for example, either vandalism or bag-snatching.

The solid basis of this consensus over serious crimes in public opinion is clearly substantiated by looking at the breakdown in terms of age, race, gender and income.

It is often argued that we live in a culturally pluralist society where different sections of the population have widely varying forms of behaviour. However true this may be of differences of dress, accent, language and cuisine it is plainly not true in terms of the prioritization of serious criminal offences. All sections of the community, young, old; black, white; male, female; high income, low income; Council house tenant and home owner view, for example, street robbery as a very serious offence which should be high on police priorities. And this is also true of all the major offence categories. There is no difference, for example, in the very high priority which women and men give to the policing of sexual attacks against women. There are variations, of course, between the categories in Table 3.2 but they occur almost totally with an overall agreement as to the top five categories of offences. Young people, for example, are more likely to prioritize sexual assaults on women, heroin abuse, and racialist attacks than are the older age range. But all age ranges take these crimes very seriously. Burglary, as one might expect from the victim statistics discussed in Chapter 2, is not an exclusive concern of the home owner or the rich but is major concern of all income groups, of home owners and squatters, as well as Council tenants.

Similarly, there is a consensus as to those offences which the police should spend least time on. Prostitution, cannabis, rowdyism in the street, shoplifting, and company fraud consistently came at the bottom of all lists of priorities whether it is by age, race, men or women. There are a few deviations to this generalization: for example, older white people are distinctively less tolerant of cannabis use. But, in general, the scale of priorities from those which the police should put at a high premium to those which should be of least concern is widely shared within all sections of the community.

It might be argued, however, that such a simple pluralism is not the problem. Rather that what has occurred is that certain sections of the population because, perhaps, of economic and social deprivation, are marginalized from the vast majority of the community, and it is in this region that one might find subcultures which have radically different views on the nature of crime. Of all the groups to which such an ascription is usually made, none is more frequently cited than young blacks. Let us, therefore, compare their priorities to those of the general population.

The profile that young blacks have in terms of the crimes to which the police should give most attention are as follows: (1) racialist attacks (77.9%), (2) sexual attacks on women (74.9%), (3) robberies in the street where violence is used (65.3%), (4) use of heroin (64.3%), (5) burglary (50.3%), (6) drunken driving (33.8%). These are exactly the top six crimes prioritized by the population as a whole and the ordering is identical, with the understandable exception that racialist attacks move into first place and that, in common with all young people, sexual attacks on women are seen as the highest category of assault. Does this look like a subculture which is alienated from the wider community? Does this look like an alien minority who despise the notion of policing in principle? It might be argued that we are pitching the sub-cultural differences at too high a level. Instead we should be asking about more minor matters, say drugs or attitudes to boisterousness in the streets.

With regard to "hard" drugs it should be noted that black youths – like the general population – see heroin as one of the major police priorities. Indeed slightly more see it as a top five priority than the general population (64.3% c.f. 59.1%). But let us look at how young blacks compare with the total population on a range of offences of which it is deemed that the police spend "more time" than necessary.

Table 3.4   A comparison of young blacks and the total population on opinions as to offences on which the police spend more time than necessary

%	Young Blacks	All
Rowdyism	10.8	10.8
Sexual assaults on women	0	1.2
Bag snatching	7.4	4.1
Burglary	0	1.8
Street robbery with violence	2.1	1.8
Cannabis	37.3	24.3
Heroin	4.2	3.4

On all the more serious offences young blacks agree with the general population. They are slightly more lenient about cannabis but then so is the general population as a whole: indeed it is only the over 45 year old whites who have a particularly anti-cannabis disposition. 51.6% of those under 25 feel that the police should spend least time on cannabis, 49.0% of those from 25-44 but only 14.2% of those over 45.

Thus there is little indication that the profile of police priorities held by young blacks is different on most offences from the public as a whole, both in terms of high priorities and areas where deprioritization is advocated.

To conclude this section it is useful to look at a breakdown in an area where the figures reveal extremely high levels of public concern. Sexual attacks on women are of course a top public priority: 69.3% of the population place this offence in the top five offences. If, however, we do a breakdown by gender, age and race, we see wide variations albeit usually still within the level of high prioritization.

As can be seen, young white women have an extremely high level of prioritization which probably reflects their high victimization rates. So, of course, do young white men – although to a lesser extent – which demonstrates the principle that it is not so much actual victimization *per se* which shapes attitudes as knowledge of victimization to people that one knows closely.

Table 3.5 **Prioritization of sexual attacks on women (by age, race and gender) (% placing in top 5 offences)**

| | White | | | Black | | | Asian | | |
	16–24	25–44	45+	16–24	25–44	45+	16–24	25–44	45+
Women	90.6	80.2	52.8	81.7	69.0	76.2	82.4	57.6	46.7
Men	83.2	79.8	60.0	65.2	75.0	62.5	52.3	35.6	48.0

Public assessment of the police: ability to deal with crime

"Public surveys conducted by independent research groups at our request are an instrument of growing sensitivity and therefore offer more accurate and credible findings. Whilst it would be wrong to deny that we look at the ratings of satisfaction with our services, consistently in the region of 75 per cent, with some degree of pleasure, it is also emphasised that we scrutinise with great care and interest the 25 per cent level of dissatisfaction (which includes those who are merely undecided) and the difference between areas, ages and opinions."

(K. Newman, *Report of the Commissioner of Police to the Metropolis*, 1984, p8)

As an independent research group, let us look at the Islington public's rating of police services.

In order to audit the public's assessment of the police efficacy in dealing with crime we asked them to evaluate police performance in seven areas ranging from sexual assault to street fights. The results were as follows:

Table 3.6 **Public evalution of the police as being unsuccessful at dealing with various crimes**

		%
1.	Mugging/Street robbery	61.5
2.	Burglary	65.7
3.	Teenage rowdiness	45.3
4.	Street fights	29.8
5.	Vandalism	65.9
6.	Sexual assaults on women	56.9
7.	Women being molested or pestered	61.7

In terms of the Commissioner's own criterion of dissatisfaction (25%), the public would be clearly extremely dissatisfied with police performance in each of these categories of offence. But less us take a less stringent

50% – that is whether a bare majority of the public were satisfied.

As can be seen we have included three of the crimes in the high public priority category (street robbery, burglary, and sexual assaults on women), one in the intermediate priority category (vandalism), two which relate to rowdiness, the least in terms of public priorities (teenage rowdiness and street lights) and a further question on sexual harassment in general (women being molested or pestered).

In five out of seven of the offences a majority of people interviewed see the police as unsuccessful in dealing with crime. These five include the three public priority crimes, vandalism and sexual harassment. The two crimes which the police are seen to be successful by over 50% of the population are dealing with teenage rowdiness and street fights, and only barely in the case of rowdiness. Furthermore, these types of crimes come very low in public prioritization of police activity. As far as we have seen, only 10% of the population prioritize street rowdiness in terms of police activities.

This would seem on the face of it a very severe public criticism of police effectiveness. It is as if an end of term report written by the people of Islington on police performance in seven major subjects, failed them in five, narrowly passed them in one and gave a clear pass in the least deserving area. And all of this involving a pass mark half as stringent as the Commissioner himself recommended.

Once again, a better understanding of the situation and the extent of the problem can be illuminated by breaking down the population by age, race and gender. Thus Table 3.7 allows us to map the differences and agreements of public assessment of police performance.

Table 3.7   Public evaluation of police performance for seven offences (age, race and gender) (% who see police as unsuccessful)

Offence	All	Age			Race			Gender	
		16–24	25–44	45+	White	Black	Asian	Male	Female
Mugging or street robbery	61.5	68.6	71.9	50.4	61.4	63.1	57.6	68.4	55.0
Burglary	65.7	67.7	77.9	55.6	65.1	69.5	71.7	70.8	60.9
Teenage rowdiness	45.3	51.1	51.4	38.2	43.5	58.4	55.3	48.6	42.0
Street fights	29.8	37.8	30.5	25.7	28.4	37.5	44.7	32.2	27.4
Vandalism	65.9	77.2	74.9	54.5	65.4	68.8	69.6	70.7	61.5
Sexual assaults on women	56.9	68.7	67.0	43.3	55.5	66.0	71.3	57.2	56.6
Women being molested or pestered	61.7	73.0	71.3	48.7	60.0	71.7	75.6	63.0	60.6

Given Newman's criteria (25%) there is simply no group which sees the police as successful in any of these offence categories. In terms of our less stringent 50%, a public assessment of the police's inability to deal with crime is revealed in every category of age, race and sex for mugging, burglary and vandalism. It is perhaps more interesting if we look at those categories which have a higher appraisal of police efficacy. One group clearly stand out and that is the over 45s. They are the only group in which a majority see the police as being successful at dealing with sexual assaults on women and sexual harassment. True, over 50% are dissatisfied with police performance in terms of mugging and burglary but they are much less critical than the younger age groups.

In contrast, if we examine these groups which have an exceedingly sceptical level of police ability to tackle crime (say over 66% seeing the police as unsuccessful) we find that we have in the case of:
 – mugging: everyone under 45, all whites and blacks, all men.
 – burglary: everyone under 45, all blacks and Asians, all men.
 – sexual assault: everyone under 45, all blacks and Asians.

In general those under 45 are more sceptical than those who are older, blacks and Asians more than whites, men rather than women.

It is the older age groups which have, of course, the lowest victimization rates which help depress these figures even at the very highest level of assessment of police ineffectiveness. Thus if one turns to the area of sexual assaults on women (Table 3.8) we can plainly see how the already high levels of dissatisfaction are, in fact, depressed by the category of older white women. Both black and Asian women have extremely high levels of dissatisfaction irrespective of age, and white women and under 45s are in marked contrast to these in the older age group.

Table 3.8   Women's assessment of the police's inability to deal with sexual assaults on women (by age and race)

	All Women	White Women			Black Women			Asian Women		
		16–24	25–44	45+	16–24	25–44	45+	16–24	25–44	45+
Sexual assaults on women	56.6	71.5	64.9	39.0	75.0	67.4	73.7	72.7	73.9	80.0
Sexual molestation of women	63.0	73.6	70.6	40.3	79.7	71.5	78.9	71.5	88.5	83.4

In terms of actual victimization rates, as we have seen in Chapter 2 (Table 2.29), white women over 45 are much less likely to be sexually assaulted than those under 45 and thus there would seem to be some relationship with beliefs in police efficacy. And the same would be true of older Asians who have high rates of sexual assault. However, the patterning of assessment of police effectiveness and sexual assault rates is not at all 1:1 as is demonstrated by the high rate of scepticism in young black women and black women over 45 despite their low victimization rates.

The high rate of scepticism of young women about the police ability to deal with sexual assault is illustrated if we up the criteria of success even further and ask whether the police have any success *at all* at dealing with sexual assault. A full quarter of young white women believe the police are not at all successful at dealing with this offence and this rises to one third of young black women.

As can be seen from Table 3.9 people's beliefs in the effectiveness of the police on each of these individual offences declines with the degree to which they have been criminally victimized *in general*. Thus, whatever crimes committed against them, people become more sceptical about the police ability to deal with each specific offence whilst the rank order of ineffectiveness from vandalism/burglary down to rowdiness and street fights remains relatively independent of the degree of victimization.

**Table 3.9   Beliefs in police effectiveness (by extent of victimization)
(% believing police unsuccessful)**

	Extent of Criminal Victimization		
Offence	*0*	*1 or 2*	*3+*
Mugging or street robbery	53.7	63.0	69.8
Burglary	58.0	66.0	74.2
Teenage rowdiness	37.5	42.4	55.2
Street fights	26.3	29.8	33.8
Vandalism	57.1	66.5	76.0
Sexual assaults on women	49.4	56.3	66.0
Women being molested or pestered	53.4	61.5	71.3

The paradox of public priorities and police successes

If we rank (comparatively) public estimation of police effectiveness against crime, public perceptions of the changes in frequency of various crimes and public priorities regarding policing, we can see the extraordinary disparity between public demand on policing and public perceptions of policing.

As we can see, there is a tendency for the public to see the police as unsuccessful at dealing with those crimes which they prioritize and see as becoming more common, and vice versa (see Table 3.10).

Public use of 999 calls

999 calls are the most vital emergency link between the police and public. They are not the major route of contact – other telephone calls and personal visits to police stations are more predominant – but even on a

quantitative level they are not far behind (20% c.f. 16%). Furthermore, as we see, the public place police response to 999 calls as the very top of their priorities (9% perceive this as a very important task) (Table 3.11).

Table 3.10   Public views on policing successes, changes in frequency of offences and policing priorities

	'The police are not successful'	'Offence has become more common'	'The police should prioritize'
Mugging	70.2	60.7	70.7
Vandalism	65.8	53.0	26.8
Burglary	65.5	67.6	58.1
Women being molested and pestered	61.7	47.8	–
Sexual assaults on women	57.0	48.1	69.3
Rowdiness	45.2	44.3	9.8
Street fighting	29.8	31.0	–

Table 3.11   Public perceptions of policing priorities

	Tasks Perceived as Very Important %
Immediate response to 999 calls	98.6
Crime investigation	93.2
Deterrent presence on the streets	87.0
Control sports grounds & public meetings	80.1
Contact with children at schools	73.5
Crime prevention advice	69.9
Keep a check on shops & offices	64.8
Traffic control	54.2
Youth community projects	49.5

The proportion of people making 999 calls in the last year in Islington was 16%. This is higher than the proportion for London as a whole, of which the PSI report remarked "a remarkably high proportion of people – 11 per cent – said they had made a 999 call to the police in the past 12 months" (D. Smith, 1983a, p85). Of these a third were dissatisfied with the result – twice as many as in London as a whole (35% c.f. 17%). *Thus the demand on the police in terms of emergency calls is considerably higher in Islington than in London and the dissatisfaction with the results even more so.* The population in terms of ethnic groups, whether white, black or Asian, make calls in almost identical proportions. Furthermore, there is no great difference in general between the levels of satisfaction by different sub-groups although older people are, to a degree, more satisfied. What is crucial is the level of victimization. In general those who have never been criminally victimized have a high level of satisfaction with 999 calls (presumably they made service related calls) whilst those who have been multiply victimized show very high levels of dissatisfaction (see Table 3.13).

Lastly, it should be noted that the highest level of dissatisfaction with the police lies in the area of 999 calls. In general the less urgent the matter the more satisfied are the public (see Table 3.13).

Table 3.12   Proportion of population dissatisfied with police responses to 999 calls (by age, race, gender and level of criminal victimization)

	All	*Age*			*Race*		
		Under 25	*25–44*	*45+*	*White*	*Black*	*Asian*
% dissatisfied	34.5	34.7	41.0	25.9	33.6	37.1	42.2

	Gender		*Victimization*		
	Male	*Female*	*0*	*1-2*	*3+*
	39.0	38.7	18.0	33.1	40.4

Table 3.13   Levels of public satisfaction with the police (by different methods of contact)

Public-initiated Contact	*Dissatisfied*
999 calls	34.5%
Other telephone calls	25.6%
Personal visit to police station	23.7%
Approaching police officer	10.9%

The secret social service?

"The average citizen thinks of the police as an organisation primarily concerned with preventing crime and catching criminals. When the crime rate goes down or criminals go uncaught, the conventional public response is to demand more or better policemen . . . for some time, persons who run or study police departments have recognised that this public conception is misleading. The majority of calls received by most police are for services that have little to do with crime but a great deal to do with medical emergencies, family quarrels, auto accidents, barking dogs, minor traffic violations and so on." (J.Q. Wilson, 1985, p61)

Thus writes James Q. Wilson, President Reagan's adviser on crime and, internationally, perhaps the most influential scholar writing about the police and policing. Such an approach to policing has had considerable impact in Britain on the thinking of certain key Chief Constables, on the Home Office and on the majority of sociologists working in the field. Broken down this portion suggests:

(i) That the public view of the police is primarily as a crime control organization.

(ii) That public demand on the police is in the majority of instances concerned with tasks of a "non-criminal" kind. Thus Wilson's classic study of citizen's complaints radioed to patrol vehicles in the American city of Syracuse had the following breakdown of calls (excluding information requests).

Citizens' Complaints Radioed to Police Vehicles, Syracuse Police Department

Service Calls (eg "accidents, lost animals, lost property")	48.1
Order Maintenance (eg "gang disturbance, family trouble, assaults, neighbour trouble)	38.6
Law Enforcement (eg burglary, check on car, making arrest)	13.2

(Source: Wilson, 1968)

(iii) That success at this service role has to be recognized as an important indicator of police performance. Thus Morris and Heal write in the Home Office Research Study *Crime Control and the Police*: "it is important to recognise that police *effectiveness* and *crime-control effectiveness* should not be confused. The importance of this distinction can be recognised by considering that one consequence of measurement in any organisation is for members to concentrate on those activities that are capable of being measured – in the present case recorded crime, arrests, clearance rates etc – at the expense of those less tangible areas of activity which are difficult if not impossible, to measure, such as crime prevention, social assistance and the maintenance of public order" (1981, p15).

Let us look at these propositions in terms of the logic of their argument and in the light of the data from the Islington Crime Survey.

(a) *The prioritization of crime control*

We have seen in the last section how the public prioritize crime control. The problem is that they are dissatisfied with the police's ability to achieve these crime control goals.

(b) *Crime control as a minority demand on the police*

It is argued that the public – despite prioritizing crime control, in fact, make only a minority of their demands on the police in this area and have a misconception as to the complex role that the police play. This notion of the role of the police has become a conventional wisdom of extraordinary tenacity particularly in Home Office circles. Thus Ekblom and Heal write in their study *The Police Response to Calls from the Public*:

> "The data confirmed the by-now well established finding (Punch and Naylor, 1973; Comrie and Kings, 1974; McCabe and Sutcliffe, 1978; Hough, 1980) that only a small proportion of calls for police assistance are related to crime matters. Of all calls received from the public over six days at the sub-divisional control room studied only 18% required the preparation of a fresh crime report. Calls relating to 'plight' (locked out of car or home, lost property, person missing from home), administrative matters (sudden death, various licence renewals or the revision of alarm keyholder records), disputes (commercial and domestic), disturbances and nuisance (eg rowdy children or noisy neighbours) made up by far the greater proportion of demand."
> (1982, p3)

More recently, Southgate and Ekblom in their review of the BCS findings on contacts between police and public write

> "Like other studies, the BCS clearly shows that most public contacts with the police are apparently unrelated to crime. Public demands for the provision of general advice and assistance, the resolution of conflict and the control of nuisance and disorder greatly outnumber requests for dealing with crime and enforcing the law."
> (1984, p25)

Indeed, earlier they summarize the basis for this seemingly rock-hard generalization

> "A number of studies have analysed the nature of public calls made on the police, consistently showing crime-related calls to be in the minority. The greater proportion of demand consists of service calls dealing, for example, with lost property, missing persons, sudden deaths, licensing, and order problems (including disturbances, nuisances and disputes). Within this overall pattern, however, there is some variation in the size of the crime to non-crime ratio observed, a variation that probably reflects differences in the definitions used to classify requests to the police, many of which are complex in nature. Thus, Ekblom and Heal (1982) found that of all calls received at one subdivision, only three out of ten were crime-related; Punch and Naylor (1973) found only 41% of requests for police help relating to law enforcement; Comrie and Kings (1975) found 34% of calls to be concerned with crime; Hough (1980) found that 36% of incidents attended by patrols involved crime; Jones (1983) found that 43% of contacts made by the public were crime-related."
> (1984, p11)

Let us first examine this portion in terms of its logic. In order to assist this process we have summarized the existing data in Table 3.15.

The crucial data are the ratio of non-criminal-related to crime-related public requests of the police in the final column. The ratio is generally acknowledged to show a majority of non-crime-related requests. Two exceptions to this are the new town in Punch and Naylor's study of three Essex towns and the recent controversial finding by the MCS of a ratio directly in contradiction to the conventional wisdom on the subject.

As the *Howard Journal of Criminal Justice* put it with regard to the MCS, "one unexpected finding from Merseyside is the high proportion of police-public contacts which are crime-related, far more than in the British Crime Survey" (Vol 24/2) May 1985, p136). Indeed, for a while there were a flurry of exchanges between scholars and other interested authorities casting doubts on the findings of the MCS and in particular the accuracy of the calculations involved. As we shall see the importance of this debate is not merely scholarly – it has quite crucial implications in the policy field.

Before we look at how the results of the ICS help clarify this matter, it is necessary first of all to clear up some of the confusion in the area. For even at first glance the table displays the rather shaky basis of the conventional wisdom. Firstly, the stage in the process of policing and the routes of public-police demand are extremely mixed. Wilson, for example, bases his classic work on citizen's complaints which have already been filtered at the police station then radioed on to police vehicles; Hough's work concerns incidents being attended to by police vehicles; Ekblom and Heal concentrate on telephone calls from the public; whilst Punch and Naylor focus on all public contacts. Secondly, the distinction between crime and order-related incidents is extremely confusing. Wilson's list of order offences includes, for example, "assaults", "gang disturbances" and "family trouble". It is difficult to see how these are not in the majority of cases crime-related. Surely what has happened is that the criminologists are merely reflecting the distinctions often made by police officers between "real" crime and "rubbish" crime? (See D. Smith, 1983b). And if the police deprioritize certain crime such as domestic disputes, there is no reason why the criminologist – or the concerned member of the public for that matter – should follow suit. Thus the arbitrary distinction between crime and order offences systematically reduces the correlated figure. Thirdly, the distinction between order and service demands is also suspicious. What, for example, are we to make of Punch and Taylor's remark that "Obviously, some calls did not fall easily into this (law enforcement) category. For instance, family quarrels or noisy parties are potential breaches of the peace but, as they rarely result in prosecution and often require the exercise of social skills, we put them in the service category" (1973,p358). It is, of course, the police unwillingness to prosecute in instances of domestic violence that has led to con-

Table 3.14 Summary of research on public initiated contacts with the police

Author(s), Date	Area of Study	Part of Policing Process	% Crime Related	% Order Related	% Service Related	Ratio Non Crime to Crime (Ratio)
J.Q. Wilson, 1968	Syracuse, USA	Citizens complaints radioed to police vehicles	13.2	38.6	48.1	6.6 :1
Punch and Naylor, 1973	New Town, Essex Old Town, Essex Country Town, Essex.	Personal and telephone contacts from public	50.7 38.9 27.0	49.3 61.1 73.0		0.97:1 1.6 :1 2.7 :1
Comrie and Kings, 1975	England and Wales	Incidents attended by patrols	34.0	17.0	49.0	1.9 :1
Hough, 1980	Strathclyde	Incidents attended by patrols	36.0	19.0	45.0	1.8 :1
Ekblom and Heal, 1982	Humberside	Telephone calls from the public	30.0	70.0		2.3 :1
Jones, 1983	Devon and Cornwall	Public contacts	43.0	57.0		1.3 :1
Southgate and Ekblom, 1984 (BCS)	England and Wales	All public initiated contacts	22.4	77.6		1.3 :1
R. Kinsey, 1984 (MCS)	Merseyside	All public – police contacts (minus social)	57.0	7	36.0	0.8 :1

siderable criticism (see Hanmer and Saunders, 1984). But a considerable proportion (28.5%) of Punch and Naylor's "service" calls are domestic disputes. Indeed it is the most frequent of all their service categories. Thus once again the "non-crime"-related calls are artificially inflated. Lastly, these breakdowns derive from very different settings: different countries, different parts of the country, large towns and small towns and rural and urban areas. This may explain the wide variation in non-criminal to criminal incident ratios and, of course, the "exceptional" findings of a comparatively low ratio in the new forum in Punch and Naylor's study and a much lower ratio in Merseyside.

The central question which the Islington Crime Survey is able to cast light upon is: what is the public demand pattern in an inner-city area? Or more directly, what is the pattern of public demand in those areas of high criminal victimization where the public have high demands on the police and where the majority of police resources and manpower are centred? In the ICS we have been scrupulous to restrict service demand to non-criminal areas and, whilst retaining for comparative purposes the category of order demands have strictly avoided including those events – such as domestic violence – which are clearly criminal.

In Table 3.16 we have divided up public-initiated contacts with the police by the rate of contact. Following the usual practice, we have calculated the ratio of non-crime-related to crime-related contacts (Ratio 1). This ratio has almost invariably indicated a majority of non-crime-related contacts ranging up to the region of 3:1.

As can be seen immediately from Table 3.15 the primary pattern of public contact with the police in Islington is crime-related and the majority of public initiated contacts are about crime, and this narrow majority is transformed when one looks at the different types of contact. Telephone contact – about half of the total – is predominantly crime related. 66% of all telephone calls are about crime and this rises to 76% if we include public order complaints. This flies totally in the face of studies such as Ekblom and Heal who find only 30% of telephone contacts to be crime related. What it does corroborate, however, is the MCS which found that 57% of all public calls (*excluding* social calls) on police time were about crime and an almost identical pattern of contact to the ICS in terms of the various routes. It would seem, therefore, that the conventional wisdom with regard to police-public contact in terms of the inner city, which is the major focus of police activity and resources, is incorrect.

The ratio we find in the ICS is basically 1:1, that is in contradiction to the majority of the previous work with the exception of the MCS. The generalization about the high rate of crime-related public requests in uban settings would seem to hold both in Islington and Merseyside. The controversial Merseyside finding would still seem remarkably atypical, however, and at 0.8 to 1 it is considerably lower than the ICS finding. But,

Table 3.15 Public initiated contacts with the police (by various types of contact)

	All	999	Non-999 Telephone	Calling in Police Station	Approaching Police Officer
% of all contacts	100.0	22.4	28.5	27.7	21.6
A. Crime related	50.8	65.9	65.0	44.0	25.0
B. Public order related	5.6	16.0	7.0	–	–
C. Service related	40.8	18.0	28.0	56.0	62.0
D. Social	3.0	0	0	0	14.0
Ratio 1 $\left(\frac{B+C+D}{A}\right)$	1.0	0.5	0.5	1.3	3.0
Ratio 2 $\frac{(C+D)}{(A+B)}$	0.8	0.2	0.4	1.3	3.0

there are two simple reasons for this – one, the MCS did not include social calls (a minor reason) and, more importantly, the MCS includes a miscellaneous category of "difficult to code" reasons which was subsequently distributed equally between the crime, order and service categories. If these were placed – as is more likely – in the service category we find results of 1.1:1; that is virtually identical with the ICS findings. Furthermore, we have continued to follow the conventional practice of having order as a separate non-criminal category. If we were to include order in crime, given that a majority of public order occasions are potentially criminal, then we would have ratios which show that the public relation with the police is predominantly crime-related (see Ratio 2, Table 3.15).

(c) *The policy implications of a finding of high public crime-related demand on policing*

Let us first spell out the policy implications of the conventional wisdom that the police have a majority service role. It is argued that there is a peculiar cognitive lapse on the part of the public – on the one hand that they expect the police to be predominantly crime fighters but, on the other, they demand a wide range of services from the police. The police are – as Maurice Punch nicely put it – "the secret social service" (1979). This results, as members of the BCS urge, in a situation where there is divergence of priorities between the police who emphasize (among the lower ranks, at least) dealing with serious crime, and the public, who expect a far wider range of services. Thus they conclude "much avoidable misunderstanding can be removed by ensuring that myths and selective views of policing are kept in check by a wider and more realistic knowledge of the entire spectrum of police-public contact" (Southgate and Ekblom, 1984, p33).

The next stage in this process is the notion that there is a link between such a predominant social service role and the low performance levels of the police at clearing up crime. A Canadian author, John Hagan, spells this line of thought out very clearly:

"The problem, it seems, is that when in doubt or desperation, we call the police. As a result, the police become our front line gatekeepers of deviance, responding to all kinds of day-to-day variations from the norm, and deciding at this point of entry which of these many acts require further agency attention. Two factors encourage the police to persist in this role. First, it allows the police to avoid an exclusive image as oppressive keepers of the law (instead, they are able to perform a social service role as well). Second, the police frequently are the only 24-hour service agency available to respond to those in need. The result is that the police handle everything from unexpected childbirths, skid row alcoholics, drug addicts, emergency psychiatric cases, family fights, landlord-tenant disputes, and traffic violations, to occasional incidents of crime. The latter wording is deliberate, for Canadian and American studies agree that relatively little police time is spent on actual criminal cases. A Montreal study reported by Evans (1973): indicates that the police of that city

spend as little as 13 per cent of their total working hours on 'anti-criminal' activity. Similarly, across Canada, Evans estimates that the average police officer brings criminal charges against only 1.25 individuals every month. Even in a major city like Toronto the volume is not much higher – with district detectives and patrol officers averaging 15.5 criminal charges per year. The explanation of this pattern seems to lie in the character of the requests the police receive. Thus, in an American study, Wilson (1968) reports the following distribution of calls: 21.1 per cent asking for information; 37.1 per cent requesting service; 30.1 per cent seeking maintenance of order; and only 10.3 per cent dealing with the enforcement of laws. The importance of these varied demands on police time will become apparent, that the public gets, to a surprising extent, much of what it asks for."
(1977, p144)

Such a position has been taken up readily in influential government and policing circles in this country. Because the police are seen to have a very large public demand on them, much of which is non-crime related, then this explains their low clear-up rate. For there can be no doubt there *is* an extraordinarily high level of inefficiency that has to be explained. *After all, there were only 4.2 crimes cleared up per police officer per year in the Metropolitan Area in 1984* (see Kinsey, Lea and Young, 1986). Indeed, the recent Home Office study on police effectiveness is quite clear on this subject. It reiterates the conventional wisdom

"Dealing with crime is only one of the many tasks performed by the police. They also maintain order on the streets, marshal crowds, control traffic, cope with emergencies such as fires and floods, and provide a miscellaneous round-the-clock service of help and advice to the public. And even if the police and others have laid great stress on their 'crime fighting' role, only a small proportion of the incidents they have to deal with are directly related to crime. The report does not consider the effectiveness with which the police handle their non-crime functions, though any assessment of optimum manning levels must take these into account. The research reviewed here therefore offers no direct guide to the appropriate size of the police service."
(Clarke and Hough 1984, pp2-3)

And then, after an exhaustive review of the literature, they conclude

"It could be said that limitations on police effectiveness in controlling crime should not be discussed in public because, for example, this might undermine public confidence or encourage offending by those who are deterred at present. But apart from any general arguments of openness it is important that there should be a wider understanding of what can be expected from the police and what the public should expect to do for themselves. It may not be helpful to think in terms of a 'war on crime' fought between criminals and the police, as this may increase unnecessarily public anxieties and fear of crime. The clearest implication of the research reviewed above is that there are few proven grounds for indiscriminately allocating further resources to traditional deterrent strategies. The evidence about police effectiveness, coupled with financial constraints, led some American police departments to reduce manpower in the late 1970s; the New York Police Department reduced its workforce by a fifth. One result was that recorded crime continued to rise – but no faster than before – and arrests for serious offences actually rose. Some police authorities in this country have also entertained the idea of reducing manpower. However, levels of police resources should not be assessed simply in terms of their effect on crime. Manpower is needed to perform the many functions of policing besides law enforcement, and it is doubtful whether the police could provide the same level of service with fewer officers.

Clearly a completely objective formula for deciding police resources will never be devised, but it might be possible to make decisions better informed. This will require several things to be achieved. The public must receive better information about police work and about the effectiveness of crime control efforts. There must be more informed discussion about the tasks which the police should and should not perform. (Here the police authorities and the recently established consultative committees have an important part to play.) The police must confront questions about the efficiency and effectiveness of their non-crime work. And survey techniques and other research methods must be deployed to support them in this task; developing adequate 'output measures' for the totality of police work – difficult though this may be – must therefore rank high on the research agenda."
(1984, pp20-1)

Here we have it starkly put. Although there is little real argument for extension of police resources in terms of crime control, the "predominant" service function makes it difficult to generate a very clear indicator of police performance and is a major argument against force reduction. And its conclusion that survey results are of great importance in ascertaining police performance of both a crime-related and service kind, has, of course, great relevance to the significance and uses of this first ICS.

The argument that crime control is a minority task of policing and that a substantial proportion of crimes prioritized by the public cannot be dealt with by the police (burglary, for example) has been taken up enthusiastically in London police circles. As Commissioner Newman put it "over a half of recorded crime is of a capricious and opportunistic nature, upon which police, acting without public help, would never be likely to make any serious impact" (1984, p4). Thus much of the type of policing which the public demand ("reactive" policing in response to 999 calls etc.) is liable to be fruitless and there needs to be a move towards greater service provision.

"An alternative to the reactive model, emphasising crime control, is for the police to take the initiative by acting upon the environment rather than merely responding to it and by working with the public and other social agencies to prevent crime. Within this model, the prevention of crime within the community is raised to at least the same level of importance as that of

detection; the emphasis moves away from a focus upon the individual offence and offender to more active consideration of the preconditions for offences and thought for the potential victim of crime."
(*Ibid.*, p8)

And Kenneth Newman repeats his conclusion in this year's report

"The police service has to a large extent become trapped in a reactive role based upon an understandable and conventional preoccupation with crime committed. Last year I urged the Force to move towards a greater feeling for the preventative role, which accords readily with well-documented research locating the vast majority of police work in the 'service' functions peripheral to crime investigation."
(1985, p19)

Thus the Commissioner very neatly acknowledges the existence of a large service provision of the police, together with the low performance in crime control, by arguing for an *expansion* of the service provision, a movement away from a role-reactive to public demands *vis à vis* crime as the only way forward in crime control.

This movement towards a focus on the service rather than the crime control aspect of policing is reinforced by a parallel shift from a focus on crime control to order maintenance. Here, once again, the influence of the work of James Q. Wilson is influential in British policing policy. Once again the Home Office Research Study *Crime and Police Effectiveness* sums up this viewpoint well in the context of the current argument about community policing:

"Community policing provides a rationale for 'putting bobbies back on the beat' in terms of better relations between the police and public. Recently a second – and to some extent conflicting – rationale has been offered in terms of the foot patrol officer's task of maintaining order on the beat. This suggests that certain levels of disorderly behaviour (on the part of drunks, tramps, rowdy youths, prostitutes and other undesirables) can trigger a spiral of neighbourhood decline, with increased fear of crime, migration of the law-abiding from the area, weakening of informal social control and, ultimately, increases in serious crime. According to this view, beat policemen should be assigned long terms to areas at risk to break the spiral, clamping down in the 'incivilities' which lead to decline.
Such ideas amount to an extension – or at least consolidation – of the police function of 'order maintenance' at a time when many have argued that this aspect of police work should be performed with a very light touch (especially in the multi-racial inner cities). At the risk of distortion it might be said that the beat policeman would arrest offenders or move them on, whilst the community constable would shepherd them back to the fold. Thorny issues about civil liberties and due process arise with informal policing of the local 'roughs' on behalf of the local 'respectables' – especially in areas where there is little

consensus about acceptable public behaviour. There is nevertheless some support for the hypothesis. (A Study) in Newark found that the introduction of foot patrols led to reductions in fear of crime, because, the authors argue, they secured a marked reduction on levels of public disorder – patrols moved on drunks, vagrants and beggars, for example, and youths were not allowed to gather in rowdy groups on the street. A more recent study also found that the presence of street disorder stimulates crime levels and fear of crime, and erodes informal control processes."
(Clarke and Hough, 1984 p17)

This is the basis of the Wilson–Kelling hypothesis (see Wilson, 1985, Ch.5) which argues that, although the police's effectiveness in directly dealing with crime is limited, the regulation of order in a community can stimulate the weak informal systems of social control back into action and thus in the long run begin to help the community regulate itself for more serious offences (see Kinsey, Lea and Young, 1986). It is easy to see how this argument corresponds with Newman's conception of prevention through community intervention and the service role rather than the direct control of crime.

Fairness to different groups

We now turn from questions of police efficiency and public priorities to questions of police legitimacy – the public's evaluation of their ability to work within the rule of law.

"A community consenting to be policed by its own members gives constables an implied mandate to preserve the peace, to prevent crime and to bring offenders to justice. Such consent rests upon the legitimacy – both actual and perceived – of the methods used by the police to discharge their mandate and of the styles of policing employed in doing so, both of which must be consonant with the demands of a vigilant and energetic democracy.
    The level of police professionalism will be gauged by the extent to which the service is able to establish that legitimacy in the eyes of the people."
(K. Newman, 1985, p1)

We asked our sample whether the police in the area treated all sorts of people fairly and equally. This is a crucial question in that it points directly to the degree of equality demanded by the law and, in terms of these groups which see themselves as unfairly treated (whether because of age, or race, or class), it provides a potential basis for alienation from the police. A full one third of respondents thought that such unfairness occurred, which is roughly equal to that found in the PSI Survey of all Londoners. This sizeable proportion varies widely when we examine the main background variables.

Table 3.16   Police do not treat all people fairly and equally

		%
AGE	16–24	54.1
	25–44	46.6
	45+	13.5
RACE	White	29.4
	Asian	30.2
	Black	61.1
GENDER	Male	32.2
	Female	32.6
EMPLOYMENT STATUS	Employed	38.6
	Unemployed	45.2
ALL		32.5

One of the most striking differences is with age, in that very few people over 45 see the police as being unfair whereas over half of 16-24 year olds do as well as 46.6% of those in the 25-44 age group. *The other remarkable difference is with race. For whereas white and Asian respondents are almost identical in their appraisal of police fairness, over twice as many blacks – two thirds in all – view the police as acting unfairly.* If such a question is an indication of police fairness by minority groups then it might be noted that the wide differences between Asians and blacks would suggest very difficult relationships with the police. For although a sizeable proportion of Asians maintain that there is police unfairness, a substantial majority – 70% – do not.

In terms of gender there is little difference between the assessment of the police by men and women, whereas the unemployed are somewhat more likely to see the police as unfair when compared to the employed.

How do these relationships appear when we control by age, race and gender? If we look at Table 3.17 we see that the groups which see the police as most unfair are young blacks and that there is little difference between men and women. It is startling that three quarters of this section of the black population believe the police to be unfair.

At the other extreme, it is whites over 45, irrespective of gender, who have the highest confidence in police fairness. This rate of 90% confidence in police fairness is not approached by any other category.

Over 45 non-whites do not exhibit this high level of confidence. The high black lack of confidence in the police in respect to fairness occurs at all ages and in both genders. The most startling difference in the black population is between over 45 men and women, the latter having a considerably lower confidence. We have discussed the exceptional case of older black women earlier in Chapter 1.

The confidence of white people in the police, in general, is not high, just under half of all men and women under 45 perceiving them as acting unfairly – it is only the very high rates of confidence of the over 45s that brings the overall figure down to 29%. Asians have a higher estimation of police fairness than whites in all categories, except the over 45s, and a much higher estimation than blacks in every category.

Table 3.17 Belief that the police treat some groups unfairly (by age, race and gender)

	White	Black	Asian
Male 16–24	46.5	77.5	32.0
Male 25–44	48.8	57.7	25.0
Male 45+	10.1	43.5	28.6
Female 16–24	53.5	75.0	45.8
Female 25–44	44.5	54.8	23.1
Female 45+	9.9	64.7	36.4

Unemployment and perceptions of unfairness
As we have noted, unemployment has overall an effect on perceptions of police unfairness. The relationship becomes clearer when we break down by age and race.

Table 3.18 Belief that the police treat some groups unfairly (by age, race and work status)

			Race	
	Age	White	Black	Asian
Employed	16–24	48.8	70.9	20.7
	25–44	45.8	56.1	27.0
	45+	8.3	52.9	30.7
Unemployed	16–24	51.3	80.3	49.7
	25–44	47.5	55.8	23.5
	45+	12.9	51.6	33.2

The considerable proportion (about a half) of whites aged 16-44 and blacks over 25 who see the police as unfair, is not particularly affected by unemployment. There is, however, a difference between unemployed and employed young blacks – 80% compared to 71% perceive police unfairness. But both these figures are very high and the fact of being young and black is obviously of much greater relevance than work status. Where unemployment does have impact, however, is with young Asians where more than double those unemployed compared to those employed perceive police unfairness.

Relationship between income and perceptions of police unfairness
To note that there is greater tendency for unemployed people to say that
the police are unfair does not mean that within the ranks of the employed
that those better off are more inclined to believe in police fairness. In fact,
a higher income *tends* to *increase* the public's perception of police unfairness irrespective of the race of the person concerned (see Table 3.19).
Young blacks, for example, with incomes greater than £8,000 a year tend
to have extremely high (80%) tendency to suspect police unfairness, and
the highest proportion of whites who perceive the police as unfair are
those aged 25-44 who earn over £12,000. Those groups with the lowest
proportion of people believing that the police are unfair are both over-45,
but they present a sharp contrast – 65% of the poorest whites and 40% of
the highest income blacks.

**Table 3.19   Belief that the police treat some groups unfairly (by income,
race and age)**

Income/Age		White	Black
	(16–24	47.1	70.4
£3,000–	(25–44	41.2	53.4
7,999	(45+	6.5	46.4
	(16–24	51.4	83.4
£8,000–	(25–44	43.6	66.7
11,999	(45+	14.5	55.7
	(16–24	51.4	82.2
£12,000+	(25–44	57.8	67.0
	(45+	16.5	40.0

Table 3.20 below indicates belief in the fairness of the police by our three
scales.

**Table 3.20   Belief that the police treat some groups unfairly (by scales
A, B & C)**

	High	Medium	Low
A. Satisfaction with neighbourhood	5.6	25.9	53.4
B. Fear of crime	31.3	32.7	37.1
C. Likelihood of crime	40.9	32.6	21.7

Thus people who are highly satisfied with their neighbourhood are very
unlikely to see the police as acting unfairly whereas those who are dissatisfied are more likely to be critical of the police on this score. Import-

antly those who believe themselves likely to be victims of crime are much more likely to doubt the fairness of the police than those who see victimization as unlikely. The level of fear of crime itself is unrelated to views on police fairness.

The disquiet felt about police fairness by those who see themselves as likely to be victims of crime is underscored by the data concerning those who have actually been victimized (see Table 3.21).

Table 3.21 Belief that the police treat some groups unfairly (by incidence of criminal victimization)

	Personal Victimization	*Household Victimization*
0	21.8	27.4
1 or 2	35.7	34.4
3+	43.2	51.2

Here we see dramatically that beliefs in the unfairness of the police increase with the chances of being criminally victimized. Such a close relationship between multiple criminal victimization and doubts as to the fairness of the police is true when one controls age and race. For example, if we look at young people by levels of victimization, we see the following:

Table 3.22 Belief in unfairness of the police (by degrees of criminal victimization and race amongst 16–24 year olds)

Victimization	*White*	*Black*	*Asian*
Nil	43.3	65.2	27.6
Multiple	56.5	82.7	40.9

Here we have the same pattern of a rising degree of dissatisfaction with the police from Asians to whites to blacks. And, in each case, there is an increase in belief in unfairness rising to an extremely high 82.7% amongst multiply-victimized young blacks.

Lastly, we find that the number of contacts with police relate closely to public evaluation of the police reacting unfairly to certain groups. Thus:

Table 3.23 Police reacting unfairly to certain groups (by contacts with police)

		%
Contacts	0	19.5
	1	39.3
	2+	45.7

132 *The Islington Crime Survey*

Police understanding of problems in the area

Overall one third of the sample did not think the police had a good understanding of the problems of the area. This was considerably larger (36% c.f. 25%) than the proportion of people at Merseyside asked the same question. Once again it varied with the main social characteristics.

Table 3.24   Belief that police do not have a good understanding of the area (by age, race, gender and employment status)

		%
AGE	16–24	58.7
	25–44	44.7
	45+	20.6
RACE	White	33.6
	Asian	41.6
	Black	54.6
GENDER	Male	34.6
	Female	34.7
EMPLOYMENT STATUS	Employed	40.5
	Unemployed	50.6

As with the public judgement of the fairness of the police to different groups, the pattern is repeated. By age, it is the 45+ age group who are exceptional in their belief in the understanding of the police. Almost half the 25-44 age group do not and this rises to 59% with the under 24s. In terms of race a substantial one third of whites doubt police knowledge of Islington and this rises to over half (55%) in the case of blacks. Asians are in an intermediate position. The unemployed are more doubtful about understanding than are the employed and, once again, there is little to choose from between men and women.

In terms of our three scales an almost identical pattern to the previous section occurs (see Table 3.25).

Table 3.25   Lack of good police understanding of the area (by scales A, B & C)

	High	Medium	Low
A. Satisfaction with neighbourhood	4.7	31.3	53.6
B. Fear of crime	39.3	35.3	31.7
C. Likelihood of crime	51.0	33.7	28.2

Once again people with a high satisfaction of their neighbourhood have an extremely high confidence in the police and those with low satisfaction are much more doubtful. Fear of crime does not vary as much – although high fear of crime is more likely to be combined between one's estimation of the likelihood of being a victim of crime and doubts as to police under-standing of the area.

Table 3.26   Lack of good police understanding of the area (by criminal victimization and contact with the police)

	0	1 or 2	3+
Personal victimization	26.6	39.9	44.5
Household victimization	30.5	39.0	53.1
Contacts with police	26.9	36.6	47.0

Once again, doubts in the abilities of the police increase with the degree in which members of the public experience criminal victimization. And the more the public have contact with the police the less they feel the police have an understanding of the area.

Serious police misconduct

Following the PSI report for London as a whole, we asked a series of questions in Islington as to public beliefs with regards to police mal-practices. The four areas of serious misconduct we will examine are: the use of undue force in the arrest situation, violence on people held at police stations without undue reason, police officers planting evidence and officers taking bribes.

Table 3.27 reveals that about one half of the survey believe that such malpractices occur and a substantial minority of those interviewed be-lieve that they occur on a regular basis: 1 in 5 believe this is true of use of undue force and planting evidence, 1 in 6 that the police use undue viol-ence at police stations and 1 in 8 that the police take bribes. *Furthermore, there is a consistent difference between the ICS and PSI results – people in Islington are more likely than those in London in general to believe that police malpractices occur.*

About one half of those interviewed believed that undue force on arrest and at the police station was on the increase, and one third that plants and bribes were more frequent today. All of those figures are sub-stantially greater than those obtained by the PSI and suggest that, as far as Islington is concerned, there is a particularly acute perception of deter-iorating police standards within the Borough. We have chosen through-out this chapter on policing to use the PSI report as a backcloth. Substan-tively, this is because it allows a comparison with all of London but it must also be noted that the PSI itself recorded a substantial level of criticism of the police and a considerable belief in the drop in standards. It is for this reason that politicians, criminologists, police officers and journalists have taken its results so seriously. For the ICS, then, to indicate considerably greater problems of public confidence in the police within an inner-city area underlines the dramatic nature of the present survey's conclusions.

It might be argued that these beliefs in police malpractices are merely a function of a sensationalist mass media which emphasize a high level of police violence and deviation from official standards, but it is difficult to understand why beliefs about the high frequency of police misconduct are more prevalent in Islington than in London as a whole. It surely cannot be a result of a greater addiction to the mass media in the inner city.

A telling piece of information as to formation of such beliefs as to police malpractice is the replies to the question "how have you come to know about it?". The answers are as follows:

Table 3.28   Sources of information with regard to police using undue violence on arrest

	%
Actually happened to you or someone you know	39
You or someone you know seeing it happen to someone else	45
Seeing news pictures on TV of it happening	87
Hearing it discussed on radio or television	84
Reading about it in the newspapers	83

Thus one moves along a continuum from direct experience to reports in the mass media. What is important to underline is the large number of people who claim that it actually happened to them or someone they knew. *Thus a full 39% of those who believe that the police use unfair force on arrest base this on actual experience.* A much greater proportion (over 80%) have also received information from the mass media with regard to the police using undue force. On one level this dismisses the common conspirational (or functionalist) notion that the mass media are a force largely supportive of the *status quo* on all issues. For if this were so why should over 87% of those who believe that the police have acted beyond the bounds of the rule of law have received information to the contrary via the "establishment" mass media? But it might be argued that the quantity and quality of such information is extraordinarily distorted within the media. After all, police drama is a major genre on television and it involves quite extraordinary ideas of the high level of clear up rate of the police and the prevalence of investigative police work (J. Young, 1986) combined with a literary structure which justifies undue violence in the course of the common good (J. Palmer, 1978). And, if there were only a small proportion of direct experential information about police work in the context of the undoubtedly large and distorted mass media input, then we could easily talk of public fantasies with regard to police work which have little relationship to reality. But, in fact, we find that there is a substantial *rational core* to the public's belief in police violence which is

Table 3.27 Police malpractices: a comparison of ICS and PSI

%	Undue Force on Arrest		Violence at Police Stations		Plants		Bribes	
	ICS	PSI	ICS	PSI	ICS	PSI	ICS	PSI
Never/hardly ever	45	68	50	64	53	57	45	44
Sometimes	34	18	34	23	35	33	42	47
Often/very often	21	14	16	14	21	10	13	9
Happens more than it used to	58	23	48	20	33	20	30	28

Table 3.29 Belief that police use more force than necessary (by age, race, gender, contact and level of victimization)

	All	Age			Race			Gender		Contact			Victimization		
		Under 25	25–44	45+	White	Black	Asian	Male	Female	0	1	2+	0	1 or 2	3+
Never/hardly ever	45.2	24.3	28.9	65.4	47.2	23.3	49.8	44.1	46.0	54.6	40.1	34.4	54.1	44.7	34.8
Sometimes	34.3	38.8	42.9	26.1	34.1	36.0	39.1	34.2	34.4	32.6	36.0	35.9	33.4	33.3	35.7
Often	20.5	36.9	28.1	8.4	18.8	40.7	11.2	21.6	19.6	12.9	24.0	29.7	12.6	22.0	29.4

based on actual experience. Thus the mass media are effective because they play on existing anxieties, however distortedly, but they seldom create public concern where there is no concern to play upon (J. Young, 1981).

The above figures refer, of course, to the proportion of the population who do believe the police use undue force. The proportion of *total informants* who claim that they have direct or semi-direct experience of undue police violence is as follows:

– actually happening to you or someone you know 24%
– you or someone you know seeing it happen to someone else 28%

These are exactly double the figures found in the PSI report of which David Smith drily commented "12 or 14% are not large proportions, but they represent a large number of Londoners – perhaps 700,000 – who will be hard to convince that this kind of misconduct does not occur" (1983a, p260). Well 24 or 28% *are* sizeable proportions – a quarter of Islington's population, some 30,000 people, and there can be no doubt that such experiences leave an indelible mark on police-public relations in the Borough. But, of course, these beliefs as to police malpractices are not equally spread across the population. They reach much higher levels in terms of particular sub-groups.

In terms of age, Table 3.29 illustrates that there are extremely wide variations: 37% of those under 25 believe the police use undue violence on arrest as against only 8% of over-45s. This reproduces the differences that we have already seen in terms of attitudes to the police with regard to fairness between different groups (see Table 3.19). Once again the over 45s present a very different picture when compared with the rest of the population. As far as race is concerned there is a very substantive difference between blacks and other groups with, as usual, Asians being less critical than whites. Important here is the fact that beliefs in the police using excessive force rise with contacts and with the extent of criminal victimization. Thus, the general rule is substantiated that the public are more critical of the police in those instances where
(a) they have a high degree of contact with them
    or
(b) they are subject to a high level of criminal victimization.

If we further break down our analysis into age, race and gender we find that the belief in the police using excessive violence is extraordinarily high in young blacks, over a half of men and women believing such violence occurs. The proportions of young whites is also considerable although not as great; one third of men and women having such knowledge of violence occurring. Of course, such beliefs may be fantasies but, as we have seen, they would seem to be based to an important extent on a rational kernel of direct or semi-direct experience. The most simple question must be asked: how can it be that there is such a wide variation between sub-groups of the population? Is it that white males and females over 45 with their miniscule beliefs in police violence (7% and 6% respectively, see Table 3.31) are correct whilst the beliefs of both black and white young people are fantasies, or is it that they reflect qualitatively different police-public encounters in the Borough? Is not the likely cause that these wide-spread differences within the population represent quite radically different experiences of encounters with the police?

If we look at Table 3.30 we find a very interesting split between direct or semi-direct experiential contact with the police compared to information obtained via the mass media. Nearly 80% of all sub-groups claim that they have obtained information with regard to undue force being used by the police from the mass media. But claims to experiential knowledge vary widely between sub-groups. Thus the mass media becomes a constant unvarying background of information. But direct experience of violence varies widely and it increases precisely in terms of those people who have either directly or indirectly (in terms of relatives and friends) a great deal of police attention focussed upon them.

Table 3.30 **Sources of information with regard to undue police violence (by age and race)**

Information Route %	All ICS	Age			Race		
		Under 25	25–44	45+	White	Black	Asian
Actually happened to you or someone you know	38.9	58.6	39.8	21.8	37.8	51.5	18.6
You or someone else you know seeing it happen to someone else	45.4	64.7	48.8	24.9	44.6	55.1	28.8
Seeing news-pictures on TV of it happening	86.9	83.9	85.9	90.7	87.5	85.7	78.0
Hearing it discussed on radio or TV	83.7	81.4	83.6	85.9	83.7	85.5	80.8
Reading about it in newspapers	83.3	79.4	81.6	88.9	84.2	81.3	67.4

Deterioration in police-public relations over time

Lastly, if we look at the sample views on whether police-public relationships have deteriorated over time with respect to undue violence (Table 3.32) we find that the number of people who believe that there has been an improvement is minute, regardless of age, gender or race. But those who believe it has worsened are in the majority of cases over half of the population. What is important here, perhaps, is that older people experience the situation as having worsened. Particularly noteworthy is that

Table 3.31 Belief that police often use excessive force (by age, race and gender)

	White Male			White Female			Black Male			Black Female			Asian Male			Asian Female		
	16–24	25–44	45+	16–24	25–44	45+	16–24	25–44	45+	16–24	25–44	45+	16–24	25–44	45+	16–24	25–44	45+
All	36.4	29.0	7.4	34.5	26.0	5.6	61.1	40.5	37.5	51.5	38.4	25.0	11.3	15.2	3.8	18.7	8.8	14.3

All: 20.5

Table 3.32 Belief that police use undue violence more today than in the past

	All	Age			Race			Gender		Contact with Police			Level of Criminal Victimization		
		Under 25	25–44	45+	White	Black	Asian	Male	Female	0	1	2+	0	1 or 2	3+
Less	2.8	3.7	3.0	1.9	2.5	4.0	5.3	3.0	2.7	3.0	2.3	2.9	2.7	4.3	2.4
About the same	13.0	36.8	37.9	42.9	38.4	39.4	53.9	41.3	37.0	42.9	42.7	33.7	44.8	36.6	35.2
More	58.2	59.5	59.1	55.4	59.1	56.6	40.8	55.7	60.4	54.1	55.0	63.4	52.5	59.1	62.4

contact with the police or experience of criminal victimization increased views of deterioration.

Willingness to cooperate with the police

In order to gauge the degree to which the public are willing to cooperate with the police we have followed the format of the survey PSI in presenting our sample with three hypothetical situations:

A. If you had seen a traffic accident in which someone had been badly hurt and the police were looking for witnesses. . .

B. If you had seen a couple of youths knock a man down and take his wallet and the police were looking for witnesses. . .

C. If you had seen a couple of youths smash up a bus shelter and the police were looking for witnesses. . .

In each situation the interviewee is asked would they (a) tell the police what they had seen? (b) be prepared to identify the people who had done it? (c) be prepared to give evidence in court about it? Thus we have three graduated types of offence from a traffic accident, to a less serious criminal act such as vandalism, to a fairly serious street robbery, coupled with a graduated degree of involvement with the judicial process – from helping the police, through identifying the offender(s), to witnessing in court.

It is vital to stress here the crucial nature of such public involvement in the judicial process. As we have seen in Chapter 2, the vast majority of offences are made known to the police by the public – something in the region of 95%+ – and the process of judicial enquiry depends very largely on public witnessing. Successful policing demands high public cooperation; where this is missing the whole process becomes unstuck.

If we examine Table 3.33 we can immediately discern distinct trends. Our very first category – the case of letting the police know about a serious accident – is a useful base line of cooperation. Here we can see that with the exception of the Asian sample – of which more later – there is no great variation (at least on this level of analysis) between the various groups. Regardless of age, race, gender or income, all groups would be willing to tell the police of the incident at a level of 95% or above (ie 5% or less unwillingness to cooperate).

As would be expected, willingness to cooperate with the police declines quite dramatically with the level of involvement in the judicial process. This is true for all social groups and all categories of offences. Thus, even in the instance of the traffic accident – where the police have the highest degree of cooperation – there is much less willingness to cooperate as witnesses in court and a much greater variation between the different groups. As would be expected of the three offences, the serious accident evokes the highest degree of public cooperation, followed by the fairly serious criminal offence and lastly the instance of youthful vandalism.

Table 3.33   Unwillingness to help the police: three situations (by age, race, gender and income)

Incident	% Lack of Cooperation	PSI Comparison	ICS All	Age			Race			Gender		ICS Income £			
				Under 25	25-44	45+	White	Black	Asian	Male	Female	Under 3000	3000-7999	8000-11999	12000+
A. Serious accident	Unwilling to tell police	3	4	3	2	5	3	4	17	2	5	5	4	2	1
	Unwilling to identify offender	–	7	8	4	8	9	12	23	5	8	10	7	4	2
	Unwilling to give evidence in court	9	13	18	7	15	11	20	33	8	17	17	14	8	5
B. Youths robbing a man of his wallet	Unwilling to tell police	4	7	9	5	8	6	13	25	6	9	9	9	5	4
	Unwilling to identify offender	9	15	21	10	15	12	29	35	11	19	18	17	11	7
	Unwilling to give evidence in court	16	22	31	15	23	19	40	49	16	29	27	25	15	13
C. Youths smashing up a bus shelter	Unwilling to tell police	17	27	40	21	26	26	34	34	24	30	31	30	22	16
	Unwilling to identify offender	23	36	51	30	35	35	46	48	30	42	43	39	29	23
	Unwilling to give evidence in court	29	44	61	38	41	42	56	58	35	51	52	47	34	30

Let us look next at the overall figures. They reflect, in every instance, a greater degree of lack of public cooperation with the police in Islington than the PSI figures which cover London as a whole. This corroborates the PSI findings that there is a lower rate of cooperation in inner-city Boroughs of high deprivation (PSI, p200) but the differences are much more striking than found in that Report. Thus, if one looks at unwillingness to appear in court, it is 44% greater in Islington than in London as a whole for serious accidents, 38% greater for street robbery and 52% greater for vandalism. In its more marked form it is striking that 1 in 5 of the inhabitants of Islington would be unwilling to give evidence in court with regards to a violent street robbery and 1 in 4 would be unwilling to even tell the police about the vandalism of bus shelters.

In this context of the markedly greater lack of police-public cooperation, it is useful to look at the differences between social groups. In terms of age, young people (under 25) are the least willing to cooperate with the police, followed by the over 45s, with the 25-44 age group the most willing to cooperate. As David Smith noted in the PSI report this is probably due to a greater hostility on the part of youth and a higher fear of reprisal on the part of the elderly (*ibid.*, p198). As far as race is concerned, we find that blacks are less likely to be willing to cooperate than whites. Thus 40% of blacks would be unwilling to testify in court with regards to street robbery as against 19% of whites. This is an early indicator of what we shall see is a marked level of alienation which corroborates the PSI findings. The most dramatic figures, however, are for the Asian population. Here just under 1 in 5 would not tell the police about a serious accident, a half would be unwilling to testify in court about street robbery and nearly 1 in 3 would not inform the police about vandalism. This is in sharp contrast to the PSI report which found only a slight difference between Asians and whites as to willingness to help the police.

In terms of gender we see clear differences. Women in general are less likely than men to cooperate with the police, particularly at the level of court room involvement. Presumably, in the case of traffic offences this is merely about the embarrassment of public appearances but in terms of criminal offences most probably this is about fear of reprisals. Lastly, there is a distinct rise in cooperation by income. The top income group (over £12,000) is the most likely to cooperate across the board with the police when compared to any other group on our chart.

What can we make of these differences? There seems to be a pattern such that those groups which have a comparatively high view of police fairness (women, the elderly, Asian) and yet a lower level of willingness to cooperate are probably worried over fear of reprisals. Whereas those groups which have a very critical view of police fairness (young people, blacks) and a low level of cooperation are less willing to help police because of a greater degree of alienation. Further research is necessary to substantiate this hypothesis but there are indications that this is correct if we further refine our analysis in terms of age, race and gender.

If one examines Table 3.34, we can examine the degree of cooperation with the police with much greater precision. If we set up arbitrarily a criterion that a reasonable degree of cooperation would be if 90% of the public were willing to help the police (ie a 10% refusal rate) then we find that public cooperation of the subsamples is reasonably high. Nine (one half) of the subsamples fall into this category and we can increase this to eleven if we include the two groups which are only just marginally outside.

This gives us the categories groups inside our criterion:
– All white groups
– All black groups apart from young men and women
– Only middle-aged male Asians
and outside
– All Asians apart from middle aged males
– Young black males and females.

What we have, therefore, is a distinct unwillingness on the part of the Asian community and of young blacks to cooperate with the police. There are clear indications that this may be a product of fear of reprisals and alienation from the police respectively. It is significant that in the Asian community it is women who are less cooperative than men and older people than younger people.

In contrast, in the black community it is young males who are exceptionally alienated and the majority of the black community is willing to cooperate with the police. There is, for example, no difference between elderly black and white women and precious little difference between elderly men. Furthermore, if one looks back to Table 3.18 where we documented the age, race and gender breakdown by beliefs that the police act unfairly towards certain groups, we find the ranking of perceptions of unfairness closely corresponds in blacks with their degree of unwillingness to cooperate with the police. There is no such correspondence of rankings amongst white or Asian sub-groups.

It should be noted that we have found no difference between black youths and the rest of the community in terms of their views as to the seriousness of street robbery. *What we have is not an alienation of young blacks from the community so much as their alienation from the police.*

It could, of course, be argued that the alienation of young blacks is simply a function of their higher offence rate, particularly in the area of street robberies. There are many problems with such an argument. Firstly, it is obvious that much unwillingness to cooperate with the police occurs in groups with very low offence rates. It is difficult to imagine a group with a lower rate of street robbery than Asian women over the age of 45, but they have the very highest rate of lack of cooperation. Secondly, although casual delinquency is common amongst all adolescent males, only a very small proportion of any sub-group would commit ser-

Table 3.34 Unwillingness to help the police in the case of street robbery (by age, race and gender)

% Lack of Cooperation	ALL	White Male			White Female			Black Male			Black Female			Asian Male			Asian Female		
		16–24	25–44	45+	16–24	25–44	45+	16–24	25–44	45+	16–24	25–44	45+	16–24	25–44	45+	16–24	25–44	45+
Unwilling to tell police	7	6	3	5	5	6	10	33	8	6	16	11	10	21	11	28	31	29	40
Unwilling to identify offender(s)	15	17	5	9	15	10	20	55	16	24	34	29	28	33	23	42	43	42	60
Unwilling to give evidence in court	22	25	8	10	25	16	33	70	32	29	51	35	43	39	46	40	63	50	67

ious crimes such as mugging. Thirdly, this is borne out by the fact that such a high proportion of young blacks rate robbery as a very serious crime. Fourthly, although there is undoubtedly some difference between the offence rates of white and black youths, it is nothing like as different as the popular mass media sometimes make out with their gross stereotype of the "black mugger" (Lea and Young, 1984). It certainly would not be reflected in the extraordinary difference between the willingness of white and black youths to cooperate with the police on this simple level of "telling the police what you had seen" – 33% of black youths would not cooperate with the police in this respect compared to only 6% of white youths (see Table 3.34). All of this points tentatively to very different relationships between police and public in the cases of black and white youths.

Table 3.35   Ranking by blacks of perceptions of police unfairness and unwillingness to cooperate with the police

Unwillingness to Cooperate with Police	Belief in Police Unfairness to Specific Groups
1. Young Male	1
2. Young Female	2
3. Middle Aged Male	4
4. Middle Aged Female	5
5. Older Female	3
6. Older Male	6

If we look at the highest level of public involvement in the judicial process – giving evidence in the courts – there are signs of a much greater unwillingness to cooperate. We must remember that street robbery is an offence which is given a very high policing priority by all sections of the community (see Table 3.1). Yet the only sections of the community willing to cooperate to the level of 90% are white men aged over 25 (ie Groups 25-44 plus 45+). Every other one of the eighteen sub-groups is unwilling to cooperate on this level and indeed fifteen of the groups have over a quarter of their members unwilling to give evidence in court. It should be stressed that such a lack of cooperation does not split on white/ ethnic group lines. If white males aged 25-44 with their remarkable 97%, 95% and 92% *willingness* to cooperate on each of the three judicial levels are perhaps the ideal typical witnesses, other white sub-groups are much less so. Thus a quarter of young whites both male and female are unwilling to cooperate, as are a third of all white women over 45.

The problem at its most severe is encountered when we turn to the highest level of non-cooperation, where we have over half of Asian women unwilling to cooperate, half of young black families and a stagger-ing 70% of black youths. Much has been written on the dire consequences on policing of public unwillingness to communicate evidence to the police (Kinsey, Lea and Young, 1986) but the hiatus in cooperation at the court level is of much greater severity. Its consequences are virtually to cripple the criminal justice system; and as can be seen from Table 3.34, the level of unwillingness to give evidence in court is even greater for minor offences such as vandalism. Even in the case of the most wealthy group of individuals who are exceptionally liable to cooperate with the police, one third would not, whilst nearly two thirds of those under 25, over half of the blacks and the Asians and of the poorest income groups would not cooperate. All of this makes it exceedingly difficult for policing to pro-duce results. For the essence of good policing is public cooperation at each level of the judicial process. Without it, clear-up rates must inevit-ably fall and protection against crime severely diminish.

Stop and search

Policing is conventionally divided into *reactive* and *proactive* policing. Reactive policing is in response to public demand, proactive policing is initiated by the police themselves. As we have argued, a large amount of the demand on police time stems from public demand particularly given that 95% of crimes are reported to the police by the public. As for the other 5% this is crime within the scope of proactive policing. Part of this process involves the police stopping and searching members of the public. There is considerable debate as to the efficacy of stop and search as a method of crime control. The PSI report presents the dilemma very clearly:

> "The findings certainly show that the present stopping policy produces a sig-nificant 'yield' and make it clear that there would be a substantial price to be paid if the policy were to be suddenly abandoned and nothing put in its place. At the same time, the cost of the present policy, in terms of the relationship between the police and certain sections of the public, is shown to be substan-tial, and most stops are wasted effort, if they are seen as purely an attempt to detect crime. The findings therefore suggest that the police should look for other more efficient and less damaging methods of crime detection to replace those stops that are currently carried out for no very specific reason."
> (D. Smith, 1983a, p117)

Therefore, on the one hand, stops in London as a whole "yield" an es-timated 45,000 non-traffic and 75,000 traffic offences a year whilst, on the other, the great majority of people stopped are innocent people who are liable to be annoyed and alienated by this process. *As far as public dis-satisfaction with stop and search is concerned, we found that 41% of those stopped in Islington were dissatisfied with the conduct of the officer con-*

cerned. This is a far higher figure than the 19% found dissatisfied by the PSI in London as a whole. Further, at searches a half of all people stopped on foot thought there was insufficient reason, as did 47% of those whose car was searched.

All of this might be neither here nor there, if the yield from such stops were sufficient. It is often suggested that the percentage of those arrested as a result of stop and search is so low that this automatically invalidates the procedure (L. Christian, 1983; P. Hillyard 1981). In fact the 11% of stops resulting in an arrest in the London area is surprisingly high. If it were any higher it would suggest that the police were guilty of telepathy or of even worse offences. What has to be looked into is the *quality* of yields. For if the yield of stop and search were high in terms of crimes such as sexual assault, burglary and violent crime, we might justifiably argue that it was worth alienating some sections of innocent people. But there is no evidence that this is the case. For example, in the notorious Swamp 81 operation in Brixton 943 stops were made of which only 22 people (2.3%) were arrested for the offences of robbery, theft and burglary at which the operation was supposedly aimed. Similarly a study in the *Guardian* of stops in Brixton found the most common categories for arrest were drugs, drunkenness and offensive weapons. The largest category by far were cannabis violations. The article commented "It sounds like a doubtful crusade against petty crime, with cannabis smokers elevated to public enemy number one. What about the most worrying local crimes – robbery and burglary?"
(*Guardian*, 19.4.83, See the commentary by L. Christian, 1983, Section C).

Further, as Louis Christian points out

"Another factor is the extent to which stop and search creates crime. This could be measured in part by counting the number of offences, such as obstruction or assault on police, which can be said to arise out of the stop and search itself."
(1983, p37)

The yield then is derisory not because of the numbers nor the percentage of these arrested but from the quality of the results. Note that one of the major offences which stop and search reveals is possession of cannabis – one of the crimes which a substantial proportion of the people of Islington believe the police should spend less time in tackling. There is an obvious reason why stop and search is an ineffective exercise and this lies in the nature of serious crime itself rather than in any reflection on the abilities of the police officers concerned. Namely, that although the number of crimes in the inner city is high, the number of people at any one time who have just committed a crime is extremely low. Further, even if they are in the most unlikely event stopped within an hour of committing their crime it is extremely unlikely that they will be carrying substantial evidence

Table 3.36 Stop and search rates over the last 12 months (by age, race, gender)

	ICS All	Age			Race			Gender	
		Under 25	25–44	45+	White	Black	Asian	Male	Female
A. % Population stopped	12.1	24.2	13.1	5.4	10.9	19.1	8.5	16.9	6.9
B. % Population stopped and searched on foot	4.0	12.7	3.4	0.4	4.0	4.6	1.4	6.6	1.6
C. Population cars searched	3.1	7.5	3.7	0.8	2.6	7.9	2.5	4.9	1.5
D. Total population searched* (B+C)	7.1	20.2	7.1	1.2	6.6	12.5	3.9	11.5	3.1

Excluding home searches

around with them. Burglars simply do not walk the streets with stolen television sets in their arms and stolen money is very difficult to identify. Similarly, violent offenders only use weapons in a minority of offences, and therefore there is simply nothing to be found on searching them. There are exceptions to this rule – young people may frequently carry around cannabis for their own consumption – but this is a crime which the public sees as extremely minor. Heroin dealers, in contrast, would scarcely parade their wares in the street, and would be unlikely to be picked up by these procedures. More positively, drunken driving – which *is* rated as a major crime by the public – can be detected by police stops and the use of the breathalyser. The important lesson is to distinguish between those activities which result in a low quality of yield because of the nature of the crimes which are ostensibly being pursued and those which justify stop and search.

Stop and search in Islington

Let us now examine the pattern of stop and search in Islington. The results show that 1 in 9 of the population of Islington have been stopped by the police in the last twelve months (see Table 3.36). Particularly affected is the under-25 age group, a quarter of whom have been stopped. In terms of race, blacks are twice as likely to be stopped as whites, and in terms of gender, men are over twice as likely as women. Asians overall have a very low stop rate. More seriously, the proportion of people stopped and searched varies remarkably by age; you are seventeen times more likely to be searched if you are under 25 than over 45, whilst you are four times more likely to be searched if a man rather than a woman. By race, blacks are twice as likely to be searched than whites and Asians have a search rate of one third of blacks and 70% less than whites. It is noteworthy that the difference between black and white search rates is largely due to the fact that the former have a high rate of car searches – the two groups do not differ in terms of searches whilst on foot. If we continue to subdivide by race and age we can gauge the degree of focus of police stops. As we can see from Table 3.37 the focus is on youth. A quarter of white youths are stopped but this rises to one third in the case of black youths (Asian figures are not sizeable enough, in this instance, to make a comparison).

Table 3.37   Rate of stops: comparison of white and black (by age)

Age	% White	% Black
Under 25	23.4	35.1
25–44	13.3	12.2
45+	5.0	10.9

Even more revealing, however, is if we control by gender – because the focus of police attention on the streets is the young male.

Table 3.38   Under 25, male stop and search

	% Stops	Search whilst on Foot	Search in Car	Total Searches	% Searched
Black	52.7	24.4	19.1	43.5	82.5
White	31.6	19.9	8.9	28.8	91.1

Thus fully one half of young black males and one third of whites have been stopped in the last year. In common with all young people a high proportion who are stopped are searched (84% of all young people male and female are searched compared to 22% of those over 45). This focussing of the police on young people, and black youths in particular, is a stark fact of policing. Thus we might contrast the white male over 45 where under 7% are stopped in a year and under 2% searched, with the black male under 25 where over 50% are stopped and 44% searched. If we find sharp differences in attitudes to the police amongst our population we must remember that different sub-groups live in totally different universes of policing.

Public opinions of stop and search
Such marked differences in the populations targeted for stop and search is reflected in widespread differences in opinions about the practice. (Table 3.39). Thus only 8% of those over 45 believe stop and search occurs often in their area compared to a quarter of those under 25. Similarly, criticism of stop and search increases with youth, with black rather than white and with the degree of contact with the police and the number of times a person has been a victim of crime.

Complaints against the police

"I am encouraged by the continuing research into public attitudes towards the police; the findings of the National Opinion Poll survey carried out in the spring of 1984 identify a positive public endorsement of our performance. The other major overall indicator I believe to be of worth is the level and seriousness of complaints. There have been substantial falls in the volume of both serious and less serious complaints, assisted in the latter case by the early experiments with conciliation. When considered alongside the rise in recorded crime and other workloads and the results of opinion surveys, the fall in complaints suggests that the performance of Metropolitan Police Officers in a difficult working environment is received with some understanding and favour by the general public."
(K. Newman, 1984, p16)

We have seen how our survey shows no such level of endorsement of police performance in general. Let us, therefore, turn to the second indicator – complaints against the police.

Table 3.39 Public beliefs with regard to stop and search (by age, race, gender, contacts with police and levels of criminal victimization)

	All	Age			Race			Gender		Contact			Victimization		
		Under 25	25-44	45+	White	Black	Asian	Male	Female	0	1	2+	0	1 or 2	3+
Stop and search occurs often in the area	16.8	25.3	22.9	7.6	15.4	29.5	17.6	16.6	16.9	–	–	–	–	–	–
Stop and search should occur less	20.6	32.1	28.0	9.0	17.8	46.2	16.8	–	–	12.6	25.8	28.3	14.5	21.4	26.9
Stop and search occurs without sufficient reason	38.4	59.4	51.9	19.5	37.0	55.0	26.8	38.7	38.1	–	–	–	–	–	–

What is of interest is that despite the level of dissatisfaction and annoyance with police performance there exists a substantial minority of people who would not make a complaint against a police officer if they were "seriously dissatisfied".

If we examine Table 3.40 we can see the level of the problem. Although, in general, only a small minority of people would not complain to the police when seriously dissatisfied, if we break down by sub-group a much greater level of unwillingness to complain is revealed. Thus, just under a quarter of all those under 25 would not complain, a quarter of all blacks, a third of young blacks, and from a quarter to half of all Asians. The paradox here is, of course, that the people who would most willingly complain to the police are those most satisfied with the police and vice versa. Thus it may well be true that over 90% of whites aged 45 and over would complain to the police if seriously dissatisfied but, of course, this group has very little to be dissatisfied about. *The main social groups from whom the bulk of complaints should emanate are the most reluctant to complain.* Lastly, we should note that contact with the police tends to diminish willingness to complain as does the level on which the respondent has been a victim of crime.

All in all, this evidence makes it difficult to recognize the level of complaints against the police as an effective indicator of police-public relations. Some explanation for its inability fully to gear into the problems of the most relevant publics is no doubt the fashion in which such complaints are dealt with internally by the police force and which have extraordinarily low levels of conviction (Kinsey, Lea and Young, 1986, Chapter 3).

Who should control the police?

We asked the interviewers who should be in control of the police, giving them the alternatives of the police themselves, the Council, the Home Secretary, local people and a combination of all of these. As we can see from Table 3.41, the existing political situation, namely that control of the London police is vested in the Home Secretary, received a derisory level of approval. Only 3% of the total population thought the Home Secretary was appropriate and in no subsection of the population did this rise above 5%. As for control by the police themselves – a situation which many claim that in terms of the majority of policy is in fact the case – only 17% overall thought that this was desirable. But there was a variation here, in that this was a policy which was upheld by a quarter of the over 45s but was unpopular particularly amongst the young (12% in favour) and blacks (9%). What is significant is that there was a marked decline in opinions favourable to police control of the police depending upon the more contacts the public has with them and, also, the more they had been criminally victimized.

Sole control by the Council was not at all popular, but control by the local people had the same support as control of the police by the police. Almost a quarter of young people wanted control by local people and the popularity of the option increased both with victimization and the amount of contact the individual has with the police. By far the most popular option was a combination of control: over half of the people plumped for this mode of control.

Table 3.40   **Percentage of the public who would not make a complaint against a police officer if seriously dissatisfied (by age, race, contact with the police and level of victimization)**

All		15.3
Age	Under 25	23.3
	25–44	16.3
	45+	11.4
Race	White	13.6
	Black	25.1
	Asian	35.7
White/Age	Under 25	21.6
	25–44	14.8
	45+	9.7
Black/Age	Under 25	30.2
	25–44	27.7
	45+	18.5
Asian/Age	Under 25	28.8
	25–44	24.2
	45+	51.5
Contact with police	None	12.4
	One	15.4
	Two+	19.2
Level of victimization	None	12.9
	One or two	13.6
	Three+	18.9

How can we translate these findings into viable policy alternatives? If we divide the various choices into three packages:
(a) *Present Situation* (police plus Home Secretary): approximately the present state of affairs.
(b) *Radical Democratic*: Council plus local people – a decentralized direct democracy.
(c) *Police Authority*: combination of options, which to the extent that it involves a degree of actual control by the Council and local people would be more democratic than the existing Police Authorities outside of London.

As is obvious from Table 3.42, the idea of a Police Authority is by far the most popular option. The least popular preference is for the situation we

Table 3.41 Who should decide how the local area is policed (by age, race, gender, contact with police, level of criminal victimization and income)

	All	Age			Race			Gender		Contact with Police			Level of Victimization			Income			
		Under 25	25–44	45+	White	Black	Asian	Male	Female	None	One	Two+	None	1 or 2	3+	Under 3,000	3000–7,999	8000–11,999	12,000+
The police	17.0	8.2	11.7	24.8	17.9	7.8	19.4	18.4	15.8	20.6	17.1	12.1	21.8	17.2	11.5	21.5	16.3	15.0	13.3
The Council	7.6	6.4	7.1	8.5	7.6	7.6	8.9	9.0	6.4	8.0	6.7	7.6	8.0	5.4	8.1	9.3	8.5	6.1	5.7
The Home Secretary	3.2	1.2	2.2	5.0	3.4	3.3	1.4	4.7	2.0	3.1	3.3	3.6	3.4	2.1	3.6	2.4	3.0	2.9	4.8
The local people	17.8	22.5	19.6	13.5	16.6	22.2	23.2	17.1	17.6	15.6	17.0	20.0	14.5	14.2	21.9	19.1	19.0	15.9	13.0
Combination of above	54.8	61.6	59.4	48.2	54.5	59.1	47.1	50.9	58.2	52.7	56.0	56.7	52.3	61.0	54.9	47.7	53.1	60.1	63.3

Table 3.42 Three policy alternatives in terms of control of the police (by age, race, gender and income)

Policy Options	All	Age			Race			Gender		Income			
		Under 25	25-44	45+	White	Black	Asian	Male	Female	Under 3,000	3,000-7,999	8,000-11,999	12,000+
A. Present situation	20	9	14	30	21	12	21	23	18	24	19	18	18
B. Radical Democratic	35	29	27	22	25	29	32	26	24	28	28	22	19
C. Police Authority	55	62	59	48	55	59	47	51	58	48	53	60	63

have at the moment. Indeed the radical democratic model is 75% more popular than the present system and is more popular for every subsection of the population we investigated, apart from the over 45s.

A clear mandate arises, therefore, for a change in the system and it points in the direction of a Police Authority with a considerable measure of direct democratic input.

Our findings should be put in the context of a major shift in public opinion among Londoners on the question of who should control the Metropolitan Police Force. A recent Marplan Poll found that 59% of Londoners were in favour of a "Democratically Elected Police Authority" for London and that 80% of a separate poll of blacks and Asians were in favour (*Guardian* 14.10.85). A *Times* newspaper poll (30.9.85 and 2.10.85) found that 60% of Londoners favoured "Local Control of the Police" compared to 33% in a similar poll taken in 1981. Clearly, a majority of Londoners favours a change from the *status quo* and some kind of locally orientated, democratically elected Police Authority, but all research polls to date, including this survey, have failed to pinpoint public views on the range and scope of powers that should be exercised by a democratically elected London Police Authority. However, it is clear that public opinion envisaged a democratically elected police authority having greater power than police authorities outside London set up by the 1964 Police Act, and would not support the inclusion of an undemocratic element, such as Magistrates.

Public perception of the term "control" needs to be more sharply defined as do, in the case of the ICS, terms like "combination of above". Although over half of the respondents favouring a "combination of above" specified the "council and local people" it would be erroneous and premature to draw any firm conclusions from that. In fact, this raises a number of further questions. Is the term "local people" in the minds of some people synonymous with "the Council" or vice versa? Does the coupling of the two imply a distance between "the Council" and "local people" in some people's minds? Does this further imply a desire for some kind of decentralization of some powers from the Town Hall? Only future research will reconcile these contradictions.

In conclusion, our question on control of the police was not finely tuned enough to go beyond ascertaining definite public support for a change in the *status quo* in a democratic direction. The precise policy parameters favoured by the public are yet to be ascertained. Future surveys will have to be designed to establish public opinion, not only on the general question of a democratically elected police authority (for London) but also on public perception of what should be its terms of reference, functions and powers.

4 Women, Crime and Policing

Introduction

Because women very rarely find themselves in the criminal statistics as offenders compared to men, they have often been ignored on discussions of crime and policing. The lack of gender in analyses of crime, however, does not mean that women are less affected than their male counterparts by crime and policing trends. In fact, as the data in Chapter 2 illustrated, it is women who are at the greatest risk for a number of offences, so that as victims of crime their experiences should not be ignored. (This is not to suggest that their experiences as offenders do not deserve consideration. Rather, because the survey is a study of victims on the one hand, and people's attitudes on the other, very little attention has been devoted to offenders in this report.) Not only are women more subject to risk on a number of personal crimes, such as theft from person (a fact which both the ICS and the BCS have uncovered), but there are a number of crimes which, although directed at both male and female victims, are largely directed at women. Crimes such as sexual assault and domestic violence are examples.

It must also be pointed out that because of their relative vulnerability, women must take precautions to ensure their own safety much more often than men. Furthermore, crimes which are for the most part directed at women are not usually effectively dealt with by the police. Domestic assaults are often down-crimed or ignored, and investigations of sexual assault reports often leave the victims feeling that they have been the offenders. For example, Chambers and Millar found that in their sample of victims of sexual assault who reported their crime, 22% of the cases were no-crimed, 24% of the cases remained unsolved, no proceedings were instituted on 16% of the cases, 15% resulted in conviction on the original charge, 10% of the cases resulted in a conviction of another charge, while the balance resulted in either an acquittal or some other court outcome (1983, 10). Although women are much less the targets of heavy-handed policing or arrests, as Chapter 3 illustrated, there is very little gender difference in terms of attitudes to the police. It might by hypothesized that negative attitudes, when they are observed, are in part due to women finding the police less responsive to their particular needs as victims. When the needs are not met, this could lead to a more negative view of the police and a greater unwillingness to report offences to them. The consequence of this process might be that women are forced to take the responsibility for their own safety, even though Islington residents pay approximately eight million pounds annually to the Metropolitan Police to ensure everyone's safety.

These kinds of issues have been gaining increasing attention by the media, the public, and women's groups, and it was felt that the ICS should attempt to measure, where possible, the differential impact that crime and policing has for women compared to men; the effects this might have on their perceptions and behaviours in relation to safety; and the extent to which the particular needs of women in terms of public safety are either being met or ignored by the criminal justice apparatus.

In order to accomplish this, it was felt that a number of specific questions needed to be asked during the interviews so that a subsequent breakdown by gender could be carried out and measures of the differences between men and women could be established. The BCS has yet to produce any substantive analysis of gender on either of its sweeps. With the exception of Maxfield (1984), who basically analyses differential fear of crime by sub-populations, very little attention has been given to women and certainly none of the publications contains a substantial gender-specific analysis. Possibly due to the very low frequency of sexual assault which the BCS uncovered, only lip service has been paid to the needs of women and again only in relation to fear as the following citation illustrates:

> "For rape, the BCS can say little, except that in comparison to crimes such as burglary, the risks of rape – and particularly of rape committed by strangers – are very low. This does not necessarily mean that women are 'worrying about nothing'. In general, one would expect rape to have a very serious impact on victims' lives – and there is nothing irrational in worrying about an occurence which may be very unlikely to happen but is exceedingly distressing if it does." (1985, 35)

Without a more thorough investigation into gender roles, gender differences, and overall exposure to violence *and* potential violence, observations such as the above citation remain hollow.

Unlike the BCS, the PSI used gender as a distinctly important variable in the analysis of people's experiences with the police and attitudes towards them; however, it failed to undertake a substantive analysis of criminal violence or other forms of harassment directed at women.

The ICS has incorporated a number of measures of non-criminal street violence towards women. It was felt that not only are women subject to criminal victimization in some classifications more frequently than men, but they are also subject to forms of street violence and sexual harassment which are not, strictly speaking, criminal. Sometimes women have to endure lewd comments in the street, the persistence of kerb crawlers, and unwanted sexual advances, both from strangers and acquaintances. Sometimes women find themselves in frightening and potentially volatile situations, such as being followed by strangers, where the threat of physical harm due to sexual or physical assault is present. Such forms of non-criminal street violence, together with the threat of criminal victimization aimed strictly at women, serve to produce a very different reality for women than for men, and it was felt that this reality probably has an effect on both women's attitudes and their behaviours. Therefore, the survey attempts to measure and analyse both material gender differences and their consequences.

Also, because the survey found a comparatively high frequency of sexual assault and domestic violence, it was felt that the experiences gleaned from the survey regarding these offences should be presented in more depth. The impact of such offences and the victims' experiences with the criminal justice system as a consequence of their victimizations deserve special attention.

The chapter will begin by looking at the observed gender differences in perceptions of risks for women and fears for personal safety. Secondly, we will examine the gender differences observed by the survey as they pertain to avoidance behaviours. Next, we shall look at the impact that crimes directed at women have on their victims. Finally we will examine the gender differences on non-criminal forms of street violence.

Perceptions of risk

There were two specific strategies which we followed to identify personal perceptions of risk. We asked a number of questions which measure how much the respondent worries about specific crimes that may happen to them. The composite measure of these items was used as an indicator for fear of crime, and this variable has been used throughout the report as a control variable in the analysis. A similar procedure was followed for constructing a composite measure for people's perceptions of the probability of being a victim of the same types of crime. The first scale is called 'Fear of Crime Scale' or Scale B, while the second is called 'Perception of Victimization in The Next Year Scale' or Scale C.

While the first scale measures people's fear of crime, the second measures their perceptions of risk in the next year. By breaking these two scales down by gender, we observe the results in Table 4.1.

Table 4.1 shows that some differences do exist between men and women for fear of crime and perception of risk, although the differences are not that striking. Women certainly have a higher fear of crime than do men, but when this is taken into consideration, they are relatively less likely to see themselves as being victims of crime in the next year. This difference may mean that although women worry more about crime happening to them than men, they have a more realistic understanding of the probability of victimization than men do. Gender roles in the family structure often restrict women from going out in the evening and, as was illustrated in Chapter 2, outings are directly related to victimization. Because the survey did not ask why people did not go out, we cannot comment upon the extent to which gender roles are related to outings, although we recognize a relationship is present. Alternatively, it may mean that women, because of their higher fear, take greater precautions to protect themselves and therefore place themselves in a risk situation less often. One way in which this might be accomplished is by staying in during the evenings more often. Table 4.2 breaks down the number of evening absences from home by gender in order to illustrate any differences between men and women in restricted activities:

Table 4.1 Fear of crime and perceptions of risk (by gender)

Scale		Males	Females
Fear of crime	Low	12.3%	8.9%
	Medium	64.7%	51.6%
	High	23.0%	39.5%
Perception of risk	Low	13.1%	14.8%
	Medium	71.2%	67.3%
	High	15.7%	18.0%

Base: All respondents weighted n= 9386

Table 4.2 Evening outings from home (by gender)

Outings per Week	Males	Females
None	10.0%	25.8%
One-two	40.5%	44.8%
Three plus	49.5%	29.5%

Base: All respondents weighted n= 9386

Table 4.2 shows that women are much more restricted to home during the evenings than are men. It should also be pointed out that the information in Table 4.2 varies by age and by race as well as other background variables. It is probably because women stay in more than men that they are less victimized by burglary as was shown in Chapter 2. Nevertheless, women appeared to be victimized more often than men on all other crimes followed up by the survey and reported in Chapter 2. It would seem, therefore, that women have a greater understanding of the relative risks of victimization and take more precautions than their male counterparts, although it is questionable whether staying in during the evenings is a successful strategy given the rates of victimization in Chapter 2. Unfortunately, the survey cannot answer this question. It may also be that given the frequency of domestic violence, some women may be protecting themselves from criminal victimization outside the home only to subject themselves to domestic violence inside the home.

A second indicator of the perceptions of risk is the fear that people display in going out in the evening. In relation to this, the following two questions were asked:
1. Do you think there are risks for women who go out on their own in this area after dark?
   If so how likely is it that something will happen to them?
2. Do you yourself ever feel worried about going out on your own in this area after dark?

Variations of these questions have been asked on much of the American research and BCS as well as the PSI as measures of the perception of personal risks. In this way, we can measure the differential between the risks men perceive for women as contrasted to themselves.

A final measure that we incorporated and which was also investigated by all of the major surveys in the United Kingdom measures the perceived risks of being at home:
   Do you ever feel unsafe in your own home because of the possibility of crime?

This question measures the perceived risk of crime while being at home and probably is a measure of the way in which the respondent not only worries about personal safety, but also about the safety of other family members if there are any.

Table 4.3 breaks down the perceived risks as measured by the above three questions by gender and by age.

Table 4.3   Perceived risks (by age and gender)

	% Feeling there are Serious Risks for Women after Dark		% Feeling Worried about Self after Dark		% Feeling Unsafe at Home	
	Males	Females	Males	Females	Males	Females
16–24	55.7	57.9	14.7	70.5	9.3	35.2
25–44	54.9	62.7	16.3	69.9	15.9	40.1
45 plus	62.0	62.2	39.3	75.7	21.7	33.8
Total	58.5	61.6	27.1	72.6	17.4	36.4

Base: All respondents weighted n= 9386

The data in Table 4.3 illustrates that there are slight gender differences for the perception of risks for women who go out on their own after dark. The relationship with age is not direct in that the middle age category for men is least likely to perceive risks for women after dark and this same category for women is the most likely, although the differences are very slight. Contrary to the view of some, therefore, men appear to be as likely as women to perceive risks for women. However, there are substantial gender differences on the perception of risk for one's self after dark. Men are consistently less likely to perceive risk for their own safety than they are for women, and younger men are much less likely to be worried for themselves than older men, perhaps illustrating why younger men are much more likely than either women or older men to go out during the evenings. Given that specific gender roles restrict women to the home more often, it is not surprising that they find going out after dark threatening.

The findings in Table 4.3 are similar to the PSI, although its findings on the risks for women show men are less likely than women to perceive risks and he concludes: ". . . in other words, men do not do for women as much as women do themselves" (1983, 31). The probable reason for differences on this question between the ICS, and PSI is that our survey is restricted to one inner-city borough, while the PSI takes into consideration all of the Metropolitan Police District which includes a number of areas outside of the jurisdiction of the Greater London Council. In those areas, it is likely that the risks for women are not seen to be as great by male respondents, as they are by men in the inner city.

The differences between men and women on the third indicator of perceptions of risk in Table 4.3 are also substantial. Women are less likely than men to feel safe in their homes due to possibility of crime, which is not surprising since men are home less often. Of significant interest is the middle age category of women which shows the highest anxiety while for men the relationship with age is direct. It must be remembered, however, that this is the age category in which respondents are most likely to have dependent children and the increased anxiety for some women in this age group may well be an expression of their concern for other family members more than it is for themselves.

The PSI in examining the race and gender differences for perceptions of risk concluded that:

> "These findings may reflect a feeling among West Indians that they are being made the scapegoats for street crime; they may wish to deny that a serious problem exists because their own group is held responsible for the problem." (1983, 33)

Here the PSI is referring to the differences displayed between whites, West Indians, and Asians. In order to compare its work with that of the ICS, Table 4.4 breaks down the indicators of perceptions of risk by gender and by race.

The findings presented in Table 4.4 do not differ greatly from that of the PSI. Although the levels of fear are lower for each group as measured by the PSI, and the measures in Table 4.4 are higher, the same relative levels of perception of risk are observed. Whereas white men are less likely to perceive risks for women than their female counterparts, black males are more likely to perceive risks for women than their female equivalents. The greatest gender difference, however, is with the Asian sample in which women are more likely to perceive risks for women than Asian males. One may only speculate at this point on the gender relations and family patterns specific to each culture and the impact that these have on perceptions of risk for women.

In terms of the worry expressed for oneself, white women are the most concerned for themselves and black males are the least concerned. Once more the gender differences on this question are staggering, indicating that *gender is a much more important determinant of perception of risk than is race*. These figures are even more staggering when one also takes into consideration the age differences illustrated by Table 4.3.

Table 4.4   Perceived risks (by race and gender)

	% Feeling there are Serious Risks for Women after Dark		% Feeling Worried about Self after Dark		% Feeling Unsafe at Home	
	Males	*Females*	*Males*	*Females*	*Males*	*Females*
White	60.0	63.4	27.0	73.3	16.5	34.5
(Total)	(61.8)		(51.4)		(26.1)	
Black	50.6	45.4	23.7	68.6	22.5	50.2
(Total)	(47.8)		(46.6)		(36.6)	
Asian	43.1	57.7	33.2	67.4	23.5	34.8
(Total)	(49.0)		(46.4)		(27.6)	
Other Non-White	54.6	54.6	35.5	65.3	23.3	52.1
(Total)	(54.6)		(50.5)		(38.2)	

Base: All respondents n= 9386

On the third question in Table 4.4, the same relative differences between men and women are illustrated with one major exception. Black females as a group are less likely to feel there are risks for women who go out on their own after dark than women staying at home. A full 50% of this group feel unsafe in their own homes due to the possibility of crime whereas only 45% feel that there are risks for women who go out on their own after dark. This is probably due in part to the fact that young black women are the most likely of all groups to be living alone, 38% of women 16-24 and 48% of those 25-44 are living by themselves, whereas the figure for young white women living on their own (the next highest category) are 31% and 35% respectively.

It was shown earlier in the chapter that women have a higher fear of crime than men and are relatively less likely to perceive the probability of crime happening to them in the next year. Table 4.5 breaks down the perceptions of risk by gender and by the scores measured for each of the scales – satisfaction with the neighbourhood, fear of crime, and perception of probability of crime in the next year – in order that comparisons can be made between men and women who display the same levels on each of the scales:

Table 4.5   Perceived risks (by gender and scale scores)

	% Feeling there are Serious Risks for Women after Dark		% Feeling Worried about Self after Dark		% Feeling Unsafe at Home	
	Males	*Females*	*Males*	*Females*	*Males*	*Females*
Scale A[1]						
Low	79.3	71.0	34.7	75.3	24.0	48.1
Medium	53.2	59.8	25.6	72.8	16.3	32.7
High	22.6	12.0	6.5	33.1	2.6	0.
Scale B[2]						
Low	33.7	37.3	9.1	42.6	5.3	16.4
Medium	55.7	53.4	22.5	67.6	12.8	23.0
High	79.1	78.2	49.0	87.0	36.9	57.8
Scale C[3]						
Low	41.2	57.3	15.8	68.7	15.2	26.2
Medium	58.5	57.1	25.6	70.8	15.2	31.5
High	71.8	79.4	40.1	82.3	29.0	58.3

Base: All respondents weighted n= 9386

1. Satisfaction with neighbourhood
2. Fear of crime
3. Perception of the probability of crime in next year

While the differences between men and women on the perception of risks for women who go out on their own after dark remain about the same, some interesting changes emerge when controlling for the scale scores. Men who have either a high or low satisfaction with the neighbourhood are more likely than their female counterparts to perceive risks for women after dark. Also, males who have a medium to high fear of crime as well as males with a medium score on the think scale are more likely to perceive risks for women after dark than women in the same groups. It would seem that the differences on satisfaction with the neighbourhood are probably due to social class – this will be examined in a later table – whereas the differences on the fear of crime show that men may project feelings for their own safety on to their female counterparts.

The differences between men and women for the second question are still quite high when controlling for the scale scores and the relationship between concern for personal safety and the scale scores are all in the predicted direction. People show a negative relationship with satisfaction with the neighbourhood: the less satisfied they are with the neighbourhood, the more concerned they are with their personal safety at night. The other two scales display a positive relationship with concern for personal safety: the greater the fear of crime or perception of crime in the next year, the greater the concern for personal safety. While this finding may seem banal to some and totally expected, it does provide evidence to suggest that the measures incorporated by the ICS for all three of the scales and the measures of risk are all valid indicators, and that other findings in this report in relation to these measures are probably valid and accurate.

The relationships on the second question hold for the third question in Table 4.5. Of interest here is that while the relative differences between the sexes remain, they appear to be both similarly affected by their perceptions measured by the scales, except in the odd instance of women who have a high satisfaction with the neighbourhood. Not one respondent in this category expressed a worry about crime happening to their home. This is probably more due to the small group who are highly satisfied with the neighbourhood than it is to gender differences.

Absences from home during the evenings, contacts with the police in the last year and the number of victimizations in the last year per household have all shown to bear some relationship with each of the variables examined so far in this report. Table 4.6 breaks down each of these by gender and perceived risks.

The first question in Table 4.6 once more shows little variation across gender on perceptions of risk for women after dark. Men who go out three or more times per week are more likely to perceive risks for women than their female counterparts, as are men who have experienced victimization in the last year or had more than two contacts with the police. It may well be that the quality of contact with the police is quite different for men than it is for women leaving them with different perceptions of risk. The odd categories are women with one contact with the police and women and men with one victimization in the past year. In the former case it seems for women one contact with the police is reassuring and reduces anxiety slightly whereas repeated contact increases anxiety. In the latter category it seems that one victimization for women decreases anxiety while for men it increases, and repeated victimizations for women increase anxiety while for men they decrease anxiety. It may well be that for men one victimization is unnerving and repeated victimization mean they get used to the idea that most crime is not too serious. Women on the other hand may find that one incident of trivial crime reduces anxiety but several incidents become threatening. In either case, a similar pattern for this category can be observed on the question about personal risks. For this question, again the gender differences hold, and the variation in perceptions of risk, except for the categories of risk mentioned above, are in the predicted direction.

The differences in the final question on Table 4.6 show that the more people go out in the evening the less likely they are to feel unsafe in their home.

Table 4.6 Perceived risks (by gender, absences from home, contacts with police and number of victimizations)

	% Feeling there are Serious Risks for Women after Dark		% Feeling Worried about Self after Dark		% Feeling Unsafe at Home	
	Males	Females	Males	Females	Males	Females
Absences						
None	56.4	62.7	45.0	80.2	21.6	39.1
1-2	61.6	65.0	32.4	74.5	20.6	39.5
3 plus	55.7	53.0	17.3	62.2	12.6	29.8
Victimizations						
None	55.0	59.4	31.3	73.7	17.3	27.8
One	63.3	59.2	25.7	66.8	15.5	39.5
Two plus	60.3	65.1	22.9	73.5	18.3	45.4
Police contacts						
None	52.6	60.9	30.8	73.3	17.9	33.1
One	54.9	58.9	32.0	68.2	18.9	34.7
Two plus	66.2	64.5	21.1	74.2	16.4	43.1

Base: All respondents weighted n= 9386

Table 4.7 illustrates that those most likely to perceive risk are the lowest income categories on all three questions. For men and women both the highest level of perceived risk on the first question is in public and private rentals. Women, however, are more concerned with their own safety in private rentals than in public rentals. For men, however, this relationship is reversed. On the second and third questions it is public rentals which create the highest concern for personal safety in both men and women, and as was demonstrated in Chapter 2, it is precisely these two categories which are most at risk for the personal crimes of theft from person, assault, and sexual assault.

By way of a summary for this section, the breaking down of perception of risk by gender and other indicators has demonstrated that:

1. Women and men show little difference on perceptions of risk for women after dark, and in some cases where indicators such as fear of crime are held constant, men are more likely to perceive risks for women than women themselves.
2. Women are much more likely than men to perceive risk for themselves when going out after dark, and this difference holds across all groups investigated.

3. Women are more likely than men to worry about being safe in their own homes.
4. Black women feel on average more unsafe in their own homes than they do being out in the street after dark.
5. The perceptions of risk appear to be in line with the reality of risk rates as measured in Chapter 2.
6. Women are more restricted than men in their activity as a consequence of perceived risks for safety and restrictive gender roles.
7. The actual risks as measured in Chapter 2 seem to bear a relationship with perceived risk as measured here.

Table 4.7   Perceived risks (by gender and socio-economic indicators)

Indicator	% Feeling there are Serious Risks for Women after Dark		% Feeling Worried about Self after Dark		% Feeling Unsafe at Home	
	Males	*Females*	*Males*	*Females*	*Males*	*Females*
Income						
Under 3000	55.6	65.4	31.6	75.2	20.9	34.8
3000-7999	63.1	64.5	29.6	74.5	18.5	40.0
8000-11000	63.3	60.3	19.3	68.7	14.5	38.9
12000 plus	51.8	51.9	23.7	67.7	14.1	29.4
Tenure						
Owned	47.9	48.2	25.2	66.3	21.9	32.1
Public rent	60.9	62.9	29.8	75.6	17.9	37.1
Private rent	59.8	70.9	18.9	70.0	11.5	35.9
Squat	46.5	32.2	37.6	23.6	25.9	22.3
Work Status						
Unemployed	58.9	60.9	32.5	74.5	19.1	36.8
Employed	58.9	62.5	22.5	70.5	15.9	36.4

Base: All respondents weighted n= 9386

We have already seen that women stay indoors during the evenings more often than men. In part this "curfew on women" is due to their structured positions in the home which do not allow them the same access to activities outside the home which men enjoy. However, risks for women's safety are also a concern. The recognition of potential harm and the desire to avoid it certainly contribute to the restriction of women's activity as well. We have also seen that the perceptions of risk are probably more accurate than other research suggests. In the next section we shall see what gender differences exist in terms of other forms of avoidance behaviours measured by the ICS.

Avoidance behaviours
A number of questions were asked on the interview schedule which attempted to measure the kinds of precautions which people take in order

to reduce their risk of victimization. Table 4.8 presents the questions and the gender differences measured by them:

Table 4.8   Avoidance behaviour (by gender[1])

	Never		*Occasionally*		*Often*		*Always*	
Question	*Male*	*Female*	*Male*	*Female*	*Male*	*Female*	*Male*	*Female*
Avoid going out after dark	73.5	29.2	12.6	17.1	7.0	16.9	6.9	36.7
Avoid certain types of people	52.2	32.6	32.9	31.3	10.3	22.9	4.7	13.2
Avoid certain streets or areas	61.6	36.0	21.9	24.4	11.9	22.3	4.6	16.1
Go out with someone else instead of alone	73.4	27.3	13.5	20.3	9.2	29.1	3.9	23.3
Avoid using buses or trains	85.5	59.9	9.4	21.9	3.4	11.6	1.8	6.8
Use a car rather than walk	81.1	55.5	7.7	14.3	5.7	16.5	5.5	13.7

1. Expressed as percentages of respondents

Base: All respondents weighted n= 9386

Table 4.8 clearly illustrates that there are substantial differences between men and women in terms of the precautions which they take simply to avoid the possibility of crime. 37% of all women never go out after dark whereas only 7% of all men avoid going out after dark simply as a precaution against crime. The differences are all quite high for each of the indicators of avoidance behaviour investigated by the survey. These gender differences, by way of comparison, are also observed by the 1984 DCS, although its treatment of the first BCS data is sketchy in relation to gender. The overall percentage for items 3 and 4 above are reported in the second BCS as 41% of women avoid certain streets or areas *after dark* usually or always, and half the women went out with someone rather than alone usually or always (Hough and Mayhew, 1985, p40).

These figures do not lend themselves to a proper comparison of the two survey's findings. The MCS found that 96% of the men under thirty, 93% of the men between the ages of 30 and 49, and 77% of older men never avoided going out after dark as a precaution against crime. Women on the other hand reported that 19% under 30, 21% between the ages of 30 and 49 and 46% of older women always avoided going out after dark as a precaution against crime (Kinsey, 1984, p91).

For purposes of simplicity of analysis and presentation of data, all of the measures or questions asked on the survey regarding avoidance behaviour were collapsed into one composite measure which we called the scale of avoidance behaviour. From this composite measure we determined which groups of people were either low, medium or high on the scale of avoidance behaviour, and we were then able to break this down by a number of key variables. Table 4.9 breaks down the scale scores for avoidance behaviour by gender, in order to grasp an overall difference between men and women in terms of this type of behaviour:

Table 4.9   Avoidance scale scores (by gender[1])

Avoidance	Men	Women
High	3.4	20.2
Medium	36.1	64.2
Low	60.5	15.6

1. Expressed as percentages in each category

Base: All respondents weighted n= 9386

As can be predicted from the previous information, the differences between men and women are high and indicate that women are forced to take the responsibility for their own safety themselves much more seriously than do men. The difficulty with Table 4.9, however, is that it does not make allowances for the variations which occur across age and race which were observed in the tables in the previous section on perceptions of risk. In order to control for the variables of race and age, Table 4.10 gives the break down of avoidance behaviour as measured by the scale by race, age, and by gender.

Table 4.10 illustrates some very important relationships which must be further elaborated. There can be little doubt that women are much more likely than men to avoid potentially threatening situations, and the differences between men and women seem to reduce as age is increased. As people get older they tend to take more precautions regardless of gender or of race. The only exception to this general trend is that of black males who almost never avoid specific situations and in the medium avoidance category the middle age black males are a higher percentage than older males. There are, however, some very substantial differences between women of different race. 18% of all white women, 34% of all black women and 44% of all Asian women almost always avoid specific situations as a precaution against crime. By way of comparison, it must be remembered from Chapter 2 that while women were more likely than men to be victims of personal crimes, such as theft from person, assault and sexual assault, it was clearly black women, generally, who were more at risk than white women, except for sexual assault in which white women were more at risk, and theft and assault where white women were more at risk in the youngest age category. As can be seen from Table 4.10 it is the youngest age group of white females who are the least likely to avoid specific situations and are, therefore, the most at risk.

It is difficult to speculate what impact less avoidance behaviour displayed by black women would have on their victimization rates. It may well be that by avoiding situations they are avoiding a certain level of victimization. On the other hand, they may well be exposing themselves to more victimization by staying in during the evenings and avoiding strangers, in that it may well be acquaintances which are victimizing them. In either event, it is clear from Table 4.10 that women generally, and particularly older and black women, feel it is necessary to restrict their behaviour and avoid certain situations as a precaution against crime. *In this sense, the Islington Crime Survey helps to illustrate that a "curfew on women" appears to be implicitly operative.*

Table 4.10   Avoidance behaviour (by age, race and gender[1])

	Low		Medium		High	
	Males	*Females*	*Males*	*Females*	*Males*	*Females*
White						
16–24	69.0	15.3	29.9	69.8	1.1	14.9
25–44	72.9	16.1	26.3	64.3	0.8	19.6
45+	51.6	16.2	42.7	65.5	5.7	18.3
Total	61.9	16.0	34.9	65.8	3.2	18.2
Black						
16–24	60.9	16.9	39.1	53.5	0.0	29.6
25–44	56.8	12.1	43.2	60.3	0.0	27.6
45+	56.3	9.5	43.8	42.9	0.0	47.6
Total	57.6	13.1	42.4	53.3	0.0	33.6
Asian						
16–24	45.5	14.3	45.5	54.3	9.1	31.4
25–44	40.4	14.7	53.2	44.1	6.4	41.2
45+	30.8	13.3	53.8	26.7	15.4	60.0
Total	38.0	14.1	51.5	41.5	10.5	44.4
Other						
16–24	77.8	11.1	22.2	66.7	0.0	22.2
25–44	44.4	11.1	48.1	63.0	7.4	25.9
45+	69.2	7.7	7.7	61.5	23.1	30.8
Total	58.9	9.8	27.9	63.2	13.2	27.0

1. Expressed as percentages in each category

Base: All respondents weighted n= 9386

As suggested earlier, however, simple avoidance behaviours may not be a successful strategy in that there appears to be a level of aggression directed at women from people whom they know. Furthermore, as the above data suggest, avoidance behaviour increases with age when the actual risks of criminal victimization decrease with age. It was shown in Chapter 2 that the risk curve for women reaches a peak in the younger years, and this finding corresponds to all the known research of this kind. While some writers such as Hough and Mayhew (1983, 1985) and Maxfield (1984) suggest that this is an anomaly, we feel that the level of violence to which women are subjected during their younger years (in part a consequence of less avoidance behaviour comparatively) makes them more cautious with age. Furthermore, in a sexist society younger women are perceived as sexual objects and are more subject to forms of sexual harassment accumulating over time. This point will be further explored in the final section.

There can be little doubt that many women experience violent criminal victimization when younger, and they learn that not only is violence an unpleasant experience to say the least, but it is something about which little satisfactory institutional support is available leaving the responsibility to women to take their own precautions. This will be explored in the next section. We feel that the differentiation as portrayed by the BCS between risk and avoidance is due to two reasons. The first is that the BCS is only concerned with occurrences in the previous year. If a woman, for example, were the victim of rape three years ago it may be safe to assume that the experience had an effect on her both in terms of victimization and increased avoidance behaviour. While the BCS would not capture the case of rape, they would capture the fear and avoidance behaviours, leading the authors to the conclusion that these were out of proportion to risk. A second reason is that where the BCS focusses on the individual, we focus on the household. In this manner we can actually relate people's fear and avoidance with other householders' experiences. Unlike the BCS which assumes that people live in isolation and are not affected by the experiences of other family members, we are concerned with the social impact of crime on the entire household. For example, if two sisters living together had the experience of one of them being sexually assaulted, and it was the one who was not that was interviewed by the BCS, then they may conclude that the respondent's fear was out of proportion to risk. We, on the other hand, would have captured the incident and established the relationship between fear and avoidance and the incident of the sexual assault for the other sister.

In order to examine more closely the nature of some offences directed at women, the following section will briefly focus on the level of aggression that the female respondents of our sample experienced in the last year for the two most common criminal victimizations directed at women specifically – sexual assault and domestic assault.

The impact of sexual and domestic assault
Unlike other surveys the ICS revealed a high proportion of sexual and domestic assaults. The following two examples selected from the des-

criptions of offences given by respondents will help to illustrate some of the more violent incidents to which women were subjected.

1. Domestic assault, white female

"My husband and I are separated now. I asked him to leave. It was stupid, we started arguing, it was to do with cards and women. He became very angry and lost his temper, he started hitting me and throwing things about, kicking the dog. He punched me down the stairs, I was quite badly hurt. He only ever gets like that towards me, he says, because he loves me. He's polite and nice to other people, that's why they never suspect any trouble and he takes it out on me."

2. Sexual assault, white female

"I was collecting up empty glasses in the bar just after closing, when a drunken lout, seeing that I had both hands loaded up with a pile of glasses, grabbed me from behind, and pushed his hand inside my bra and grabbing hold of [my breast] very hard. He then bit into my neck at the back, as I was calling for my husband who was in the other bar. He then moved his hand and pinched [me] between his nails. His other hand at the same time reached around the other way pulling up my skirt and clasping [me]. He pulled up sharply which stretched the knickers tightly through my crotch until the elastic snapped and they tore through. All the while he was biting into my neck harder and harder against the bone at the back just above the shoulder blade and pinching my breast. He then dug his nails and fingers into my vagina, and then it was over as suddenly as it started when my husband arrived from the other bar and pulled him off.

I'd say that all this happened in the space of about twenty seconds or less. I remember the whole thing so vividly and I was thinking absolutely clearly – wide awake and I knew that with 12 or more glasses piled inside each other in both hands, that if I tried to struggle or pull away I would most likely have tripped and fallen forwards onto the glasses causing myself a very nasty injury."

These two examples show that there is a very real level of violence to which some women are subject and that to make the attempts to avoid them from happening, or to be frightened that they may occur, is not an unrealistic response.

In virtually all of the measured occurrences of sexual assault and domestic violence the victim could give information about the assailant, with only 5% of the victims of sexual assault being unable to do so. All of the victims of domestic violence claimed to have known their assailant before, which is hardly surprising due to the definition of domestic violence, while 18% of the rape/attempted victims and 25% of the sexual assault victims knew their assailants. This figure seems low since it is a common assertion in the literature that very few sexual assaults are committed by strangers. It is quite probable that the ICS was more successful in capturing cases of unknown assailants than it was in discovering cases in which the assailants were known. Nevertheless, our data indicate that most of the cases of sexual assault which we found involved assailants that were unknown to the victim.

In order better to illustrate the level of violence used and the type of injury sustained we have partitioned out the data for the offences of domestic assault, rape/attempted and sexual assault. Because of the low number of actual rape or attempted rape cases, generalization from these data is not warranted. Table 4.11 is the types of violence used by offence:

Table 4.11   Type of violence used (by offence[1])

	Domestic Violence	Rape Attempted[2]	Sexual Assault
Grabbed/Punched	74.5%	73.3%	67.7%
Punched/Slapped	92.1%	83.4%	14.3%
Kicked	56.9%	46.2%	4.5%
Weapon used	19.7%	24.7%	–
Raped	–	26.3%	–
Attempted rape	.7%	73.7%	–
Sexually assaulted	2.2%	–	100%
Other	5.5%	–	14.1%

1. Multiple responses asked of respondent.
2. Indicates other types of violence in combination with the rape or attempted rape (this applies to all subsequent tables).

Base: All victims weighted data.

From Table 4.11 it can be seen that a substantial level of violence is used on all offences but particularly domestic violence. Even more dramatic is that the level of physically injurious violence seems higher for domestic assault than it is for rape/attempted since in all categories, except for the use of a weapon where the difference is slight, the proportion of cases reporting a specific form of violence is higher than for rape. In the cases where other forms of violence were reported, the interviewers recorded such things as strangulation, cigarette burns, pinched and bitten, stabbed in the face with a cigarette, spat at, hair pulled and head-butted.

It is clear from Table 4.11 that a high level of violence is directed at women in the commission of these offences, but in order to determine what injuries are sustained from these assaults Table 4.12 breaks down type of injury by type of offence.

From Table 4.12 it can be seen that at minimum nearly all respondents reported bruises. Surprisingly, almost 10% of all domestic assaults resulted in broken bones, indicating that while the survey under-estimates domestic violence, it is probably the most serious cases which have been disclosed to interviewers, so that generalization to all cases of domestic violence may not be warranted. Nevertheless, there appears to be sufficient violence in the cases disclosed to warrant concern. Other types of injury recorded by the interviewers included, sprained ankle, sprained wrist, sore breast, loss of hair, burns, bite marks, dizziness, bloody nose, tooth knocked out, bruised vocal chords, damaged back, broken vein in ear, bumps on head, "internal damage", concussion and partial loss of hearing.

Table 4.12 Injury sustained (by offence[1])

	Domestic Violence	Rape Attempted	Sexual Assault
Bruises/Black eyes	96.3%	100%	86.5%
Scratches	62.2%	19%	56.0%
Cuts	45.0%	19%	13.5%
Broken bones	9.8%	–	–
Other	15.2%	25%	48.9%

1. Multiple answers asked of respondent

Base: All victims – weighted data.

Weapons were used in 22% of the cases of domestic assault on female respondents, and on 52% of the victims of rape/attempted. There were no weapons used in any of the cases of sexual assault uncovered by the survey. Use of weapons in domestic violence was restricted to whites and blacks. It would appear that white males are much more likely than black males to use weapons in domestic disputes since of the cases in which weapons were used 76% were white and 18% were black, with the balance falling into the residual category. Table 4.13 illustrates the type of weapon used by the three offences and the frequency of cases in which each weapon type was reported:

Table 4.13 Type of weapon (by offence[1])

Percentage of Cases in which Weapon was Used

Weapon	Domestic Violence	Rape Attempted	Sexual Assault
Bottle or glass	32.6%	46.2%	–
Knife or scissors	21.2%	28.0%	–
Stick, club or blunt object	28.3%	–	–
Firearm	–	–	–
Other	17.0%	25.8%	–

1. Refers to female respondents only

Base: All victims reporting a weapon weighted data.

In those cases where other types of weapons were reported, a variety of implements were used indicating the degree of innovation which males have during assaults. These included tools, bunches of keys, shoes, umbrellas, hammers and shovels, as well as a variety of sticks and blunt objects.

As a consequence of the violence and weapons used on females during the commission of the offences and the injuries sustained by the victim, 45% of the victims of domestic violence, 45% of the rape/attempted victims, and 5% of the victims of sexual assault found it necessary to seek medical attention. Whereas none of the rape or sexual assault victims were required to stay in hospital overnight, 24% of those cases of domestic violence which did seek medical attention (or 12% of all cases of domestic assault), were required to stay in hospital at a minimum of overnight. Table 4.14 provides a list of reasons why victims of the three offences found it necessary to seek medical attention:

Table 4.14   Reasons for attending doctor (by offence[1])

| | *Per Cent Reporting Yes* | | |
| | *Domestic* | *Rape* | *Sexual* |
Reason	*Violence*	*Attempted*	*Assault*
Physical injuries	93.5	41.6	–
Difficulty sleeping	34.6	41.6	–
Worried, anxious, nervous	46.2	100	100
Felt depressed	39.7	75	–
Shock	41.0	75	100
Headaches	37.1	–	–
Nausea	24.4	–	–
Other	5.1	58.3	–

1. Based on respondents more than one answer encouraged

Base: All victims seeking doctor's attention, weighted data.

Other reasons that were given by respondents included: pregnancy tests to prove that rape had occured, anger and frustration, heart trouble, police statement, hearing tests, and the possibility of a lost pregnancy. When all the factors are taken into consideration, *it would seem that domestic violence of the sort uncovered by the Islington Crime Survey can be extremely violent and results in more explicit physical injury than the type of rape uncovered by the survey*. On the other hand the psychological injury of rape was much more severe than for domestic assault.

Even in cases where the rape victim did require medical attention it was often due to the evidence required legally in order to prove rape had occurred rather than to physical injury, despite the psychological effects experienced by the victims. This fact must also be considered when assessing the overall impact of submitting oneself to medical examination for evidence required by the courts as opposed to physical injury. The procedure must generate even more anxiety in a victim who is already experiencing negative psychological effects due to the violation of rape.

The notion of having to seek medical attention for purposes of generating evidence brings us to the assessment of the institutional responses that the victims of these offences receive when reporting an offence of this kind to the police. For domestic violence, all respondents reported that the police found out who did it, which is not surprising since the respondent would have told them when reporting the offence. Victims of rape reported that in 69% of the cases the police found out who did it whereas for sexual assault the police found out who the offender was in one third of the cases. It would appear that from these statistics the police were quite successful in clearing up those cases which were brought to their attention. It must be remembered, however, that these figures only reflect those cases which were reported to the police, and since in some cases of rape and sexual assault the respondent knew the offender previously, it would not require a great deal of detective work to find out who the offender was. Perhaps a more significant measure of police effectiveness in dealing with the victims of these kinds of crime would be the respondent's satisfaction with the police response. Table 4.15 gives the responses on satisfaction with the police given by those respondents which reported the offence:

Table 4.15   Satisfaction with police (by offence)

	Offence Domestic Violence	Rape Attempted	Sexual Assault
Highly satisfied	42.4	00	00
Satisfied	24.0	00	00
Dissatisfied	20.2	15.8	33.3
Highly dissatisfied	13.3	84.2	33.3

Base: All victims reporting the offence, weighted data.

It can be seen from Table 4.15 that the police have a dismal record in terms of satisfying reporting victims of sexual assault or rape. This fact is even more important when one compares the figures for these offences given in Chapter 2 on rates of reporting. It may very well be that the lack of satisfaction which women feel from the police on sexual offences is related to their reluctance and unwillingness to report the offences. A full two thirds of cases of domestic violence however, expressed some satisfaction with police response. However, because the survey results probably over-represent the serious cases of domestic violence in relation to the less serious ones, this figure should be interpreted with extreme caution. It may very well be also that women reporting the less serious cases tend to be dissatisfied and less willing to report as a consequence.

Table 4.16   Time lost from work (by offence)

	Domestic Violence		Offence Rape/Attempted		Sexual Assault	
	Respondent	Other	Respondent	Other	Respondent	Other
None	67.4	95.7	100	100	82.4	100
1 day	7.4	2.1	0	0	13.4	0
2 days	9.9	0	0	0	0	0
3 days-week	9.7	2.2	0	0	4.2	0
1 week-1 month	5.7	0	0	0	0	0
Over 1 month	7.1	0	0	0	0	0

Base: All victims weighted data.

Table 4.16 illustrates that domestic violence is much worse than the other categories in terms of lost work. Not one of the rape victims reported lost time from work, although a number of these may have been unemployed and may have lost time from work had they been employed.

Another measure used by the survey to assess the impact of the offence was the question: "How much effect would you say the incident had on you or other members of the household?" Table 4.17 provides the answers to this question by offence:

Table 4.17   Impact of offence on respondent and household

	Domestic Violence	Offence Rape Attempted	Sexual Assault
Very big effect	95.7	100	100
Quite a big effect	2.1	0	0
Not much effect	0	0	0
No effect	0	0	0

Base: All victims weighted data.

It can be seen from the above table that all of the offences had a very big impact on the respondents and on their households and the figures speak for themselves.

Before concluding this section, it will be useful to examine where and when these offences take place. It should be pointed out, however, that while respondents were not specifically asked these questions, interviewers were to probe for details of the incident, and only in few cases did the information get transmitted. As a consequence, generalization may be risky. Table 4.18 gives the break down by offence of the location for those respondents from whose descriptions of offence the information could be gleaned:

Table 4.18 Location of offences

Location	Domestic Violence	Offence Rape Attempted	Sexual Assault
In or around respondents home	77.1%	–	1.8%
In or around friend or relatives home	9.3%	33.1%	–
In or around a strangers home	–	18.7%	–
Tube, bus, train or public transport property	–	–	11.4%
Work	–	–	13.5%
Place of business	–	–	–
Neighbourhood street	5.1%	8.0%	33.4%
Non neighbourhood street	2.2%	16.6%	33.1%
Pub	–	–	–
Other	6.3%	23.6%	–

Base: All victims providing information on location of offence, weighted data.

While most domestic violence occurs in the home it is not restricted to home. Sometimes it occurred in friends' or relatives' homes and sometimes in the street, either inside or outside the neighbourhood. Most rapes/attempted occurred either in a friend's or stranger's home or in the street. While most sexual assault occurred in the street, a substantial proportion occurred both at work and on public transport property. These findings are in line with other studies, although the sample size of those providing this information has been substantially reduced.

Table 4.19 breaks down the time of day by offence in order to ascertain any patterns for the three offences.

Table 4.19 Time of offences

Time	Domestic Violence	Offence Rape Attempted	Sexual Assault
Daytime – week	1.7%	2.0%	–
Evening – week	–	6.5%	–
Night – week	6.9%	7.6%	13.2%
Daytime – weekend	2.9%	2.9%	–
Evening – weekend	5.8%	3.0%	–
Night – weekend	–	6.5%	29.2%
Time not specified	82.7%	53.5%	57.7%

Base: All victims, weighted data.

By way of summary to this section, it is very obvious from the data generated from the ICS that there is a considerable level of criminal violence used against women in the forms of domestic assault, rape/attempted and sexual assault. The most frequent and the most harmful in terms of obvious physical injury was observed for domestic violence. Psychological effects were most frequent in rape cases. Institutional responses were judged to be unsatisfactory on all cases of sexual crimes, and the impact that all of the offences produced for the victims was strikingly severe. There can be little doubt that many women face a significant level of criminal violence, especially in their younger years, so that it is not surprising, in fact, it should be expected that older women display a fear of leaving their homes during the evening. The anomaly is that due to the levels of domestic violence, women, in using avoidance behaviour as a precaution against crime, may be subjecting themselves to risks of domestic violence.

Still, there may be sceptics who feel that women's fears are out of proportion to their risks of criminal victimization. The next section examines the frequency of non-criminal street violence directed at women in order to establish the relationships if any between these kinds of violence and women's avoidance behaviours.

Non-criminal street violence

A number of questions were asked of all respondents concerning a variety of possible encounters they may have experienced in the last year, to the extent that the experience made them upset.

It was felt that there are a number of situations in which people find themselves and which, although not criminal in nature, may be upsetting and, therefore, encourage avoidance behaviour in the respondent. While it would be impossible to cover all such situations, we felt the measures included in the survey were sufficiently representative of the total types of situations to act as an overall measure.

While it may well be that women are more likely than men to experience such things as sexual harassment, it is also the case that sometimes these situations may have racial connotations, and for this reason men would be exposed to unpleasant situations which they may wish to avoid as well.

It was also felt that the frequency of experiences in relation to these kinds of incidents would be related to people's fear or anxiety. The purpose of the questions, therefore, was twofold. Firstly, we wanted to measure the frequency of these incidents, and secondly, we wanted to be able to compare these experiences with attitudes and actual behaviours. Because the frequency of these encounters is quite high, we decided to report the frequencies as simple dichotomous variables. Table 4.20 provides the frequencies of those respondents who reported experiencing an incident at least once, and breaks this down by question, age and gender:

Table 4.20   Non-criminal street violence (by age and gender[1])

	16–24		25–44		45+	
	Males	*Females*	*Males*	*Females*	*Males*	*Females*
Being stared at	11.3	28.6	6.6	12.6	2.4	1.7
Being followed	5.1	30.8	3.8	13.8	1.4	3.2
Being approached and spoken to	8.5	23.3	4.0	12.0	1.1	2.9
Being shouted at or called after	9.1	22.2	9.8	12.1	2.0	2.4
Being touched or held by anyone	2.7	14.2	1.9	5.9	0	1.0
Kerb crawling	0	21.3	0	13.5	0	2.5
Being confronted	14.0	19.3	10.9	10.6	3.0	2.5

1. Percentages indicate those repondents experiencing one or more incidents

Base: All respondents weighted data.

Table 4.20 illustrates that women are much more subject to non-criminal forms of street violence than men. There also appears to be a considerable inverse relationship with age for both males and females. The older people get, the less likely they are to experience these kinds of incidents, and this is probably due to going out less and taking more precautions in form of avoidance behaviours as illustrated by Table 4.10. Furthermore, there can be little doubt that younger women are much more likely to be the targets of sexual harassment. In a primarily sexist-orientated culture where younger women are perceived as sexual objects their exposure to sexual harassment in the street is more frequent, even if outings are controlled for. Nearly one third of all young women reported being followed to the extent that they were upset at least once in the last year and one in five had been upset by kerb crawlers in the same age group for the same period. By comparison only one in 30 elderly women were followed to the point of being upset and only one in 40 complained about kerb-crawlers. Being confronted to the point of being upset was the situation which showed the least difference by gender, indicating that this type of threatening behaviour may not be as closely related to one's sex.

Because there are a number of questions, and because the number of incidents was so high per individual reporting in the affirmative, it was decided to collapse all of the questions into one simple dichotomous variable which for purposes of this report we have called harassment. Also, because of the implicit sexual connotations of much of the encounter types, we also included the measures of any sexual offence and sexual pestering. The total of the measures for these variables was then taken and collapsed into the categories of harassed at least once and not harrassed at all. In this way we can make some aggregate comparisons across a number of variables for simplistic presentation.

Table 4.21 gives a breakdown by age, race and gender for those respondents who reported at least one incident of harassment in the last twelve months:

Table 4.21   Harassment (by age, race and gender[1])

	16–24		25–44		45+	
	Males	*Females*	*Males*	*Females*	*Males*	*Females*
White	21.8	60.9	24.0	40.8	7.3	8.9
Black	43.3	72.0	24.3	43.4	12.8	18.6
Asian	33.3	42.4	35.4	47.6	19.6	14.3
Other	44.4	64.7	37.1	33.3	15.2	30.0

1. Percentages indicate those respondents experiencing one or more incidents

Base: All respondents weighted data.

The observed gender differences in the above table are quite staggering particularly in the younger age categories. Women are much more subject to threatening situations than men are. There is also a considerable difference between the levels reported by whites as opposed to blacks, indicating that not only is much of this interaction probably sexist, but is almost certainly racist as well. More than twice as many black males reported an incident than their white counterparts in the youngest age category, as was previously demonstrated. Whites in this category are more likely to perceive themselves at risk in the evenings than their black counterparts.

However, when we compare the figures for women in the same categories, we find that the differences are much less, indicating even further that this type of incident is almost certainly sexist motivated.

Not only are there substantial gender differences on harassment as shown in Table 4.21, but the frequencies of multiple incidents also display substantial gender differences. Because the above tables only include those people reporting at least one incident, they serve to mask the frequency somewhat, in that women are much more likely than men to have these experiences more than once. Table 4.22 breaks down the percentage of respondents reporting more than one incident of those that reported at least one, by age, race, and gender. In this way, we can make comparisons of the level of multiple victimization for harassment incidents.

Table 4.22 indicates that not only are women much more likely than men to experience more than one of these incidents in all categories but one, but younger people are more likely than older people to experience multiple victimizations. Furthermore, white males are much less likely than black males to experience these incidents more than once. As with criminal victimization, non-criminal victimization is much more likely to keep happening to the same people over and over again, and the most likely population to have multiple experiences is women.

Table 4.22 Multiple harassment (by age, race and gender[1])

| | 16–24 | | 25–44 | | 45+ | |
	Males	Females	Males	Females	Males	Females
White	63	89	52	84	50	62
Black	80	86	89	76	50	76
Asian	73	93	77	90	77	100
Other	25	45	69	91	0	78

1. Percentages indicate those respondents answering in the affirmative

Base: All respondents weighted data.

A final strategy which we adopted for purposes of this report was to restrict the number of incidents for each respondent to two, in order to calculate the number of incidents occurring for different sections of the population. In this way, we could compare gender differences across other variables used for control purposes throughout the report. Table 4.23 provides a breakdown of the number of incidents per 10,000 population observed by the survey, by fear of crime, evening outings per week and income:

Table 4.23 Frequency of harassment (by gender, fear of crime, outings and income)

		Males[1]	Females[2]
Fear of crime	Low	1472	3100
	Medium	2619	5195
	High	3461	6957
Evening outings per week	None	1127	2522
	1–2	2250	5029
	3 plus	3416	9744
Income	Under 3000	1924	4254
	3000–7999	2656	5515
	8000–11999	2829	7720
	12000 plus	3476	7915

1. Expressed as rates per 10,000 males
2. Expressed as rates per 10,000 females

Base: All respondents weighted data.

Table 4.23 shows considerable differences once more between men and women when these variables are controlled for. In almost every category, women are at least twice as likely as men to experience these incidents and in some categories nearly three times as likely. There is a direct relationship with all three variables. Women who have a high fear of crime have a high risk of experiencing these kinds of situations. Women who go out in the evenings more often are more likely to experience harassment, and women earning more are exposed to these incidents more often that women earning less. It is clear that exposure to threatening situations contributes to women's fear of crime, and the increased risk of exposure created by going out in the evenings places women in threatening situations more often than women who stay in. The relationship with income is probably due to women in the higher income categories being more sensitized to threatening situations and they are probably more likely to report in the interview situation than women in the lower income categories. Furthermore, they have more opportunity to go out and would find themselves in risk situations more often. Since a substantial portion of sexual assault was shown to take place in the work place, it is not unreasonable to assume that higher levels of sexual harassment may also be observed in the work place.

It is extremely clear from the data presented in this section that women are much more likely to experience situations which are threatening to the point where they are upsetting, and these situations are not necessarily criminal. Nevertheless, they have the potential to severely frighten at worst and extremely annoy at best. Given the frequency of exposure that women experience, it is hardly surprising that they engage in more avoidance behaviour and express higher levels of fear. It is precisely these kinds of frightening, threatening or annoying situations which further contribute to the curfew on women.

Summary and conclusions

This chapter criticized the BCS for exhibiting a number of conceptual difficulties in its treatment of the relationship between fear of crime in women and actual risk of victimization. Firstly, the BCS implicitly assumes that any experience of violence directed at a woman will somehow only last for one year and then be forgotten. Secondly, it implicitly assumes that people automatically compare themselves to their cohort, which we feel is slightly unreasonable. If a female victim of violence is observed by the community, it is doubtful that community members only take notice if they are similar on all characteristics. For example, if an elderly black lady falls victim to violent attack, it is doubtful that observers are relieved if they are young, white females. Finally, because the BCS does not measure high levels of violence against women, either criminal or non-criminal, and because it does not carry out a sufficient analysis by age and gender, it misses the frequency of violence with which young women are forced to persevere and for which they must take their own responsibility.

The ICS has shown that not only are women more fearful than men but they have very good reasons for this. An examination of the criminal forms of violence directed specifically against women showed that there was a high level of both physical and psychological injury sustained by women very frequently. The survey illustrates that women receive very little institutional support of a satisfactory nature and must take responsibility for their own protection as a consequence. This means that they must engage in more avoidance behaviour than men which restricts them in their activities more often, especially at night.

The survey also shows that there is a much higher frequency of non-criminal forms of violence directed at women than at men, particularly younger women, which contributes to higher levels of both fear and precaution by women.

From the survey data it would seem that older women are more fearful than younger women despite the fact that they are less at risk of both criminal and non-criminal violence. Rather than being an anomaly, we see this as being the consequence of the combination of two material facts. Firstly, younger women go out much more often than older women and are, therefore, more often at risk of victimization. Secondly, because of the high levels of violence which younger women face, over time they learn not only how to be more successful in avoiding it, but also, that they are at risk of serious violence. Because the effects of violent attack and harassment are prolonged, the fear of crime measured in older women is the product of a lifetime of threatening to violent encounters and the expression of the accumulation of experiences. Younger women, although more at risk, and although experiencing more incidents of violence in the previous year, have not experienced as many incidents over the course of their lifetime as have older respondents. For this reason, older women engage in more avoidance behaviour, exhibit more fear, and are less at risk than their younger counterparts. While there are undoubtedly restrictions on women's activity which stem from gender roles and family structure, and which in turn contribute to heightened fear for personal safety, the survey did not investigate this aspect of women's experience.

5 The Impact of Crime Upon Victims

Introduction

In the preceding chapters it has been demonstrated that there is much more crime in Islington than comes to the attention of the police. Virtually every crime survey conducted in a variety of countries has come to similar conclusions. One difficulty of findings such as those of the ICS is that they serve to sensitize the population to the frequency of criminal victimization and the recognition that the amount of crime is even higher than is reported in the media. The danger of such information was in its potential to generate "moral panic" and public demand for more resources being directed towards combating crime.

Some researchers have attempted to deal with this danger by emphasizing the triviality of much of the crime which goes unreported to the police but which is disclosed on the crime survey. Levine (1976, 1978) has suggested that victimization data contains a large number of trivial incidents that the respondents felt were too minor to report to the police. Chambliss (1984) has argued that most of the unreported crimes were not brought to the attention of the police because the victim felt that "nothing could be done", "there was not enough proof", and "it was not important enough", and he comes to the conclusion that serious criminal victimization is still a rare event. Also, Sparks (1981) has noted that a full three quarters of personal crimes uncovered by the National Crime Survey involved attempts only.

The motivations underlying the observations of such researchers are probably more than a sincere interest in resolving the crime puzzle. On the one hand the research shows that there is a great deal of under-reporting of crime, but on the other hand, the seriousness of such crime is sometimes questioned in the interests of avoiding moral hysteria and demands for more police.

What is lacking in most crime survey research is a substantive comparison of the differential impact that crime might have on different groups of people. There are a number of difficulties in undertaking such an analysis. Firstly, there is the difficulty of what the impact of crime involves. For example, should the concept of impact of crime be considered only as material effects such as loss or damage to property and physical injury, or should it also include various psychological effects. Secondly, once the previous question has been addressed, how should those effects be considered? Should there be objective comparisons or should the comparisons be made upon subjective criteria. For example, if a £50 loss is considered to be objectively serious, is its quality altered by the financial situation of the victim or the perception of the seriousness by the victim?

On the other side of the coin, such an analysis would allow an assessment of who gets hit the hardest as a consequence of crime. Official crime data do not allow such an assessment. Even crime survey data such as those reported in Chapter 2 only allow for an assessment of which populations are subjected to most risk, but they do not allow an assessment of the differential effects that the crime might have for the victims. Although the BCS did collect information on the effects of crime, they did not report in any detail which groups of people were affected and how they were affected. Rather, their strategy was to report by offence categories what losses were incurred, what effects were reported, and on the basis of these measures an attempt was made to assess the overall costs to society by offence.

We feel that the approach taken by the BCS in reporting the impact of unreported crime serves to mystify social variation by reporting the impact of crime by offence rather than by individuals. The strategy taken by this survey, therefore, is to report by offence and by groups of people. In this preliminary report, a number of measures which were made during the survey are not reported simply due to space constraint. For purposes of this chapter, we have decided to present breakdowns of the impact of crime as measured by material effects only. While the data reported in the tables can be interpreted objectively, we shall also draw the reader's attention to the subjective impact of victimization as well. The two main sections will examine the extent of property loss and damage and the extent of personal injury as a result of criminal victimization. Because the preceding chapter investigated the impact of violent crime against women, domestic assault and sexual assault will not be covered in this chapter.

The extent of property loss and damage

Three major classifications of crime which were followed up by the ICS involved property loss or damage. For purposes of expediency, these will be reported here as: all burglary, all vandalism, and all theft from person followed up by the survey. Questions regarding the amount of loss or damage to property presented the respondents with a set of categories ranging from under £5 to over £1000.*

* These categories were used so that comparisons could be made with the BCS findings. The difficulty, however, is that the measures made by these questions are ordinal, in that the size of the interval for each category is different, making it

In total 86% of burglaries reported some loss of property, while 84% reported some damage to property. Table 5.1 reports the value of property lost due to burglary by household income:

Table 5.1   Burglary loss (by income)

	Under 3000	3000-7999	8000-11999	12,000+	TOTAL
Under £5	1.2	–	5.8	–	1.2
£5–24	13.2	8.4	3.0	.9	7.1
£25–49	8.2	5.7	2.3	5.0	5.6
£50–99	12.1	18.8	18.8	6.6	14.0
£100–249	25.2	14.3	5.8	21.5	17.4
£250–499	14.9	29.4	16.2	27.6	21.2
£500–999	7.2	8.7	14.0	19.9	11.8
£1000+	18.1	14.8	34.1	18.6	21.2
TOTAL	32.8	23.0	23.2	21.0	100
MEAN	£326	£366	£532	£483	£424

Base: All burglary victims weighted data.

It can be seen in Table 5.1 that more losses are incurred in the higher income categories. Not only is the modal category higher in the higher income categories, but the lower income categories have a higher percentage in the under £100 categories. These differences are reflected in the mean values for each income group. Two points require clarification. Firstly, it is not surprising to find higher losses due to burglary in the higher income categories since this is the group which is most likely to have items with higher property values inside the home. It makes sense that the would-be burglar is going to remove high value items where and

difficult to calculate mean losses or mean property damage by social groupings. The strategy was to calculate the mean for each category by dividing the sum of the lower limit and upper limit by two. Then for each category, the percentage of respondents was multiplied by the mean. By taking a sum of the categories and dividing by 100 an estimate of the mean loss or damage was calculated for each social grouping. There can be little doubt that this procedure involves error, although the mean for each category will produce the least errors of prediction, and unless each category is consistently skewed in a different direction for each social grouping the errors should cancel out. It is difficult to compare sets of categories by inspection alone, and by reporting the mean values, this difficulty can be overcome to some extent. While the relative values of the means should remain a good measure for comparison for social groupings, the mean values for each offence may not accurately reflect actual losses per offence and will serve as estimates only.

when they are available. Secondly, the people in the lower income categories are in the least position to sustain the loss, and as will be shown
later, they are less likely to have the property recovered by the police or
replaced by insurance.

Damage is also related to burglary. In most cases (87%) burglary involves a break-in where some damage to property is sustained. Table 5.2
provides a break-down of the value of damaged property due to burglary
by income group:

Table 5.2   Burglary damage (by income)

	Under 3000	*3000-7999*	*8000-11999*	*12,000+*	*TOTAL*
Under £25	13.1	45.0	19.1	59.4	35.0
£25–49	51.7	26.0	33.3	9.2	30.0
£50–99	11.9	7.8	20.3	7.3	11.2
£100–249	20.2	17.3	13.5	13.3	16.3
£250–499	2.0	2.6	6.9	5.9	4.2
£500–999	1.0	–	6.9	3.8	2.6
£1000+	–	1.3	–	1.2	.7
TOTAL	27.7	26.2	19.2	26.8	100
MEAN	£ 80	£ 74	£131	£102	£ 94

Base: All burglary victims weighted data.

From Table 5.2 it can be seen that the higher income categories are once
more subject to higher levels of property damage due to burglary,
although the differences are not substantial. This is not surprising since
people in this group are more likely to have their homes more secured so
that breaking in requires slightly more damage.

By way of comparison, the BCS shows smaller losses for burglary,
although the reporting categories differ. For example, because the
highest category is only one half of that for the ICS, we will show higher
losses on the average.

For vandalism, similar trends can be observed as illustrated in Table
5.3, where it can be seen that most vandalism falls below £50. Once more,
the groups most likely to experience the greatest property damage are the
higher income groups, although the factor of likely replacement of property must be taken into consideration as it will be later in the chapter.

There can be little doubt that in terms of absolute property loss and
damage the higher income categories lose more before their property
is replaced or recovered. However, this relationship reverses when we
examine losses due to theft from person. Table 5.4 provides a breakdown
of losses due to theft from person by household income of the victim:

Table 5.3   Vandalism damage (by income[1])

	Under 3000	3000-7999	8000-11999	12,000+	TOTAL
Under £25	14.9	45.3	60.0	49.3	49.4
£25–49	31.9	27.8	9.4	7.6	19.0
£50–99	15.1	14.4	9.0	17.5	14.4
£100–249	2.2	9.4	13.9	16.2	10.5
£250–499	2.2	2.4	2.9	5.6	3.4
£500–999	1.3	.7	2.7	2.0	1.6
£1000+	2.4	–	2.1	2.0	1.7
	£ 74	£ 57	£ 94	£106	£ 84

1. All vandalism followed up

Base: All vandalism victims followed up – weighted data.

Table 5.4   Theft from person (by household income[1])

	Under 3000	3000-7999	8000-11999	12,000+
Under £5	13.0	11.1	20.7	4.5
£5–24	23.4	40.0	29.8	28.2
£25–49	27.8	18.5	8.7	33.0
£50–99	22.7	12.4	22.4	17.6
£100–249	4.7	9.4	14.8	10.2
£250–499	5.0	4.6	3.5	4.2
£500–999	.9	2.5	–	–
£1000+	2.6	1.6	–	2.4
TOTAL	26.2	37.3	14.7	21.7
MEAN	£ 91	£ 91	£ 64	£ 87

1. Includes robbery

Base: All victims theft from person – weighted data.

Table 5.4 shows that on average, lower income groups suffer more loss due to theft. While the small number of large thefts increase the mean value disproportionately overall, the lower income groups report more losses as illustrated by the higher percentages in the higher loss categories. This fact is not surprising since the lower income people are more likely to be carrying cash whereas the higher income people are more likely to be carrying credit cards.

The following three tables provide a break-down of losses incurred due to theft from person by age, gender and race respectively.

Table 5.5 Theft from person (by age[1])

	16–24	*25–49*	*45+*
Under £5	12.6	9.6	15.3
£5–24	35.3	25.0	37.6
£25–49	16.9	25.0	23.0
£50–99	14.6	19.8	17.4
£100–249	13.5	10.5	3.1
£250–499	5.8	6.7	–
£500–999	–	–	3.6
£1000+	1.3	3.4	–
TOTAL	26.6	41.5	31.8
MEAN	£ 81	£105	£ 60

1. Includes robbery

Base: All victims theft from person – weighted data.

Table 5.6 Theft from person (by gender[1])

	Males	*Females*
Under £5	8.6	14.1
£5–24	36.6	29.1
£25–49	15.9	25.5
£50–99	17.4	17.9
£100–249	10.2	8.3
£250–499	5.5	3.7
£500–999	2.6	.4
£1000+	3.2	1.0
TOTAL	34.6	65.4
MEAN	£114	£ 69

1. Includes robbery

Base: All victims theft from person – weighted data.

The previous three tables show that men, and people in the 25-44 age category, are the most likely to suffer the greatest losses due to theft from person. Also, it is these who are the most likely to be carrying property of higher value on their person. Women, for the most part do not have the same access to money as their male counterparts, and people in the middle age category have the highest earnings potential. The comparison by race does not yield much in the way of differences, since the number of Asians and those in the residual category were so small that the estimates cannot be generalized.

Table 5.7   Theft from person (by race[1])

	White	Black	Asian*	Other non-white*
Under £5	13.4	3.6	20.1	7.3
£5–24	31.3	33.8	35.2	39.8
£25–49	21.9	27.5	7.5	9.5
£50–99	17.0	21.1	28.9	17.6
£100–249	9.1	9.1	–	8.8
£250–499	4.8	2.4	–	–
£500–999	1.1	–	–	17.0
£1000+	1.6	2.6	8.2	–
TOTAL	85.2	11.8	1.6	1.4
MEAN	£ 83	£ 82	£112	£165

1. Includes robbery
* Due to small number of actual cases these should be interpreted with caution

Base: All victims theft from person – weighted data.

Theft from person, averaging out to approximately £85 per occurrence, seems rather high. This is because the very few instances in which there were large values stolen bias the estimate of the mean upwards.

Sometimes property is stolen or damaged during the commission of offence which has a sentimental value to the victim and cannot be quantified. Table 5.8 provides a breakdown of those respondents reporting this kind of loss by offence and by income group:

Table 5.8   Loss or damage of sentimental value (by income and offence)

	Under 3000	3000-7999	8000-11999	12,000+	TOTAL
Burglary	51.6	58.8	56.7	46.9	52.1
Vandalism[1]	16.8	9.8	none	5.6	7.0
Theft from person[2]	31.6	26.3	39.7	42.6	36.2
Robbery	56.9	40.6	58.1	14.6*	43.6

* Too few cases to draw any definitive conclusions
1. All vandalism followed up
2. Includes robbery

Base: All victims – weighted data.

Not too many conclusions can be drawn from Table 5.8 because it is difficult to compare losses which are not quantified. However, it would seem that robbery and burglary produce the most instances of loss of property with sentimental value. For robbery, items such as jewelry, which may have been gifts etc., may be demanded by the assailant if they are worn by the victim. Most often these items could not be stolen in a theft from person incident which was not classified as robbery. Since households contain personal possessions, these may well be stolen during the commission of a burglary, but it is unlikely that property outside of the home which is subject to criminal damage would have much sentimental value.

From all of the data presented so far in this section, it would seem that when income groups are partitioned, higher income categories sustain more loss of property and slightly more damage to property than lower income groups for household offences. However, for personal offences such as theft it would seem that lower income groups are more likely to sustain higher losses.

Sometimes victims of crime have their property recovered by the police, and sometimes the property which was stolen or damaged might be covered by an insurance policy, a claim for which may replace some or all of the value. It may be misrepresentative to use the value of loss of or damage to property as indicators of who was more financially worse off as a consequence of the offence. For this reason we asked the question of the victim:

> "Bearing in mind any property that was recovered and anything that you got from an insurance company for what was stolen or damaged, were you financially worse off in the end?"

It was felt that this question would provide a more accurate measure of net loss after all other factors were considered than would the simple measures of total loss and damage. In this manner we can compare the net effects of financial loss due to crime across social groupings. Table 5.9 presents the comparisons of victims reporting net financial loss due to crime by household income:

Table 5.9   Financial loss (by income and offence)

	Under 3000	*3000-7999*	*8000-11999*	*12,000+*
Burglary	86.9	73.8	78.1	71.9
Vandalism[1]	62.5	60.1	40.3	45.3
Theft from person[2]	94.1	93.5	81.7	81.1
Robbery	94.7	86.4	78.4	100*

* One case only
1. All vandalism followed up
2. Includes robbery

Base: All victims – weighted data.

It is very clear from Table 5.9 that the lower income categories are the most likely to report net financial loss due to crime. In every classification there is a negative relationship with income – the higher the income the less the probability of net financial losses due to crime. The only slight variation falls in the two highest categories of vandalism in which the relationship reverses. These findings come as no surprise, since lower income people are least likely to have their property insured against loss or damage. Because the survey only uncovered two cases of robbery in the high income category, it would seem that this type of offence is working class.

When one moves from the objective measures of net financial loss to the subjective measure of how much that loss means to the respondent, it would be safe to conclude that because the lower income victims are least able to afford the loss they would probably feel the loss to a greater extent than the higher income victims. *In either event it can be safely concluded from the Islington Crime Survey that in terms of economic loss due to crime, the lower income residents of Islington are hit the hardest.*

Personal injury

There are a number of criminal occurrences in which violence was used during the commission of the offence. When domestic violence and sexual assault are taken into consideration, violence was used in 28% of all crimes followed up by the survey. Of these 47% of the cases were women, 59% of the cases involved victims from the lowest two income categories, 16% of the victims were from a visible ethnic minority and 85% were victims under the age of 45. From these figures, younger people are more at risk of violence, and age is the most important single predictor of violent crime. Whites are slightly less at risk than their proportion in the population would indicate, as are women. People from households where income is under £8,000 are slightly less at risk of violence overall than people from the higher income categories.

When domestic violence and sexual assault are not considered, violence is used in 21% of the cases followed up by the survey. Of these 30% of the cases involving violence are female, 51% fall into the lowest two income categories, 17% of the victims are from a visible ethnic minority, and 80% of the victims are under the age of 45.

Sometimes, burglary and vandalism involved the use of violence. If all crimes followed up by the survey are considered, 0.2% of cases involving violence were burglaries, and 0.5% were incidents of vandalism. These numbers equate to 1.2% of all burglaries and 2% of vandalism. Because these proportions are so low, these crimes will not be looked at here, although some readers may feel that they are of considerable interest.

In total, injuries were sustained in 20% of the cases followed up by the survey when sexual assault and domestic violence are included. Of these

41% of the victims were women. When domestic violence and sexual assault are not included, 16% of the cases involve injury and women are victims 20% of the time. Injuries were also observed in the lowest two income categories 60% of the time, while 17% of the injuries were sustained by members of a visible ethnic minority and 85% of the injurious cases involved people below the age of 45.

For purposes of this section, the discussion and presentation of data will be restricted to assault and robbery. Because in this survey robbery has been included in the more general category of theft from person, a brief description of the statistical victim of robbery seems appropriate. 21.5% of all robbery victims were in the 16-24 age group while 46.8% of the cases were in the 25-44 age group with the balance falling into the oldest age category. Since the younger victims form the same proportion in the sample as they do in the population, one cannot see any relationship with age. The 25-44 age category is over-represented, however, while the oldest age category is under-represented indicating that rather than the little old lady, the most likely victim of robbery is 25-44. He is most likely male as well, since 64% of all robbery victims are men. Whites and blacks are both slightly over-represented in the sample of victims indicating that in comparison to the other ethnic categories these people are the most likely victims of robbery.

Table 5.10 provides a break down of the type of violence used by the two offences and by age:

Table 5.10 Type of violence used (by age and offence[1])

	Assault[2]			Robbery		
	16–24	*25–44*	*45+*	*16–24*	*25–44*	*45+*
Grabbed/ Pushed	86%	79%	65%	100%	90%	100%
Punched/ Slapped	68%	58%	34%	25%	37%	100%
Kicked	42%	36%	29%	25%	29%	66%
Weapon	14%	29%	10%	–	25%	34%
Other	5%	10%	10%	–	–	–

1. Percents based on number of respondents reporting a type of violence and all respondents answering each question for each age category – multiple answers encouraged.
2. Does not include domestic assault

Base: all victims of assault and robbery – weighted data.

From Table 5.10, it can be seen that the most common type of violence employed during the commission of an offence is grabbing or pushing. Elderly peoplė seem to have less violence of all sorts directed towards them for assault, although these are the most likely to feel the effects of

violence most severely. It is interesting to note, however, that robberies
involve a weapon more often when elderly people are the victims than
when they are not. Even though the middle age category is more suscept-
ible to robbery, older people are more likely to report a weapon being
used, and they appear to have violence of all sorts used against them more
often than any other age group during the commission of robbery. Despite being more vulnerable, they appear to have more violence directed
towards them.

In order to illustrate the use of weapons touched upon in the last table,
Table 5.11 breaks down the types of weapons used by offence and by age:

Table 5.11   Type of weapon used (by age and offence[1])

Weapon	*Assault[2]*			*Robbery*		
	16–24	*25–44*	*45+*	*16–24*	*25–44*	*45+*
Bottle/						
Glass	26%	19%	–	64%	71%	34%
Knife/						
Scissors	24%	28%	15%	36%	11%	66%
Stick/Club						
Blunt object	38%	34%	38%	–	29%	–
Firearm	–	8%	–	–	18%	–
Other	36%	42%	48%	–	–	–

1. Percents based on number of respondents reporting a weapon and number
of cases for each age category – multiple answers encouraged.
2. Does not include domestic assault

Base: all victims of assault and robbery reporting weapon use – weighted data.

The patterns of weapon use vary from offence to offence as illustrated in
Table 5.11. Broken glass or bottles are used the most often in robberies,
while the most common weapon during the commission of assault is some
kind of stick, club or blunt object. Firearms were used in only 3% of all
robberies and they were always used on male victims and always men in
the 25–44 age group. This group is also much more likely to have weapons
used of any sort during the commission of an offence than their proportion in the population would indicate. The relatively low use of firearms
should be kept in consideration when evaluating the number of armed
police officers currently in Islington.

One case of burglary and 10 cases of vandalism involved the use of a
weapon. Sometimes vandals were observed in the act of criminal damage
using a weapon of some sort to damage property, and for this reason these
cases have not been included in Table 5.11 which reports on weapons
used against the person.

Table 5.12 provides a break-down of the injuries sustained by victims of
violent crime by offence and by age:

Table 5.12 Type of injury (by age and offence[1])

Weapon	Assault[2]			Robbery		
	16–24	*25–44*	*45+*	*16–24*	*25–44*	*45+*
Bruises/						
Black eye(s)	84%	76%	64%	50%	73%	100%
Scratches	48%	56%	24%	100%	73%	34%
Cuts	13%	61%	5%	50%	62%	66%
Broken						
bones	4%	8%	–	–	14%	–
Other	14%	5%	48%	–	–	–

1. Percents calculated on those reporting injury for each age category – multiple answers encouraged.
2. Does not include domestic assault

Base: all respondents reporting injury – weighted data.

It would seem from Table 5.12 that the elderly victims of robbery are the most likely to be injured. All respondents in this category sustained bruises or black eyes and two thirds of the elderly robbery victims received cuts. For assault, the middle age category is the one most at risk of injury. Whereas the youngest age group is more likely to be restricted to bruises or scratches (as are elderly victims), the middle age category is most likely to receive cuts or broken bones. Women on the other hand appear to be the recipients of injury more often than men for both offences as illustrated in Table 5.13:

Table 5.13 Type of injury (by gender and offence[1])

	Assault[2]		Robbery	
	Males	*Females*	*Males*	*Females*
Bruises/				
Black eye(s)	79%	75%	78%	85%
Scratches	47%	55%	60%	63%
Cuts	39%	40%	68%	48%
Broken bones	5%	9%	–	19%
Other	12%	24%	–	–

1. Percents based on those reporting injury for each gender – multiple answers encouraged.
2. Does not include domestic assault

Base: all victims reporting injury – weighted data.

It can be seen in Table 5.13 that on all forms of injury except bruises, women are more at risk than men. They receive more scratches, cuts and broken bones than men do in both offences. Given that women were the assailants in only 2% of the robberies and 11% of the assaults, there is little wonder that women are more often injured. Men are usually stronger, more aggressive, and capable of inflicting more injury than women. Most cases of female injury sustained during the course of a criminal offence, therefore, are the result of a male attacker, and it is not surprising to find that women are injured more often during these kinds of offences.

Very few respondents found themselves seeking medical attention because of the injuries sustained from all offences as illustrated in Table 5.14:

Table 5.14   Medical attention (by offence[1])

	% Seeking Doctor	% Staying Overnight
Burglary	1.5	–
Vandalism	2.5	.5
Theft from person[2]	6.8	1.9
Assault[3]	20	1.1

1. Percents are based on respondents claiming at least one household member seeking attention.
2. Includes robbery
3. Does not include domestic assault – weighted data.

A full 20% of assault victims required the attention of a doctor and this was the category for which the highest value was observed. In all other cases the proportion of victims having to spend at least one night in hospital is even lower – less than one percent of all victims. *It would seem from this data that although the level of violence appears to be quite high, as does the frequency of physical injury, the frequency of serious personal injury as a consequence of criminal victimization remains relatively rare.*

The most frequent victim of personal crime, according to the survey is not the youngest person, but rather those in the 25-44 age category. However, it is people from the 45 plus age group who appear to sustain the most severe effects of personal crime, when they are victims of either robbery or assault.

Overall impact

The previous sections have presented the impact of crime in Islington as measured by property loss and damage, net financial loss, and personal injury. This final section will examine the overall impact.

It was discovered above that it was the people from the lowest income categories who suffered the most financial loss as a consequence of crime. One other measure of the impact of crime on a victim or their household is the amount of time lost from work as a result of the crime. Table 5.15

breaks down the time lost from work for both the respondent and other household members by offence and by household income:

Table 5.15   Time lost from work (by household income and offence[1])

	Under £3000		3000-7999		8000-11999		12000+	
	Resp.	*Other*	*Resp.*	*Other*	*Resp.*	*Other*	*Resp.*	*Other*
Burglary	5.0	2.8	22.1	7.4	24.7	16.5	40.0	21.7
Vandalism[2]	0	1.8	7.2	0	15.0	10.6	13.4	7.8
Theft from person[3]	46	1.9	4.3	0	15.4	2.6	15.8	0
Robbery	37.4	16.2	18.1	5.3	36.4	16.5	46.6*	0*
Assault[4]	11.2	3.2	17.1	3.3	33.8	6.6	35.9	13.8

* Numbers too small to draw any definitive conclusions
1. Percents are based on respondents reporting any loss of work
2. Only vandalism followed up
3. Includes robbery
4. Does not include domestic assault

Base: All victims – weighted data.

While the low income categories lose more money from crime, the higher income categories lose more time from work. Firstly, people from the higher income levels are more likely to be employed than persons within the under £3000 annual income category. Secondly, it is much easier for people in better paying jobs to take time off work if necessary. People on salary do not lose financially for taking a day or part of a day off work, whereas people on wages lose valuable hours if they are required to stay off work. This idea is partly substantiated by the data. People from the higher income group take more time from work but lose less money than their counterparts in the lower income categories indicating that they do not lose salary as a consequence of the crime.

One reason why more time is lost from work by the higher income group is that they are more likely to have insurance claims to settle and would probably need to take time during the day to conduct business in relation to making claims, being interviewed by the police, and possibly replacing or having damaged property repaired. One indication of this is that the largest differences can be observed for the property crimes, and smaller differences for the personal crimes. There is much less difference for robbery victims, as an example, than there is for burglary victims.

The previous discussion made the assertion that older victims of violent crime sustained more severe effects than younger victims. Table 5.16 provides another measure in support of this assertion. Household crimes have been omitted from this table since our concern is for personal crimes, and in particular, violent personal crimes.

Table 5.16   Time lost from work (by age and offence[1])

	16–24		25–44		45+	
	Resp.	Other	Resp.	Other	Resp.	Other
Theft from person[2]	13.4	1.4	9.2	1.2	3.1	0
Punched/ Robbery	18.0	11.6	25.9	12.3	35.7	0
Assault[3]	15.7	5.9	22.2	5.4	45.5	5.0

1. Percents based on respondents reporting any loss of work
2. Includes robbery
3. Does not include domestic assault

Base: All victims of personal crimes – weighted data.

It can be seen from Table 5.16 that for the violent crimes older people are much more likely to lose time from work as a consequence of the crime indicating that they experience more severe effects of this type of personal crime. Even though people from the middle age category are at the highest risk, when violent crime is directed at older victims they feel the effects more strongly. It may well be that in losing time from work, these people also suffer lost wages, although since the survey did not ask this question, the idea remains speculative.

As a final overall measure of the impact of any of the crimes followed up by the survey we asked respondents:

"How much effect would you say the incident had on you or other people in your household?"

Table 5.17 provides a break down of those respondents who said the incident had either a very big effect or quite a big effect by offence and by selected background variables.

Table 5.17 shows that for all categories except vandalism, over half the respondents reported a high impact. Even vandalism is high in some categories, and for a crime which is so highly unreported, supposedly due to the insignificance of most vandalism, it appears to have quite an impact upon the victims. While gender differences remain minimal, except for assault where women feel a higher impact, large differences can be observed on the background variables. The older the respondent the more they are likely to report that the incident had a big effect. Lower income people are more affected by criminal victimization. Visible ethnic minorities are much more likely to report a big effect than whites on all categories of crime except for robbery: however, since it was asserted earlier that this crime is a working class crime, and since whites are less likely overall to be working class due to social inequality favouring the white population, one would expect this result from aggregate statistics.

Table 5.17   Effect of offence (by offence and selected variables[1])

	Burglary	Vandalism[2]	Theft[3] from Person	Robbery	Assault [4]
Gender					
Males	77.0	44.5	54.6	79.5	52.0
Females	79.2	48.9	64.7	77.9	89.1
Income					
Under 3000	79.4	48.0	67.9	96.8	78.2
3000-7999	87.8	57.1	58.9	66.5	61.8
8000-11999	69.1	45.6	63.8	78.4	64.7
12000 plus	74.7	39.0	59.7	100*	59.6
Age					
16-24	79.7	32.9	57.5	85.8	54.8
25-44	72.3	40.5	58.4	81.2	75.9
45 plus	84.3	63.3	68.2	71.4	72.6
Race					
White	77.8	45.7	59.6	80.6	67.0
Black	87.3	53.6	76.6	67.3	70.9
*Asian	34.9	46.5	48.5	69.8	67.1
*Other					
non-white	80.1	45.3	50.1	–	53.3
All respondents	78.3	46.9	61.3	78.9	67.5

1. Percents based on respondents reporting "quite a big effect" to a "very big effect"'
2. Only includes vandalism followed up
3. Includes robbery
4. Does not include domestic violence
* Due to small number of cases, these should be interpreted with caution.

Base: All victims – weighted data.

Summary and conclusions

This chapter makes a preliminary examination of the impact of crime on residents of the London Borough of Islington.

While much crime goes unreported, researchers whose data illustrate that the levels of crime are much higher than recorded levels of crime find themselves exposing high rates of crime on the one hand and attempting to downplay the significance of much unreported crime on the other. In part this is accomplished by making assertions that much of unreported crime remains trivial. A difficulty with this approach, however, is that the assessments of the impact and seriousness of unreported crime must take into account both subjective and objective considerations. On the low end of the scale of seriousness, a broken window caused by vandals may not be to most people a serious crime, due to the low costs of having the window replaced. This would be an objective assessment. If the victim of the crime does not have the means at their disposal to have the window replaced, or if they found the experience of the criminal damage was extremely frightening then the impact of the incident may be much higher for that person than another. This would be subjective assessment.

For purposes of this chapter, we have not made a sufficient inquiry into the nature of the impact of crime by subjective criteria. Rather, we have described the material consequences of the types of crimes followed up by the survey in terms of property loss and damage, financial losses, time lost from work, and the extent of physical injury. Where appropriate, we have compared these objective measures across different populations and indicated how they might be viewed differentially by the victims. Rather than try either to trivialize high levels of unreported crime on the one hand or to create a moral panic on the other, we have attempted to illustrate that the effects of crime are felt more severely in some groups of the population. We have neither argued for greater levels of law enforcement nor dismissed the importance of unreported crime and its impact on victims.

This brief examination produced a number of findings:

1. The initial loss or damage to property on household offences is higher in the higher income groups. Nevertheless, after taking into consideration the property either recovered by the police or replaced by insurance, the lower income groups end up being financially worse off more often than the higher income groups.
2. The losses realized due to personal property crimes are higher both before and after replacement by police or recovery by police in the lower income groups.
3. Injury is more frequent in the older age groups even though these people are less at risk in terms of the frequency of violent crime than younger people.
4. The impact of robbery is high in all groups, but it is the middle age group which is the highest risk category, especially when weapons are used.
5. Although older people are less at risk of robbery, when they are victims of this offence, they are more likely to report violence of all kinds.
6. Although violence characterizes 28% of all offences, when domestic violence and sexual assault are excluded serious physical injury is rare.
7. Women are more at risk to personal injury due to assault than men.
8. Higher income groups can afford to take more time off work than lower income groups but this does not seem to affect their losses due to crime.
9. While the majority of respondents reported that the crimes covered by the survey had at least quite a big effect, older people, women and people from the lower income groups were more likely to report that the incident had quite a big effect.
10. After all material factors have been taken into consideration, it is the lower income groups that are hit the hardest by crime.

6 Conclusions and Policy Recommendations

Summary and policy recommendations

1. *Taking the public seriously*

We have shown that crime is perceived by the people of Islington to be a problem of major dimensions. Indeed, crime and vandalism are seen as the second greatest problems in the Borough after unemployment, on par with poor youth and children's facilities and housing – and way ahead of schools and public transport.

The impact of crime is considerable and it is far from a rare event. 31% of households in Islington had a serious crime committed against them in the last year – and it shapes their lives. For example, over a quarter of all people in Islington *always* avoid going out after dark because of fear of crime and this rises to over one third in the case of women. We have here a virtual curfew of the female population. Yet it is frequently suggested that such fears are fantasies, part of some moral hysteria fanned by the newspapers and television. Thus it is often suggested that it is paradoxical that women have a higher fear of crime than men given the supposedly lower rate of crime against them. We have shown that this is simply not true: women have a higher victimization rate than men, they suffer to a greater extent from particular crimes, sexual assault obviously but also crimes like street robbery, and they suffer from a much greater rate of sub-criminal harassment. And all this is in the context of a much greater level of precautions taken. Their fears, therefore, are realistic. Similarly, we find that the degree of criticism of the police in terms of unfairness between groups and the use of excessive violence and other malpractices varies with people's actual experiences. The virtue, then, of a crime survey is that it provides us with a more realistic mapping of the impact of crime and policing, and it also reminds us that we should take seriously people's knowledge of crime. Successful policework depends on the police tapping such knowledge and the various other social agencies acting upon such a public information stock, whether it is providing suggestions as to who is committing racist attacks, which kids are the local vandals, why such an architectural blindspot is dangerous at night and what are the problems of their area.

2. *The crisis of crime control and policing*

"We appear to have remained for over 150 years very much an inward-looking organisation, largely unwilling to challenge in any active sense the large scale abdication to the police service of responsibility for law and order. And nor was this process of delegation, in my view, entirely one-way; there was also a tendency, I think, on the part of the police to corner the market in crime prevention and detection and to assume for many years that they were, indeed, the sole agency with responsibility for community order. Although this led to a strong sense of pride and esprit de corps, it fostered also a tendency to elitism – which was inclined to separate out the police officer from the community in the way that the police officer talked or dressed, or in qualities implicitly arrogated to ourselves such as infallible memories or unequalled investigative skills. It was but a short step for this tendency to separatism to be institutionalized into policies which reinforced withdrawal, introspection and self-evaluation.

As the crime rate grew and outstripped the human capacity of our officers, cracks manifested themselves in this rather brittle professional texture; criticism mounted, so further encouraging the inward-looking defensive posture in which the Force preferred to keep its own counsel and would seldom, unless cornered, admit that criticism was justified.

It was a position which could not be defended on either ethical or practical grounds. The need to change was inescapable."
(Newman, 1984, p6)

There can be little doubt that we face a crisis of extraordinary proportions in the policing of the inner city. At present the clear-up rate per officer per year in the Metropolitan Police Area is four crimes at the staggering cost of £6,076 (see M. Joyce, 1985) each crime. In areas such as Islington the clear-up rate for burglary has fallen to 9% and this refers, of course, only to the crimes known to the police. As our survey shows, many people simply do not bother to report crime because little good is likely to come from it. Meanwhile, substantial sections of the population are alienated from the police. We have traced the evidence of this in detail. It is certainly a time for change.

In a series of frank and revealing statements Commissioner Newman correctly pinpoints the tendency for people to view the police as the sole agency of social control, for the police to accept this misconception and for the whole of such a belief structure to begin to collapse under the weight of the rising crime rate and the increasing failure to control crime. Quite rightly he indicates the way in which the problem of crime control is a problem for us all, and quite certainly there has to be a multi-agency approach to crime control. What is not at all self-evident is that the police, particularly in their present structure, should form the central axis or agency to such a corporate approach to crime.

There can be no doubt that the philosophy of crime control as an issue involving wider agencies than the police, and in which the police can play only a partial role, is correct. Acceptance of this on the part of the police would be a rational response to the crisis in crime control and clear-up rate which now face them. This survey overwhelmingly accepts this philosophy and, although it is a study specifically focussing on crime and policing, it specifically distances itself from these analyses which note that there is very real and rising problem of crime and then proceed simply to pin the blame upon the police.

Crime occurs for many reasons and one of them is the problem of poverty and unemployment. Burglary, sexual assault, inter-personal violence and racial attacks all are linked to the grave problems of economic deprivation within the inner city. However, it is ludicrous to blame the police for the failure of the economy or of Government policies. If on one side there are causes of crime, on the other there are profound changes in the forces of social control both informal and formal which attempt to contain it. Social control is manifest on a whole series of fronts, on the level of the family, the local community, the tenants association, the Council, the schools *as well as* the police force. Most social control simply does not involve police action and perhaps even less police involvement than occurs at present might be possible. Furthermore, the enactment of successful policing is dependent on the public to a degree which is not conventionally realized. A full 95% of crime known to the police in Islington is made known to them by the public; direct police apprehension of offenders involves only 3.8% of cases. And, of course, successful prosecution of justice demands public witnessing in every stage of the judicial process. The police without public support are like fish out of water. This being said, the police are a vital part of the control of anti-social behaviour – they are after all, outside of the Armed Forces, the only part of society which is on any scale permitted legitimately to use coercive force. And this force is made effective both in terms of direct intervention and as a potential back-up force to various formal and informal non-coercive systems of control.

Our recommendations are, therefore, aimed at various and interrelated methods of crime control. They are directed at Islington Council in terms of initiatives which would greatly ameliorate the problems of crime, at tenants' associations in terms of procedures which might greatly help the predicament of inner-city victimization, at the voluntary bodies in terms of what they can do in order to aid victims and so on. They are also directed at the present system of policing Islington. If the proposals seem to be particularly critical of the police it is because, firstly, many of the people of Islington feel that they are getting bad value for their money and secondly in our estimation the policing component of crime control is in deep crisis. But the police do not bear the full brunt of this criticism.

3. *Public estimation of police effectiveness*

We have seen that there is widespread public scepticism about the ability of the police to combat the crimes which are of greatest public concern. This is reflected in the extremely high proportion of people who simply do not report offences to the police because they feel that it would do no good. As we have indicated throughout, the key to police efficiency is public cooperation. The standard Home Office study *Crime Control and the Police* summarizing the research noted:

> "On the basis of evidence from American and British studies, there can be little doubt that the detection and clearance of the commoner forms of crime depends for the most part upon the willingness and ability of the public to report criminal incidents to the police. Unfortunately, in their eagerness to make this point, authors have failed to draw on their research to identify those areas within which police skills may play some part. The detective has a variety of skills. These include gathering information from the public; locating suspects; interviewing and, on the basis of information derived from both the public and suspects, of preparing cases for the prosecution."
> (Morris and Heal, 1981, pp32-3)

The point to stress here is that detective work is rarely of a Sherlock Holmes variety and is much more often dependent on good public relations. Criticism of police efficiency is *ipso facto* criticism of police-public relations. It is for this reason that arguments about the necessity of the police to act scrupulously within the letter of the law and in a courteous fashion in their relations with the public, are not only important on a level of democratic sensibility. They are also so in terms of police effectiveness. This is clearly recognized in the excellent *Principles of Policing and Guidance For Professional Behaviour* published by the Metropolitan Police. Thus:

> "Any unreasonable, abrupt and over-zealous action by us will not achieve an orderly society, except perhaps in the very short term, but will rapidly lose for the Force its public support. And, since a police service without public support will not be able to police by consent, and in the long term will not be able to police at all, one of the very cornerstones of democratic government will have been put at risk.
>
> On the other hand, by acknowledging always that you are a friend, a guide and a servant of your fellow citizens, and never their master, by adopting an appropriately firm but conciliatory and helpful manner to everyone you meet, and by acting always in ways which are manifestly fair and lawful, so naturally attracting public acceptance of police activity, you and your service colleagues can help to sustain our democratic way of life and build up a store of goodwill to be drawn on in the future.
>
> It is vital therefore that you are aware constantly of the potential that each of your actions has for good or harm and of the importance for the success of policing and of democracy, not only of those actions themselves by of the style you adopt when going about your business. You are part of the complex machinery by which this country remains democratic and free – and an understanding of that should colour your every action."
> (1985, pp20-1)

4. *Public estimation of police legality and fairness*
We have seen that a considerable number of people in Islington believe the police do act illegally and unfairly towards certain groups. If this were just a *belief* it would by itself be unfortunate in its consequences, but it is all the more so in that it is backed up by *directly experienced evidence* of interviewees and their friends. Such a situation, apart from its violation of the law and the guidelines set out in *The Principles of Policing*, has two deleterious consequences in terms of crime control. First of all it alienates significant sections of the public, who become less willing to cooperate with the police. As a result clear-up rates fall and crime is encouraged. Secondly, such malpractices are directed at certain sections of the population. In particular they are directed at youth – and most of all at black youth. There is a considerable criminological literature which suggests that one of the key factors which precipitates delinquency is when young people experience police illegalities towards them. For what could be a more potent device to break a young person's faith in the rule of law than the breaking of these rules by those whom the community have charged to maintain the law? The focus of police malpractices on the groups most at risk, the young and the unemployed, is likely ironically to contribute to their delinquency – economic marginality is underscored by feelings of political marginality.

To dismantle this equation of crime we need to tackle the economic predicament of the inner city but we can deal immediately with those processes which impose upon those already economically deprived. One of these is policing: we must press for a situation where our surveys can detect little difference between the experiences of contact with the police between different sub-groups of the population – between young and old, black and white, male and female, working class and middle class, and where *all* groups have a belief in police fairness. It is not that the ideals are not there. Witness the following from the guidelines:

"When faced with malpractice by any officer your duty is clear. Although in such a case you must, of course, apply all those restraints and considerations which we have mentioned earlier as being necessary principles governing all police action, there is no room for equivocation of any kind when you see wrongdoing by a police officer, or when you obtain any other credible evidence of it.

With your growing experience of colleagues, and your knowledge of police practice, you should not have too much difficulty in differentiating between what is over-zealous, or laziness or error of judgement, or genuine mistake, and what is wickedly neglectful or even criminal.

And you may not shield yourself from your duty by closing your eyes, or falling silently behind your group loyalty.

You must speak out and ACT.

Failure to do so would not just be neglectful on your part, it would be so

serious an evasion of duty as an individual constable as to attract the most serious punishment."
(1985, pp55-6)

What are we to make of such a contrast between such exemplary ideals and the actual police practice reported by so many of the public? It is as if, at times, the Guide to Professional Behaviour was like the Constitution of the Soviet Union – full of high principles but somehow never realized in practice. Surely the solution to lapses in professionalism is a healthy leavening of democratic control.

5. *Who should control the police?*

We have shown from the results in this survey that the present system, where the Home Secretary together with the police themselves are in control of policing, commands an extremely limited public support amongst the people of Islington. Their preference is for a Police Authority which includes representatives of the community, the Council and the police. This is not only a heartfelt expression of democratic values, it is also politically sophisticated to the extent that it permits the possibility of checks and balances necessary in an institution which must preserve the rights of the minorities, allow balance between local and national needs and allow for a leavening of expert and practical opinion. Such a position does, of course, find considerable opposition in many quarters, to the extent that many think that anarchy would ensue if it were implemented. It should be noted that such a political control of the police occurs in very many cities of the United States and is supported by both right and left of political opinion, all of whom would no doubt be amused that their democratic persuasions amount to anarchy.

6. *A critique of present policing policy*

What are the lessons that we can learn from the Islington Crime Survey? What are the demands on police and policing of the citizens of a high crime rate, inner-city area? We believe that the ICS provides evidence which substantially invalidates much of current thinking and practice in the area.

In their demands on the police, the public specifically prioritize crime control. 99% – almost everyone – see immediate response to 999 calls as the major task of policing and this is followed shortly behind by 93% who see crime investigation as a major role and 87% the deterrent presence of police officers on the street. Service work such as traffic control and youth community projects come least on their list of priorities in terms of police tasks (54% and 50%). It is not that the public think these services are unimportant, it is simply *not* what they see as the major police role. And note that there is virtual consensus as to prioritization of the reactive role – where the police are reacting to public demands. This is further substantiated when we look at the types of offences which the public prioritize: four of the top six crimes are very clearly of a reactive nature. They are offences which are overwhelmingly made known to the police by the public and where a quick reaction is necessary – burglary, sexual assaults on women, street robbery and racist attacks. Furthermore, in terms of the quantity of demands on the police, a majority of the crimes which are *least* prioritized by the public are most frequently "order maintenance" areas where the police act more on their own accord – proactively – where discretion is high and where the boundary between legality and illegality is often blurred. Witness cannabis, rowdyism in the streets and prostitution.

If we turn to the quantative demand on the police by the public, we have seen that there is clearly a majority demand which is of a crime-related nature. This is true if we use the conventional division between crime, order and service demand. But it is even more clear if we include in our calculations that proportion of order demand which is of a crime-related nature (eg domestic violence). Once again, the service demand is substantial but it is not prioritized and this result corroborates the findings of the Merseyside Crime Survey.

There is no evidence, therefore, that the public in the urban areas have a majority demand of a service nature on the police. The notion of a lapse on the part of the public where, on the one hand, they envisage the police as primarily crime fighters yet paradoxically demand more of them of a service nature, is disproved. When the Home Office writers Southgate and Ekblom point to a divergence between the lower ranking police officer and the public on the question of prioritizing crime control they are clearly wrong within high density urban areas (see also Kinsey, 1985). In his recent book *The Politics of the Police*, Robert Reiner sums up the police and public attitude to the service role well when he writes:

"There is copious evidence that most rank and file policemen believe the service aspects of the work should have low or no priority. As one uniform constable summed it up: 'This idea of performing a public service is a load of cobswobble as far as I'm concerned'. Nor is there much evidence of the public seeing the police as a broad service agency (Brogden and Wright, 1979). In truth, the service work of the police is largely a by-product of their availability on a 24-hour basis, and their possession of coercive powers in order to perform their core mandate of order maintenance and law enforcement. When people call the police to a scene of trouble (even if there is no immediate obvious crime aspect) they do so not primarily because they require the services of an amateur priest, psychiatrist, nurse or marriage guidance counsellor, but because the problem needs authorative resolution, by force if necessary (Bittner, 1974). To say that the police are a crypto-social work agency because so many of their calls involve this, is like saying sociologists are professional coffee-drinkers because that is what they spend so much of their time doing (like I am now)."
(1985, pp76-7)

It is probably more accurate to say that any rift which does occur between the attitudes of public and police occurs between the public and certain senior police officers, who are backed by the dominant current philosophy at Bramshill Police College.

It is vital to note that the starkly contrasting ratios of service to crime related demands on police time found by the ICS and MCS when compared to the national BCS survey (ie 1:1 c.f. 3:1) is of greater significance than simply a contrast between predominantly urban as opposed to mixed areas. For it is in these urban areas that there is the highest concentration of police resources and the highest calls on police assistance in terms of crime. Thus the number of police officers per 1000 of the population is 3.7 in the Metropolitan Area compared to 2.3 in Humberside or 1.7 in the Thames Valley area (source, CIPFA, 1985). Researchers who base their analysis in low crime areas or on the country as a whole forget that police resources are far from equally distributed throughout the country.

Thus we can conclude that crime is a major problem for people in Islington, they make high demands of the police and prioritize crime over service demands, and they do so in terms of the urgency of the demands they make on the police. Their overwhelming disposition is towards a reactive police force responsive to public demand and overall they show little interest in most proactive order maintenance policing. A performance indicator of police effectiveness which accurately expressed the wishes of the citizens of the Borough would therefore highlight:
- clear up rates
- reactive rather than proactive capacity
- speed of response
- degree of prioritization of resources in the top six areas
- prioritization of crime over service provision.

These views are a consensus of all sections of the community and in all probability the majority of police officers. As we have seen they do not reflect current policy on policing in London.

7. *The uniform application of the law*

We have seen that there is a broad consensus on the priorities of policing across the community which is independent of age, race or gender. There is no evidence for a pluralism of standards which suggests that one part of the community should be policed differently from any other. All policing demands decisions as to the apportioning of resources; some areas of misconduct must be prioritized as foci for police action over others. In a situation of scarce resources it is, therefore, disquieting if undue police time is spent on activities which rate very low on the public's scale of concern and not enough time on those which the public quite rightly feel anxious about. The problem is not so much that the police apply different standards to various sections of the community but that, at times, they appear to be applying their own standard which is different to that of the community as a whole.

8. *The problem of opportunistic crime*

"Initial exploration led me to two predominant conclusions, which were to shape planning for 1983; firstly, that over half of recorded crime is of a capricious nature, upon which police, acting without public help, would never be likely to make any serious impact. Secondly, that the origins of opportunist crime – and probably all other – are of such social complexity that the combined wisdom and resources of society must be used to redress them.

The majority of crime facing the Metropolitan Police is of a frustratingly fleeting and transient nature. A burglary – whether from a house, a garage or from business premises – is capable of being effected within seconds where there is offered temptation and opportunity. Thefts from cars or thefts from the person, sometimes with an element of violence, are equally rapidly executed and with a randomness which suggests that the comparative ease of success and escape are the culprit's only serious consideration.

However effective the police are able to be within their existing resources against the millions of opportunities provided by parked vehicles and available premises, their achievements will appear insignificant alongside the bulk of opportunist crime.

Such considerations lead directly to the conclusion that the police cannot, alone, be held responsible for 'law and order'. They are the principal agency for achieving the maintenance of a peaceful community but if crime is a by-product of the combined influences of contemporary thought and action in society, then any solution must equally lie with the whole of the community and not simply with one appointed body within it."
(K. Newman, 1984, pp4-5)

As we have argued, such a multi-agency approach to crime is essentially correct although we disagree strongly with the central and dominant role which the police envisage for themselves within it. However, the corollaries of such a theory of opportunistic crime are a shift from reacting against crime to prevention, and a shift of emphasis from direct crime control (which in 50% of cases is not seen as very possible) to order control. Such strategies – very popular in the United States (see Wilson, 1985) – emphasize that the police by maintaining order help the community to regain its own informal system of social control so that crime itself will decline in the long run, a more "indirect" crime control. Such an approach has been given great emphasis in the recent *Principles of Policing* (Metropolitan Police, 1985, pp40-41). Most importantly, the notion of order control has been given considerable underpinning by the stop and search panels of the Police and Criminal Evidence Act 1984 and the white paper on Public Order Law (Cmnd 9510) with its detailed provisions on the control of disorderly conduct (ie as represented in The Public Order Bill, 1986).

Our objections to such an approach are twofold. First of all we dispute the notion of opportunistic crime as a justification for a policing "impossibilism". It is important to stress that the London clear-up rate is quite exceptional: at 17% it is lower than any other Metropolitan Area (41% in Greater Manchester) and half the clear-up rate of its nearest competitors in the low clear-up league (Hampshire 33%, Surrey 34%) (see M. Joyce, 1985). Over the period 1973-1983 we find the following changes compared to England and Wales in general:

	% Change	
	Metropolitan Police	England and Wales
Police manpower	+ 28	+ 22
Clear-up rate	− 13	− 10
Number of crimes cleared up	+ 7	+ 48
Number of crimes cleared up per police officer	− 18	+ 18
Cost of crimes cleared up/ crime 1983	£6,076	£1,748

(Source: Kinsey, Lea and Young, 1986, p22)

Despite the London police force being allocated extra resources compared to the rest of the country there has been markedly less effectiveness. If this is due to opportunistic crime, are we to believe that there is a similar variation throughout the country – other high urbanized areas do not seem to suffer from it to such a degree – or that opportunism has increased so remarkably in London in the last ten years?

In terms specifically of burglary, we have given clear evidence that it is not as opportunistic as is suggested. Indeed we feel that a false alternative is posed between professional burglary (committed by a small number of professionals with high skills and clear patterns) and opportunistic burglary which is random. If it were true that "amateur" burglary was committed by anyone, anytime, almost at a whim in the sense that opportunistic seems to have entered the language of policing, then, of course, it would be very difficult to solve indeed and it would be quite justifiable to relocate it in the category of unsolvable, in contrast to professional burglary which would remain in the province of policework. But, in fact, amateur burglary involves repetitive patterns – a few individuals, usually adolescent males, repeating their methods of break-in, in the same area, often to the same houses over a limited period of time. Surely it is the failure of detective work and the extremely low proportion of time that officers spend interviewing the public and following up leads which is the source of this failure (see the PSI Survey of Police Officers' Use of Time in D. Smith, 1983b and the Merseyside Study by R. Kinsey, 1985)?

As far as order offences are concerned they are an extremely mixed category, and include serious racial harassment and domestic violence as well as minor examples of disorderly conduct in the street. We know that the public distinguish quite clearly between general problems of disorderliness, which they do *not* rate as serious problems in Islington and precise areas such as racist attacks and sexual harassment of women which they certainly do. What one gleans from this is that the better implementation of specific powers against violence against women and racist confrontations would command a considerably greater public support than the introduction of blanket powers to deal with unspecified disorderly conduct.

9. *Curbing stop and search*

A specific police activity which involves largely an "order maintenance" function is stop and search. Our survey indicates that in Islington a third of young white males have been stopped in the last 12 months and over a half of young black males. The yield of such procedures is extremely low in terms of the main public priorities with regard to crime. We argue that with the important exception of breathalyser checks on suspected drunken drivers (a high public priority) that stops should be severely curbed. The likely result of the present policies is to alienate substantial sections of the population, particularly these which have information about crime which the police desperately need to fulfil successfully their role. For unwillingness to cooperate with the police coincides almost totally with the degree of such police-public encounters. As a general principle, crime control should be public initiated and reactive (where the public makes demands on the police) rather than police initiated and proactive (where the police act off their own bat).

10. *The construction of effective police performance indicators*

Given the size of the crime problem in the inner city, and the considerable amount of money such predominantly less well off communities pay for policing, it is paramount that the public gets value for its money. For this reason it is necessary to develop a series of performance indicators which are independently audited. With this in mind the regular crime survey is a useful tool into which can be built the relevant indicators. Examples of such indicators are reaction times, public satisfaction with requests for police assistance, experiences of police illegality, and levels of yield from stop and search procedures. Vital to this enterprise is the creation of a valid index of clear-up rate. At present, as the official crime rate is a function of crimes reported to the police, it is a fraction of the actual crime rate. Many crimes are not reported to the police because of the lack of public confidence in the police doing anything about them and many crimes reported to the police simply do not find their way into the crime report. The official clear-up rate is, therefore, an extremely flawed indicator. All that one can safely say, in the majority of instances, is that if the official rate is x% then the real rate is certainly more than x%. Given the low official clear-up rates of such crimes as burglary, such pronouncements certainly underscore the gravity of the situation but they, of course, lack precision. Most importantly they are useless for measuring performance over time. It could be, for example, that in a situation of rising public confidence in the police there would be more crimes reported and consequently a decline in official clear up. Such paradoxes are obviated by the figures obtained from the survey.

It is often argued that because of the service role of the police the use of crime control indicators of police effectiveness is mistaken and unfair (see Thomson and Heal, 1981). It is clear from the survey that the public expect from the police a role which is primarily that of crime control. It is, therefore, in this area that our prime indicators must be developed.

11. *Taking the pressure off the police*
The police face the problem of an annual increase in the amount of work which they have to tackle. At the same time, there is little evidence that an increase in personnel would facilitate any greater effectiveness of crime control. The recent Home Office Survey of research in this area entitled *Crime and Police Effectiveness* was extremely doubtful about this. Indeed, as we have seen, some American police departments have actually reduced their size and in an interesting experiment in New York in the late seventies the workforce was reduced by one fifth. Recorded crime continued to rise – but at the same rate as before – and arrests for serious offences actually rose. It was "industrial action" by the police rather than a failure in effectiveness which cut short this promising experiment.

A realistic appraisal of the present policing situation in the inner city must involve attempts to rationalize the present work force and its tasks in order to maximize the productivity in terms of crime control. We do not intend to enter here into the necessity of rationalizing the present management structure of the police force and the divisions between uniformed and plain clothes officers. Radical and far reaching suggestions have been made in this direction both by the PSI survey of police in London (see D. Smith 1983b, D. Smith and J. Gray, 1983) and by the Merseyside Police Survey (see R. Kinsey, 1985). The ICS, being a survey of the public rather than of police and the utilization of police resources, focuses on public assessment of the *tasks* which are most appropriately carried out by the police force. What is evident from our data is the public's assessment of the prime role of the police as tackling crime. There was little prioritization of their service role. Indeed, as we have seen, much of their role as the "secret social service" seems to have occurred merely because they happen to be one of the few agencies which maintain a 24-hour switchboard. It would be more rational if the social services task of policing were, in fact, carried out by the appropriate social services (eg social work departments for child neglect, housing departments for emergency problems in that area etc.).

Certainly such a round-the-clock service would be a great asset to the social services – its financing could be accomplished by reallocating funds from the precept.

The professional rationale behind such a move is to maintain a clear

distinction between the various roles – that it is not the job of police officers to be social workers nor of social workers to be police officers. There
are all sorts of necessary and productive tensions between the two jobs
which it is necessary to maintain within a democratic structure.

A second major area which would take pressure off the police would be
to institute wherever possible (eg community groups and tenants' organizations) methods of pre-legal mitigation between disputing individuals. Particularly in those fragmented parts of the community where
informal social control is low and the crime high, there is a tendency to
solve problems by immediate recourse to the police. Often these involve
crimes of a trivial nature and, importantly, there are often actions which
are on the edge of illegality – noisy parties, vandalism, threats of violence
and sub-criminal harassment – more anti-social behaviour than crimes.
Very frequently the complainant knows exactly who the culprit is. And
often when police help is sought in these areas it is (a) unforthcoming or if
it is (b) there is insufficient evidence to prove a criminal act, or if there is
(c) the complainant finds the proceedings, and results of the criminal
courts extremely unsatisfying and unrelated to the actual "solutions", or
justice he or she wanted in the dispute. Pre-legal mitigation – as has been
tried in many countries – affords the aggrieved complainant a chance to
meet and negotiate with the culprit. It avoids the automatic rush to police
and law which artificially bloats the crime figures.

12. *The potentiality of Neighbourhood Watch*
The institution of Neighbourhood Watch schemes throughout the
London area involves a correct reading of the present crisis in policing by
the Metropolitan Police. That is, that a major priority must be given to
increasing the information flow from the public to the police. Neighbourhood watch schemes were successful particularly in Detroit where they
have had a proven effectiveness in crime control. However, it should be
noted that this was in a context of democratic control of the police in
which the watch schemes were part of a package which included an independent civilian complaints panel, appointment of a new and more radical police chief, and a change in the ethnic composition of the police to
reflect the population of Detroit (see Lea and Young, 1984). Their effectiveness was in a particular political context and the transplant of the
Detroit Scheme into areas such as Islington involved only one portion of a
package out of the wider context.

In order to increase information flow it is essential that the police gain
the confidence of the public. As we have seen from the results of the
survey, high levels of confidence in the police exist only in restricted
pockets of the population, particularly in the over 45 age group. The
Centre for Criminology has conducted a survey of Neighbourhood Watch
in Islington which is at present being analysed (see J. Lea, 1986). Preliminary indications, however, point to the fact that such police-initiated
schemes have taken root in only very specific areas, in particular, middle

class and in close-knit housing estates containing a large measure of elderly tenants.

There is, of course, no reason to take exception to the limited success so far. However, the following problems should be highlighted: (i) there is a danger of crime being *displaced* from one area to another from a neighbourhood watch scheme to surrounding areas without neighbourhood watch. Such displacement involves not only movements of criminal activity from one area to another but the movement of police resources into neighbourhood watch areas. (ii) The crime rate in Islington or any other inner city in Britain is simply not sufficient *by itself* to provide an ongoing focus for the institution of neighbourhood watch. There is, in short, not enough to watch. (iii) As neighbourhood watch schemes are police initiated and many people particularly in areas with high crime rates are – as we have seen – suspicious of the police and unwilling to join such schemes. That is, those worse hit are most reluctant or unable to take part. Paradoxically neighbourhood watch schemes work best in those areas where there is a viable community organization yet crime is highest in those areas where the community tends to be fragmented. In terms of our general principles of a multi-agency approach to crime – a police force oriented around the police and policing alone is inadequate. For example, on the most obvious level, the housing department with its control of lighting, the physical structure of estates, and the allocation of tenancies is vital in any strategy against crime. It is for this reason that we advocate neighbourhood watch schemes being attached to the present decentralization plans for neighbourhood forums. The net of neighbourhood watch schemes should therefore be widened whilst their constitution should be changed from being police and crime centred to being consultative, multi-agency and multi-problem directed.

13. *Dealing with the impact of crime*

We have seen that it is the weakest in the community who suffer most from the impact of crime. It is here that the local Council can make a substantial contribution. First of all it should ensure that Council tenants have sufficient protection against crime in terms of target hardening (we have dealt with this in the Crime Prevention Section), secondly it should expand on the present system of Council insurance to cover all tenants. It is vital to point out that those most likely to have a severe impact from crimes committed against them are the least likely to be insured and who find insurance provisions most difficult to obtain, most expensive, and have the least available funds to pay. Furthermore, such a scheme should be expanded where possible to include tenants in the private sector both in housing associations and with private landlords. The private rented sector in Islington includes many of the most impoverished members of the community and it is a gross mistake to see this as a wealthy section of the Borough despite the fact that a small proportion of such tenants, of course, exist. A useful step in this direction would be to pressurize on a parliamentary level for legislation to ensure that private sector landlords make substantial contributions to such insurance. Of course, once again, such insurance would focus not only on crime but on the wide range of damage and disaster that can occur to housing and personal property. In particular, we feel that a system of free insurance for old age pensioners would be an extremely progressive step forwards for any Council to instigate.

The Council, then, should take a major role in dealing with the impact of crime both in the public and the private sectors. As for the police, their role is of necessity a minor one in this field, yet there are important tasks to perform. An adequate interviewing of the victim and neighbours with regard, for example, to burglary would do much to allay the victim's fears. As it is, we find a strong dissatisfaction with the police in terms of their often desultory and public relations-created dealing with such crime. Unfortunately, the notion of "opportunistic crime" has often instilled a feeling that all that the police role could possibly be is one that is cordial and generally, if fleetingly, supportive. This is not good enough, insofar as more careful interviewing can result in a higher yield and could inspire more real confidence that the police are actively tackling the matter.

14. *Crime prevention*

There is no area where a multi-agency approach is more necessary than in the area of crime prevention. What use, for example, would be advice on suitable locks, if the Council were not to ensure that the doors to its tenants' flats were tough enough to resist being pushed from their frames? And public information is vital in this sphere. In the survey we were able to pinpoint from our interviews with the public the danger spot of the Archway tunnel. Indeed our survey alone picked up one multiple rape, two robberies, and one sexual assault at this location. In order to tackle this, it is necessary to consult and inform architects and planners, so that such vulnerable locations can be "designed out" both in the present sites and in future constructions.

It is vital that the Council extend its crime prevention services. The existing finances from the Department of the Environment of £¼ million for improvement on council estates is insufficient as is the extremely small allowance of £50,000 for private sector tenancies. Certainly personnel must be extended in a multi-agency project – in particular, the two police officers allocation to Crime Prevention in Islington are manifestly insufficient.

In order to prevent and lessen the impact of crime, various specific projects are of great importance and should be strengthened and supported. Two areas, particularly, should be singled out: the activities of Women's Aid providing shelter for battered women and the Council's "Minders" scheme which recruits volunteers to protect citizens' houses and flats from racist attacks (see Race Relations and Police Sub-Committee papers, 1985).

15. *A unified crime control plan for Islington*

In order to combat crime it is necessary that all points of the community contribute towards its control. Foremost is the public itself, but also the Council with its various departments, tenants' organizations, schools, community groups and the police must play their part. To this extent Commissioner Newman's advocacy of multi-agency policing is both correct and innovative. Its failure is that it does not go far enough: it still has at its essence the notion of the police as *the* central organization of crime control around which strategies are planned and decisions made. Instead a genuine collaborative effort is needed which, whilst avoiding a corporation which blurs the boundaries between the various agencies, recognizes the fact that one-sided approaches contribute to the present lack of success in crime control in the inner cities.

As an initial stage the Consultative Committees set up in the wake of Scarman are a step in the right direction. They are handicapped in that they consist of an interface between democratically accountable bodies and those which are much less directly accountable to the public. But they at least represent a public arena where anxieties, doubts as well as strategies can be aired and where the sense of public alienation with policing and the problem of crime control in general can, to an extent, be assuaged.

What is necessary are agencies which can provide a base for a multi-agency approach to crime on the local level. The present policy of decentralization being carried out by the London Borough of Islington provides a series of neighbourhood offices in which the neighbourhood forums would be appropriate bases for such local agencies (see T. Jones, 1983). Here could be located local crime prevention panels which in the contact between local beat police officers and the public would parallel the initiatives of the Joint Consultative Committees on the macro-level. The experiment of local joint liaison on the Barnsbury Estate should be monitored in order to learn from its progress. It is at the local neighbourhood forum that the watch schemes should be centred. That is, the proposal to democratize and widen the net of neighbourhood watch should be facilitated through cooperation with the present Council's decentralization plans. At such neighbourhood forums a wide range of issues should be aired, some which bear on crime and some not – and indeed many issues could be discussed which cross the boundaries between problems of crime and other problems of area (eg leisure facilities for youth, adequate street lighting). Decisions at such a level should also be filtered up to the macro-level: the various appropriate departments of the Council (eg housing, social services) to the police and to the Crime Prevention Working Party. It is also in a neighbourhood forum grounded in substantial local support that attempts at non-financial settlement of disputes (eg noisy parties, vandalism) should be attempted (see T. Marshall, 1985).

The approach we have outlined to combating crime must therefore be multi agency, it involves reforms both in public policy and in policing, it must involve both local and Borough level initiatives and it should strive towards the greatest level of popular participation and democratic accountability.

WARDS, WARD NAMES and POLLING DISTRICTS

LONDON BOROUGH OF
ISLINGTON
STREET MAP
1983

Scale

One Mile

One Kilometre

HARINGEY L.B.

Finsbury Park

KINGSLAND

N/FD

N/FA

N/GB

QUADRANT (2)

GILLESPIE (2)

N/FB

N/GA

N/GB

N/BD

N/BC

HIGHBURY (4)

N/AB

N/BB

N/BA

N/KC

DILLINGTON (3)

N/JA

N/CB

N/CA

N/KB

N/JB

N/KA

N/IC

SUSSEX (3)

N/IB

N/IA

SS/BB

HILLMARTON (2)

HIGHVIEW (2)

N/DC

N/DB

HILLRISE (3)

N/DE

N/EE

N/HB

ST. GEORGE'S (3)

N/HA

N/DA

N/EA

N/EB

JUNCTION (3)

N/EC

Appendix 1

Demographic Composition of the Sample

The following tables have been included in this chapter for two purposes. Firstly, because they provide breakdowns of various demographic characteristics of the sample, the reader will have an appreciation for the distribution of the demographic composition of the Borough as well as the sample. This information should assist the reader in drawing conclusions about the interpretation of the findings presented in the preceding chapters.

The second purpose of the following tables is to illustrate what distribution characterises the control variables which have been used to break down the data in the following chapters. The relationships between these variables are illustrated by the tables, and readers are reminded that a careful reading of the tables should better equip them in interpreting the findings of the survey.

TABLE 1.1 to TABLE 1.35 provide percentages of respondents for each category of the selected variables. Some columns do not add to 100 due to small rounding errors.

Table 1.1   Race By Age

	White	Black	Asian	Other Non-White
16–24	17.4	30.9	27.4	16.8
25–44	34.3	32.9	36.8	43.0
45 plus	48.3	36.2	35.9	40.2

Base: All respondents weighted n = 9386

Table 1.2   Gender by Age

	Males	Females
16–24	18.3	19.4
25–44	33.8	34.9
45 plus	47.8	45.7

Base: All respondents weighted n = 9386

Table 1.3   Race By Gender

	White	Black	Asian	Other Non-White
Male	47.0	48.8	60.9	49.0
Female	53.0	51.2	39.1	51.0

Base: All respondents weighted n = 9386

Table 1.4   Household Income by Race

	White	Black	Asian	Other Non-White
Under £3000	34.2	28.7	14.7	25.9
£3000-7999	32.0	37.5	42.6	40.2
£8000-11999	16.7	19.8	18.4	17.6
£12000 plus	17.1	14.0	24.3	16.2

Base: All respondents weighted n = 9386

Table 1.5   Household Income by Gender

	Under £3000	£3000-7999	£8000-11999	£12000 plus
Males	40.0	48.0	57.0	55.3
Females	60.0	52.0	43.0	44.7

Base: All respondents weighted n = 9386

Table 1.6   Tenure by Age

	Owned	Public Rental	Private Rental	Squat
16–24	16.1	15.8	31.6	33.6
25–44	45.7	31.1	35.8	40.2
45 plus	38.3	53.1	32.6	26.2

Base: All respondents weighted n = 9386

Table 1.7   Race By Tenure

	White	Black	Asian	Other Non-White
Owned	15.4	13.7	39.0	21.1
Public Rental	65.6	70.6	35.0	51.7
Private Rental	18.1	13.9	24.2	23.4
Squat	.9	1.7	1.8	3.8

Base: All respondents weighted n = 9386

Table 1.8   Satisfaction with Neighbourhood by Age

	16–24	25–44	45 plus
High	.9	.5	2.6
Medium	68.0	68.4	80.3
Low	31.1	31.0	7.8

Base: All respondents weighted n = 9386

Table 1.9   Satisfaction with Neighbourhood by Race

	White	Black	Asian	Other Non-White
High	1.5	.7	4.9	3.1
Medium	74.9	62.3	81.7	65.5
Low	23.7	37.0	13.3	31.4

Base: All respondents weighted n = 9386

Table 1.10   Satisfaction with Neighbourhood by Gender

	Male	Female
High	0.9	2.1
Medium	77.7	70.2
Low	21.4	27.7

Base: All respondents weighted n = 9386

Table 1.11   Satisfaction with Neighbourhood by Income

	Under £3000	£3000-7999	£8000-11999	£12000 plus
High	2.6	1.1	0.4	1.8
Medium	75.6	71.7	69.7	77.4
Low	21.8	27.2	29.9	20.8

Base: All respondents weighted n = 9386

Table 1.12   Satisfaction with Neighbourhood by Tenure

	Owned	Public Rental	Private Rental	Squat
High	0.8	1.4	2.1	9.3
Medium	80.3	72.0	75.7	60.5
Low	19.0	26.6	22.2	30.2

Base: All respondents weighted n = 9386

Table 1.13   Fear of Crime by Age

	16–24	25–44	45 plus
Low	11.2	8.4	11.8
Medium	55.6	62.7	55.5
High	33.2	28.9	32.7

Base: All respondents weighted n = 9386

Table 1.14   Fear of Crime by Race

	White	Black	Asian	Other Non-White
Low	10.2	12.8	13.8	11.6
Medium	59.2	48.7	51.8	54.8
High	30.6	38.5	34.4	33.6

Base: All respondents weighted n = 9386

Table 1.15   Fear of Crime by Income

	Under £3000	£3000-7999	£8000-11999	£12000 plus
Low	14.1	8.5	6.0	13.3
Medium	53.2	57.4	61.5	63.0
High	32.7	34.1	32.5	23.7

Base: All respondents weighted n = 9386

Table 1.16   Fear of Crime by Tenure

	Owned	Public Rental	Private Rental	Squat
Low	12.5	9.8	11.3	9.8
Medium	65.2	54.9	62.9	55.0
High	22.3	35.3	25.7	35.2

Base: All respondents weighted n = 9386

Table 1.17   Perception of Probability of Crime by Age

	16–24	*25–44*	*45 plus*
Low	10.2	11.5	17.2
Medium	69.0	69.8	68.8
High	20.8	18.7	14.0

Base: All respondents weighted n = 9386

Table 1.18   Perception of Probability of Crime by Race

	White	*Black*	*Asian*	*Other Non-White*
Low	14.1	13.4	10.2	12.6
Medium	70.3	60.9	63.7	63.3
High	15.6	25.7	26.1	24.1

Base: All respondents weighted n = 9386

Table 1.19   Perception of Probability of Crime by Income

	Under £3000	*£3000-7999*	*£8000-11999*	*£12000 plus*
Low	17.8	14.3	8.6	12.6
Medium	64.7	67.1	74.8	73.0
High	17.5	18.6	16.5	14.4

Base: All respondents weighted n = 9386

Table 1.20   Perception of Probability of Crime by Tenure

	Owned	*Public Rental*	*Private Rental*	*Squat*
Low	9.8	15.2	13.3	10.0
Medium	75.7	67.0	71.3	67.9
High	14.5	17.8	15.5	22.1

Base: All respondents weighted n = 9386

Table 1.21   Perception of Probability of Crime by Fear of Crime

	Low	*Fear of Crime* *Medium*	*High*
Low	35.5	11.8	9.9
Medium	58.0	77.4	57.5
High	6.5	10.8	32.7

Base: All respondents weighted n = 9386

Table 1.22   Satisfaction with Neighbourhood by Fear of Crime

| | Satisfaction with Neighbourhood | | |
	High	Medium	Low
Low	27.5	11.4	5.6
Medium	64.2	60.2	50.4
High	8.3	28.4	43.9

Base: All respondents weighted n = 9386

Table 1.23   Satisfaction with Neighbourhood by Perception of Probability of Crime

| | Satisfaction with Neighbourhood | | |
	High	Medium	Low
Low	16.3	15.4	8.1
Medium	72.0	69.8	67.1
High	11.7	14.9	24.8

Base: All respondents weighted n = 9386

Table 1.24   Household Income by Tenure

	Under £3000	£3000-7999	£8000-11999	£12000 plus
Owned	1.7	8.8	21.0	48.1
Public Rental	81.0	69.5	61.0	33.3
Private Rental	16.5	20.3	18.0	17.0
Squat	0.8	1.4	0.1	1.6

Base: All respondents weighted n = 9386

Table 1.25   Age by Average Weekly Evening Absences from Home

	16–24	25–44	45 plus
None	5.3	8.9	30.4
One-Two	32.5	42.1	47.4
Three plus	62.2	49.0	22.2

Base: All respondents weighted n = 9386

Table 1.26   Race By Average Weekly Evening Absences

	White	Black	Asian	Other Non-White
None	18.8	11.8	21.2	13.4
One-Two	41.3	50.0	58.3	46.2
Three plus	39.8	38.2	20.5	40.3

Base: All respondents weighted n = 9386

Table 1.27   Household Income by Average Weekly Evening Absences

	Under £3000	£3000-7999	£8000-11999	£12000 plus
None	31.7	18.0	8.5	4.0
One-Two	39.6	45.8	45.7	36.7
Three plus	28.7	36.1	45.8	59.3

Base: All respondents weighted n = 9386

Table 1.28   Tenure by Average Weekly Evening Absences

	Owned	Public Rental	Private Rental	Squat
None	6.4	23.2	11.5	6.4
One-Two	44.2	43.9	36.8	46.7
Three plus	49.4	32.9	51.8	46.9

Base: All respondents weighted n = 9386

Table 1.29   Satisfaction with Neighbourhood by Average Weekly Absences

	High	Medium	Low
None	53.5	18.8	12.0
One-Two	20.6	43.1	43.0
Three plus	26.0	25.1	45.0

Base: All respondents weighted n = 9386

Table 1.30   Fear of Crime by Average Weekly Evening Absences

	Low	Medium	High
None	18.8	16.6	19.1
One-Two	35.1	40.4	49.9
Three plus	46.1	43.0	31.0

Base: All respondents weighted n = 9386

Table 1.31   Perception of Probability of Crime by Average Weekly Evening Absences

	Low	Medium	High
None	36.7	15.0	13.1
One-Two	32.1	42.8	49.1
Three plus	31.2	42.2	37.8

Base: All respondents weighted n = 9386

Table 1.32   Contacts with Police by Average Weekly Evening Absences

	None	*One*	*Two or More*
		Contacts with Police	
None	26.4	15.5	8.0
One-Two	44.9	43.2	39.4
Three plus	28.7	41.4	52.6

Base: All respondents weighted n = 9386

Table 1.33   Number of Victimisations in Last Year by Average Weekly Evening Absences

	None	*One*	*Two or More*
None	26.8	14.0	9.8
One-Two	42.2	43.5	43.0
Three plus	31.1	42.5	47.2

Base: All respondents weighted n = 9386

Table 1.34   Employment Status by Average Weekly Evening Absences

	Unemployed	*Employed*
None	28.4	9.3
One-Two	40.7	44.3
Three plus	30.9	46.4

Base: All respondents weighted n = 9386

Table 1.35   Percentage Having Friends or Relatives in the Area by Age, Race, Tenure

	Owned			*Public Rental*		
	16–24	*25–44*	*45+*	*16–24*	*25–44*	*45+*
White	76	65	66	73	65	53
Black	90	63	50	70	45	64
Asian	53	50	43	55	32	35
Other	52	67	60	48	51	54

	Private Rental			*Squat*		
	16–24	*25–44*	*45+*	*16–24*	*25–44*	*45+*
	53	56	60	66	61	100
	67	58	100	65	–	–
	65	45	81	24	–	–
	87	85	34	–	50	–

Base: All respondents weighted n = 9386

Appendix 2

Methodology

1. The Research Design

In order to carry out an in-depth investigation into crime and policing in The London Borough of Islington as requested by the Council, a number of special factors needed to be considered in the development of an appropriate research design particular to the research problem and the research environment offered by the Borough. Firstly, it was decided that the overall design of the research be explanatory rather than descriptive or exploratory. Larger studies such as the British Crime Survey (1983, 1985), the Policy Studies Institute (1983), and the Merseyside Crime Survey (1985) carried out in England and Wales have remained largely descriptive in nature. This is not to suggest that these studies were not analytical or that they did not provide much information on crime and policing processes. Rather, since no systematic multi-variate analysis was carried out on these data, the prediction of risk populations became speculative at worst and very generalised at best. Since the aim of the Council was to produce an informational basis from which policy development directed at crime and policing could be informed by the needs, concerns and experiences of the people of Islington, the prediction of risk populations seemed particularly important. From these predictions, derived from a multi-variate analysis, crime prevention initiatives could be targetted where they would be needed most and designed from the special qualities of particular areas or groups. For this reason the design of the research was such that it would lend itself to a rigorous multi-variate analysis.

The type of crime to be investigated was also an important consideration. Some types of crime require different strategies of investigation than others. For example, various corporate crimes in which members of the public are unknowably victimised must be investigated in a different manner than various types of street crime in which the victims do realise their victimisation. Due to the number of inherent limitations of official crime statistics generally, particularly problems of accuracy, reliability, validity, and scope of information, many governments in the Western

World have increasingly turned towards the Crime Survey as a way of improving upon these severe limitations. The technology which has been developing over the past two decades for purposes of doing this kind of research has been the Crime Survey. The logic of this approach is that by surveying a representative sample of the residents of a particular jurisdiction one should be able to measure the frequency and distribution of recorded, reported, and unreported crime. There are a number of criticisms which can be directed at various crime surveys, too numerous to mention here; however, these were taken into consideration when developing the design for the research. As such, the investigation restricted itself to street crime and various forms of extra-legal aggression using in-depth, structured, in-person interviews which measured some 550 variables.

Since a growing body of literature produced from victimisation studies has helped to clarify some of the correlates of victimisation, it was decided to make use of some of this information in developing the overall design. Because studies consistently show, for example that the risk of victimisation decreases with age, this fact was considered in setting out the methodological strategy.

Since an overview of the experience and views of the people of Islington was required, an effective design for producing a representative sample did not present any special problems. However, there are concerns with young peoples' relations to crime and policing, people of different ethnic groups in the multi-racial inner-city and their relations to crime and policing, and the different experiences that inner-city life produces for men and women in relation to crime and policing. For this reason it was decided that the survey should generate data on people characterised by any combinations of the values of the three variables: age, ethnicity and gender for an appropriate multi-variate analysis to be carried out. This was to be accomplished by producing an achieved sample of *n* respondents using probability sampling techniques.

The amount of resources directed towards the research also provided an important consideration for the quality of the overall design. In the spirit of cost-effectiveness, the researchers found that the budget would only allow for a maximum of two thousand interviews. The task, therefore, became one of generating the largest and most accurate data set for the parameters set by the resource allocations.

While it was decided that crime was the consequence of the three way interaction between offender, victim and law enforcement agencies, and that a host of measures should be made on as many aspects of this process as possible, it was readily apparent that the measures would have to be made on the victims of crime. Because the statistical frequency of serious victimisation remains relatively rare even in the inner cities, in order to generate a large enough target sample of victims we would have to call upon a substantially larger group of respondents. It was, therefore, decided that the questionnaire design would be such that it would measure a number of variables on all respondents and for those who had been victims of certain types of crime within the time period covered by the survey, a second questionnaire which examined the impact of the crime would be administered. For this reason the two stage design of measurement was adopted. Phase one would measure attitudes to the community, attitudes towards crime, attitudes towards penality, attitudes towards the police, experiences with crime as a victim, experience with crime as a witness, experiences with the police, experiences with other agencies that deal with crime, and all of the appropriate information on background variables. Phase two questionnaires, on the other hand, would measure the characteristics of the offence, all the related details to the offence and offender, the impact of the crime on the victim and the household, and perceptions pertaining to the most difficult aspects of the crime for the victim. Questionnaires can be found in the following two appendices.

The set of concerns for the overall research design presented itself as very similar to that of Smith's (1983) *Survey of Londoners*, although for different reasons. For Smith (1983), the concern with younger people and with ethnic minorities was in relation to their experiences with policing. It was felt that these groups should be over-represented due to their disproportionate contacts with the police. For the Islington Crime Survey, however, the issue of cost-effectiveness was a further concern. Because previous research demonstrates that these people are more likely to experience victimisation generally, it was felt that to oversample both groups would produce a sub-sample of victims which was much larger for the same costs. While a level of accuracy is certain to be lost as a consequence, a greater level of accuracy would be achieved for the sub-samples, and we would actually end up with a greater sample of victims more cheaply.

For these reasons we adopted a similar sampling strategy as that outlined by Wood (1984). The sample was to consist of two completely different exercises. The general sample was an overall sample of households using probability sampling techniques, and a multi-stage cluster design. The target population for this sample was all people over the age of 16 living in Islington. Because the electoral registers are incomplete for this population, and because demographic changes occurring since the introduction of the electoral register would create greater inaccuracy in the list of eligible persons, it was decided not to use this particular instrument. Rather, a block design was adopted in which a representative sample of households would be selected from enumeration districts which would act as the primary sampling units. From these, individuals would be selected for interview. The overall plan for the general sample is described later.

The second sampling exercise involved the generation of an Ethnic Minority Booster sample. This sample would be drawn from the population of all Afro-Caribbean and Asian people over the age of 16 using probability sampling techniques. Unfortunately, there is no such list of Islington residents from which a sample might be selected. For this reason, it was established that before a target sample could be selected, a list of eligible residents would have to be generated. This was to be accomplished by carrying out a separate operation of enumeration for purposes of generating a satisfactory sampling pool. This method is outlined later in this appendix.

Units of Analysis

The decision of which unit of analysis would be suited for the study was based upon the availability of information and theoretical considerations. Most research of the type proposed here has used the individual for the unit of analysis. We felt that this presented certain difficulties. The most obvious of these is in making comparisons of fear of crime to experiences with crime. Individuals do not live in social isolation, and there are a number of households in which there is more than one occupant. It would not be incorrect to speculate that the experiences one household member may have with crime will affect the way in which other household members perceive crime and policing, particularly the perceptions of their own risks.

A second consideration was cost-effectiveness. We were obligated to produce as large a sample of victims of selected crimes as possibly afforded by the resources available to the project. For this reason, we asked respondents if any other member of the household had experienced any of the personal crimes followed up by the survey *viz*. theft from person, assault, sexual assault. By then combining the observed measures for the respondent and for any other member of the household, we would have established all offences for the household as a unit, and could compare these experiences directly with the attitudes expressed by the respondent. By then weighting the data by the fraction expressed by $1/1+$ e, where 'e' is the number of other householders over the age of 16, we could infer the actual number of these offences using the number of households in Islington as the base.

The strategy outlined above in using households as units of analysis for personal crimes should produce a larger sub-sample of victims. In cases where another household member had been identified as a victim, the phase II questionnaire was administered to them. In short, with this approach, we could be assured of generating a sub-sample of more victims more cheaply, and we would have the added advantage of being able to compare attitudes to household incidents of crime.

In theory this particular strategy should produce the same estimate of occurences for the Borough as using individuals for units of analysis. In practice, however, we are assuming that the two measures are equally accurate which, of course, they are not. The third party measure assumes that the respondent has total knowledge of all other household members, which, of course, would not necessarily be true. Women may not tell their husbands, fathers, brothers, boyfriends, or any one else in the household, for example, that they had been sexually assaulted. Also, it may well be that the respondent would be reluctant to provide third party information on other household members as they were the ones being interviewed. In either event, the third party measure is bound to produce an under-estimate of criminal victimisations. For this reason, the combined measure of household occurrences for personal offences is surely an underestimate overall, and any inference to the population of households would be certainly less than those estimates derived from the inference of observed occurrences of respondents to the individual population. In short, the first measure is more accurate and the second will always under-estimate. Inferences from the combined measure to households in the Borough will be less accurate, and of lower frequency than inferences from the single measure to the population of people.

The research design allows for both sets of inferences to be made. In this report, however, we have used the combined measure, since that was the purpose of generating it in the first instance. In the final report both estimates will be provided and compared. For this reason, it should be kept in mind that the estimates of crimes against the individual by household are probably conservative when interpreting the results in chapter three.

For all other variables which were measured in the survey at both phases, the units of analysis have been the individual.

The General Sample Design

The target area for the survey was the London Borough of Islington, while the target population was residents over the age of 16. Whereas other research of this nature has used the individual as the unit of analysis, the Islington Crime Survey was designed to use both individuals and households as units of analysis for different variables.

Census information is available from the 1981 census which is organised at the three levels of Borough, Ward, and Enumeration District. For a number of reasons it was decided that for an in-depth survey of a concentrated area such as Islington, the most likely unit for sampling would be the enumeration district. If polling districts were used, we would not have the ability to compare census demographic measures with those obtained by the sample. Furthermore, Wards are too large an area to cover, since there are only twenty, and if we selected only a portion of these, we would end up with very large clusters which were not evenly distributed throughout the Borough. The electoral register as a listing by Ward or polling district has been used in the past. This is the strategy used by the British Crime Survey and The Policy Studies Institute Study.

We felt that despite having access to the electoral register, using it would be problematic for this survey for a number of other reasons besides the desire to use the household as the unit of analysis. The enumeration district as a primary sampling unit would produce a large number of small clusters which would be more evenly distributed around the Borough. In this way, interviewers could be assigned areas in which to work that would reduce travelling time and costs, as well as allow for closer field supervision.

Also, by using the household as the target, we would not have to worry about the changes occurring since the production of the latest electoral register. Often the interviewers find that either the elector has moved or that the composition of the household has changed so that it becomes necessary to use a grid to select one householder at random for interview along the lines of the method outlined by Kisch (1965). If selected enumeration districts were surveyed in advance of interviewing, interviewers could be presented with a list of addresses from which they would randomly select an appropriate household member for interview. In this manner, we would have an up-to-date listing of individual dwelling units for each of the enumeration districts selected for the survey, and we would also be able to save mailing costs in that the surveyor/sampler would deliver a letter to each of the households selected, drawing their attention to the fact that an interviewer would be calling for purposes of the survey. It was felt that this may help to improve the response rates, and it would certainly reduce the number of non-productive calls by interviewers in that places of business, derelict premises, and obviously vacant properties would not be included in the sampling pool.

For the reasons outlined above, it was finally decided that the enumeration district would be the primary sampling unit. From these, some households would be randomly selected, and from these, eligible household members would be selected at random for interview.

There are a total of 580 enumeration districts in Islington, and for each we had access to census information. Unfortunately, these districts are not of a uniform size either geographically or population-wise. A complete listing of these districts was generated by computer, and starting from a random point, a systematic interval was applied in order to obtain the appropriate number of sampling points for the target sample. In order to determine the number of enumeration districts to be selected, a number of factors had to be considered. The first factor was the projected response rate. For surveys of this nature carried out in the inner city, a response rate of about 60% seems likely. Because the survey was being carried out by the local authority and because we had letters delivered to households which were finally selected, we hoped thta we could improve the response rate above this. Also, interviewers were well trained in communication facillitators in order to develop quick rapport with individuals at the doorstep which, it was hoped, would also help to improve the response rate.

A second factor which was considered was the eligibility rate of those households falling in the sub-samples for age (described below). Since we were aiming at an overall sample size of 2000, and since 400 of these were allocated for the Ethnic Minority Booster Sample, we were really aiming at a target sample for the general sample of approximately 1600 not considering response rates.

When projected response rates are considered, the proportions of the target sample change. We felt that we should be able to expect a response rate of 70%. If this turned out to be optimistic, we could further sample from the point at which we finished sampling from the original listing of enumeration districts. With a projected response rate of 70%, and with an issued sample of 400 for the booster sample, we calculated that our target for the general sample would be: $2000, -.7 \times 400 = 1720$

Assuming a response rate of 70% for the general sample as well, we calculated that the issued sample should total approximately 2460 issued addresses. However, due to the oversampling of younger people we had to further calculate the number of issued addresses in excess of this figure, due to projected eligibility rates for people in the special sub-samples. For the 16 plus sample, we simply assumed that there would always be at least one eligible person per address who would respond 70% of the time. For the 16–44 sample, we assumed that we would find an eligible person 70% of the time who would respond 70% of the time. For the 16–24 sample we assumed that we would find an eligible resident 30% of the time who would respond 70% of the time.

Although these projected eligibility rates are higher than the census estimates for people in these age categories, they are similar to those found by Smith's *Survey of Londoners* (1983) reported in Wood (1984). We also felt that we would want the sample proportions to over-represent younger people in the following proportions:

Table A.1   Target Sample Proportions Compared to 1981 Census

Age	Census	Target Sample
16–24	20%	37.5%
25–44	35%	37.5%
45 plus	45%	25.0%

We accordingly calculated that we would use a total of 80 enumeration districts with an issued sample size of 42 each for a total of 3360 addresses.

Because we were oversampling younger people it was necessary to alter the design of the general sample to one which was more heavily crafted. Again, following a procedure used by Wood (1984) we divided the general sample into the three following subsamples according to the age of the target populations:

1. X sample – this sample consisted of all residents over the age of 16.
2. Y sample – this sample consisted of all persons between the ages of 16 and 44.
3. Z sample – this sample consisted of all people between the ages of 16 and 24.

Given the target values which had been calculated, the surveyor was given a list of 80 enumeration districts complete with copies of survey ordinance maps to assist him in the field. For each enumeration district, the number of individual dwelling units was identified and then proceeding from a randomly selected starting point between 0 and 9, individual dwelling units were selected and recorded on address sheets. The address sheets were constructed in such a manner as to allow for the automatic assignment of sample. Each line of the sheet had a space which indicated to which sample the address was assigned. These were arranged so that for every seven addresses, three would fall into the X sample, and two each would fall into the Y and Z samples. Furthermore, each address would be assigned a selection digit, continuing from the starting point, and these would be later used by the interviewers when selecting the individual for interview.

Table A.2 provides the breakdown of the assigned target sample:

Table A.2   Structure of Issued Sample

Sample	Issued	Expected
X Sample (16 or older)	1440	1008
Y Sample (16–44)	960	470
Z Sample (16–24)	960	202
TOTAL	3360	1680

From these target values it was discovered that a slight deviation would occur in different enumeration districts due to difference of size and the fact that the number of individual dwelling units would not always yield the exact number of 42. Also, in areas where the number of units was low, to yield 42 would mean to have to increase the sampling fraction to more than one third. In some of the larger areas, such as housing estates, in order to yield 42 issued addresses, would mean to alter the sampling fraction to less than one fifth. In order to compensate for this problem, it was decided that in no instance should the sampling fraction be larger than one third or less than one fifth. It was decided that this strategy would prevent the smaller areas from being over-represented in the final sample at the expense of larger areas. Finally, in two of the selected districts, the yield was so low that these were replaced bringing the total to 82.

As a consequence of the above strategy, the final issued sample, after the surveying of each of the enumeration districts, took the following proportions:

Table A.3   Structure of Final Issued Sample

Sample	Issued	Expected
X Sample	1418	993
Y Sample	978	479
Z Sample	944	198
TOTAL	3340	1670

For the 1670 issued addresses it was expected that the following proportions per age group would be achieved:

Table A.4   Estimated Proportions of Achieved Sample by Age Compared to the 1981 Census

Age Group	Census Proportions	Estimated Achieved Proportions
16–24	20%	572 (34%)
25–44	35%	652 (39%)
45 plus	45%	446 (27%)

While the projected sample differed slightly from the preferred sample, due to the adjustments necessitated in the field, the final expected proportions were similar enough to the preferred ones, particularly when weighting at the stage of analysis would compensate for the oversampling at any rate.

In summary, the sample was effected by the systematic selection of enumeration districts. Households were selected by the surveyor/sampler in the field who produced a set of address sheets for each district, and which contained one address per line with its corresponding sample indicator, selection digit and interval value. These were then passed along to the interviewers as their primary field documents. Finally, for each individual dwelling unit which was recorded on the address sheets, a letter was delivered to the household by the surveyor/sampler which notified the household of their selection for interview, alerted them to the fact that an interviewer would be calling, and which encouraged them to participate in the study.

Addresses were selected from each district by applying a sampling fraction as the interval, i between each address selected from a random starting point. When the surveyor/sampler reached the end of the district, he would return to the beginning again in order to include into the sampling pool those individual dwelling units which came prior to the random starting point.

The Role of Interviewer in Sampling

Figure A.1 is a replica of the address sheets which were provided for the interviewers. Along with these interviewers were provided with maps of the enumeration districts to which they had been assigned, and various field working documents.

Sometimes, it would be the case that the interviewer would find that there was more than one household at a particular individual dwelling unit. While the surveyor/sampler took every precaution to ensure that multi-dwelling buildings were listed separately, in some instances there may have been a boarder, two families, or flat shares. When this occurred, interviewers were instructed to carry out two interviews, one for each household using the same sample designation and selection digit for the original address to select the respondent.

In all other cases, interviewers would determine from their address sheet in which sample the address fell. They would then produce the appropriate respondent selection sheet corresponding to that sample. For example, if the address was designated 'X' they would use an address sheet marked 'X'. After introducing themselves, the interviewers would seek the first names of all residents of the individual dwelling unit whose age fell within the parameters of the assigned sample. If no eligible person lived at that address, the interviewer would not seek an interview, and the address would be recorded as a non-eligible.

In cases where there was only one eligible person at the address, the interviewer would seek the interview with that individual. In cases where there were more than one individual eligible for interview, the interviewer recorded the first names of the eligible householders in alphabetical order, and then by using the grid on the selection sheet would select the person with whom to seek the interview using the number of eligible persons and the selection digit from the address sheets as the reference points for grid selection. The grids were designed in such a manner as to produce a fully random selection if this procedure were followed explicitly. If the selected party were unavailable, or refused, the interviewer was not allowed to make a substitution and the address was recorded as either a non-contact or refusal whichever the case may have been.

While the surveyor/sampler took every precaution not to include vacant premises, sometimes there were addresses which were obviously vacant. In some cases this may have been because the occupant vacated during the period between sampling and interviewing, and sometimes this was due to the surveyor/sampler being unsure as to whether or not the address was occupied. In these cases, the interviewers were instructed to assign the individual dwelling unit immediately adjacent to the one recorded on the address sheet. They were further instructed to always be consistent in the direction which they accomplished this. If the next address were also vacated, then the interviewer would write this address off as being vacant. If, however, there were an occupant at the adjacent address, then the interviewer would alter the address on his sheet, and proceed to follow the normal procedure for selection using the same sample and selection digit that were assigned to the original address.

Finally, in some cases the interviewer may find that there was an insufficient knowledge of English for an interview to be carried out. In such cases, they were to record the language spoken at the home in order than an interviewer fluent in the appropriate language could be sent to seek the interview.

It was felt that all of the precautions taken above would provide the best probability sample for the resources available, and that all members of the community would have an equal probability of selection for interview.

Table A.5   Sampling Points by Ward – General Sample

Barnsbury:	AA09		AF07	Mildmay:	AN02
	AA05		AF10		AN11
	AA10		AF17		AN21
	AA19	Highbury:	AG04		AN26
Bunhill:	AB01		AG24		AN30
	AB05		AG33		AN40
	AB10		AG36	Quadrant:	AP04
	AB16	Highview:	AH01		AP07
	AB17		AH11		AP10
	AB20		AH17	St. George's:	AQ27
	AB22	Hillmarton:	AJ01		AQ36
Canonbury:			AJ11		AQ39
East	AC02		AJ24	St. Mary's:	AR02
	AC04	Hillrise:	AK02		AR05
	AC19		AK05		AR13
	AC20		AK11		AR22
Canonbury:			AK21		AR23
West	AD04		AK30	St. Peter's:	AS07
	AD10	Holloway:	AL01		AS17
	AD13		AL07		AS24
Clerkenwell:	AE10		AL09	Sussex:	AT01
	AE13		AL17		AT02
	AE19		AL18		AT11
	AE21		AL28		AT20
	AE23	Junction:	AM09	Thornhill:	AU10
	AE27		AM19		AU19
	AE29		AM28	Tollington:	AW06
Gillespie:	AF03		AM35		AW25

Fieldwork Results from the General Sample

Piloting
During the spring months of 1984 a pilot study was conducted on the Girdlestone estate as a measure for testing both the proposed methods of the fieldwork as well as the draft questionnaire. A full report of the pilot study was presented to The London Borough of Islington Police Sub-Committee on November 8, 1984. A total of 26 interviews were carried out by six interviewers, and although the purpose was not to generate any results, a number of questionnaire revisions were incorporated as a result of the pilot as were some revisions to the sampling design and field supervision strategies.

Interviewers
A total of three persons were used to carry out the survey and sampling of households in all of the selected enumeration districts. These people were well briefed, trained and supervised in the field.

A total of 58 interviewers worked on the project all of which were required to attend a series of briefings given by the principal researcher. These briefings covered a variety of topics on interviewing generally and interviewing specifically on this project. These will be outlined below. A total of 160 potential interviewers attended briefing sessions, and of those completing all the required sessions, those who seemed particularly suited to this project were selected. A total of 22 briefing sessions were given by the principal during the period February to April 1985, while the main fieldwork for the project was carried out between March and August 1985.

Results of Fieldwork
Table A.6 provides an analysis of the responses as calculated from the fieldwork documents received from the interviewers.

The most notable figure from Table A.6 is the high response rates overall. It was hoped that a high response rate would be achieved because of the general support to the council displayed by most residents, and a number of precautions taken in the fieldwork operations. Tenants associations were contacted where they existed when it was determined that they existed in the area, and in some cases the research staff made oral presentations to the associations. Furthermore, interviewers were well briefed on how to present both themselves and the project on the doorstep. In all instances interviewers were required to wear council identity cards which displayed a photo of them in order that the residents would be assured that they were on official business. Also, the interviewers were told that if there was any scepticism about their purpose to encourage the respondents to contact the field supervisor immediately. These precautions combined with people's displayed concerns for the subject of the

Table A.6   Analysis of Response – General Sample

	X Sample		Y Sample		Z Sample		Total	
Issued Sample	1418		978		944		3340	
PLUS:								
– Occupied addresses next to vacant	54		36		34		124	
– Multiple households at address	7		3		13		23	
	1479		1017		991		3487	
LESS:								
– Vacancies	100		46		40		186	
– Addresses with no-one of sample age	– 100	%	338 384	%	624 664	%	962 1148	%
Addresses eligible for survey	1379	100	633	100	327	100	2339	100
LESS:								
– No contact after 4-plus calls	105	8	42	7	29	9	176	8
– Refused to participate	268	19	98	15	48	15	414	18
– Selected person speaks language for which no interpreter is available	15	1	9	1	3	1	27	1
Total Not Interviewed	388	28	149	24	80	24	617	26
Total Interviewed	991	72	484	76	247	76	1722	74

survey and their support of this council initiative enabled 74% of respondents overall to complete the survey despite its length – a mean of 55 minutes.

Table A.7 provides the breakdown of the final results from the general sample by age, race and gender:

Table A.7   General Sample Fieldwork Results

	16–24		25–44		45-plus		Total	
	Male	Female	Male	Female	Male	Female	Male	Female
White	174	215	262	323	192	233	628	771
Black	21	43	23	43	21	9	65	95
Asian	13	9	17	16	5	1	35	26
Other Non-whites	9	17	25	25	11	12	45	54
TOTAL 1	217	284	327	407	229	255	773	946
TOTAL 2	501		734		484		1719	
PLUS 3 cases insufficient information							3	
					Grand Total		1722	

Table A.7 illustrates the proportions of each category which were achieved by the fieldwork. As can be seen from the table, there were slightly fewer numbers in the youngest and oldest categories while the middle age category had a slightly greater number of achieved responses than the original projection calculations. It is doubtful that these differences are due to changing demographic trends, but probably has more to do with the higher probability of finding people in the middle age category at home than in the younger group, and also because their higher proportion in the population compared to the younger group and their over-representation in the issued sample in comparison to the older age group.

E.D. NUMBER ☐☐☐

Street

Enumeration Survey – Main Sample Dwelling Selection Sheet

Page   Of

For This Street/Section/Block

Street No.	Flat	Sample	Sel Digit	Inter Val	Comments	Non-Contact 1st Call	2nd Call	3rd Call	4th Call	Inter Comp.	Notes
		Y				NC	NC	NC	NC	Y	
		X				NC	NC	NC	NC	Y	
		N				NC	NC	NC	NC		
		X				NC	NC	NC	NC	Y	
		Y				NC	NC	NC	NC	Y	
		N				NC	NC	NC	NC	Y	
		X				NC	NC	NC	NC	Y	
		Y				NC	NC	NC	NC	Y	
		X				NC	NC	NC	NC	Y	
		N				NC	NC	NC	NC	Y	
		X				NC	NC	NC	NC	Y	
		Y				NC	NC	NC	NC	Y	
		N				NC	NC	NC	NC	Y	
		X				NC	NC	NC	NC	Y	

QSTAAF.

Ethnic Minority Enumeration

It was decided early in the project that normal sampling techniques would not provide a large enough sample of certain ethnic minorities to allow for a rigorous analysis of either attitudes or victimisation patterns. Furthermore, we felt that it would be essential to attempt to measure the differences in the frequency and quality of police contacts for visible minorities.

Whereas the general sample design did provide for a probability sample that should yield proportions of ethnic minorities in the sample approximately equivalent to their proportions in the population, these figures would be too low for statistical inference. Furthermore, due to the large number of variables measured by the survey, it would be difficult to provide partitioned data for the ethnic minorities, simply due to the small proportion of representation.

For these reasons, it was decided that an ethnic minority booster sample should be generated. The logic underlying such a decision is easily grasped. Not only are we searching for rare elements in the population when we are looking for victims of serious crime, but the elements become even rarer when we are looking for ethnic minority victims. Writing upon the sampling methods for identification of rare elements Kish (1965) states:

> "Rare traits that are expensive to find create a predicament. Adroit applications of [some] techniques bring about a reasonable approach. When choosing between them, consider the trait's rarity, as well as the available survey resources, including knowledge about large concentrations of the trait. This could mean lists, or known geographical concentrations, or high correlations with other clear indicators." (1965:405).

One of the reasons for over-sampling the ethnic minorities was to be cost-efficient in terms of the overall survey costs. It was essential, therefore, that the most cost-efficient design for the ethnic sample be crafted. One way in which this was effected was to concentrate on visible minorities only, and within this parameter to concentrate on the two major groups of Asian, and Afro-Caribbean. While there are certainly numerous definitional problems associated with these two broad nominal categories, they were not as serious as those raised by the 1981 census.

In order to take the advice of Kish (1965), for example, and make use of existing knowledge about concentrations of the target groups, the best known source would be the census. Unfortunately, the census did not ask any questions relevant to the identification of ethnic minorities except for the very crude measure of country of birth. Table A.8 presents the population of Islington by country of birth from the 1981 census:

Table A.8   1981 Census for Country of Birth

Country	Males	Females
England	53324	58459
Scotland	1841	1639
Wales	814	893
Rest of U.K.	787	712
Irish Republic	4944	5275
Old Commonwealth	464	629
New Commonwealth	8681	8405
East Africa	432	632
Africa remainder	1249	1206
Caribbean	2475	2790
India	632	615
Bangladesh	438	231
Far East	762	683
Mediterranean	2564	2442
Remainder	129	76
Pakistan	193	137
Other E.C.	1589	1990
Other Europe	1190	1425
Rest of World	2066	2065
TOTAL	75893	81629

It can easily be seen from Table A.8 that any calculation of the proportion of visible minorities in the Borough of Islington based on the census would be speculative at best. Firstly, one must assume that people born in the Caribbean are black, for example, and that people born in Ireland are white. While these assumptions may be correct most of the time, some of the time they are not. For areas such as East Africa, for example, the problem is heightened in that persons born there who emigrated to Islington may well be of Asian, African or English origin.

A further difficulty is that people of either Asian, or Afro-Caribbean ancestry (the two groups targetted for the survey) who were born in England, will not show on the census as anything but U.K. born. Therefore, the census obviously underestimates these populations.

Thirdly, even if we were to restrict ourselves to first generation immigrants for purposes of calculating concentrations, we could easily be misdirected if, indeed, there are second generation enclaves of people from these groups, which is almost certainly going to be the case.

These factors considered, it was decided to follow the method of Focussed Enumeration, outlined by Brown and Ritchie (1981), and utilised by Wood (1984) on the Policy Studies Institute survey.

Essentially, this method involves enumerating selected areas in order to pinpoint the target population and develop a suitable sampling pool.

From this pool, a suitably sized random or stratified sample is drawn to meet the design specifications.

The problem for the Islington Crime Survey, however, was that due to the obviously low proportions of target populations for the survey according to the census, to draw an independent sample of enumeration districts for enumeration purposes may not yield large enough numbers to meet the sample target figures unless a large number of these enumeration districts were selected for focussed enumeration.

It was decided, therefore, that a list would be generated of all the enumeration districts which had a greater than 2% composition of either of the ethnic groups. This list would have two strikes against it from the outset. The first strike is the definitional problem associated with the census data on country of birth. The second strike is that any second generation enclaves would be omitted automatically from the lists if the census data were used for purposes of generating the list.

While the above strategy would obviously under-represent people of either ethnic group living in enumeration districts where there is a less than 2% concentration, this would be overcome somewhat by the general sample, and it had to be accepted as one of the limitations of the approach. It was also accepted that second generation persons not abiding in the selected enumeration districts would also have to be included in the general sample with probability proportionate to their representation in the overall population.

The lists were generated by a computer programme written to select and list the appropriate enumeration districts. For the Asian clusters were combined persons born in East Africa, India, Bangladesh, Far East and Pakistan. For the Afro-Caribbean clusters we combined persons born in the remainder of Africa and the Caribbean. Although we recognised the limitations of such crude measures of concentration, it was decided that given the budget we would have to accept these limitations. The results of the computer listing is given below in Table A.9:

Table A.9 Enumeration Districts with High Concentrations of Visible Minorites

Enumeration District Concentration	Afro-Caribbean	Asian
Under 5% but over 2%	185	159
5% or more	236	52

Since it was impossible to determine either the expected response rate or the demographic shifts occurring since the census, we used as a rough estimate for the number of enumeration districts to select, the results of the Policy Studies Institute survey reported in Wood (1984). In that study, Wood (1984) was able to identify a total of 327 Asians and 612 West Indians by enumerating 50 enumeration districts for a total of 7,634 addresses.

We felt that we would select 30 enumeration districts for each group and conduct separate exercises for each. Of the 30 districts, 20 would be from the over 5% concentration group, and 10 would be from the lower concentration listings.

These enumeration districts were selected from the lists using a systematic selection procedure and random starting point. It was felt that if these did not yield enough numbers, we would select more using the same interval proceeding from the last enumeration district, previously selected.

In fact, it was discovered after being well into the fieldwork that the yield was so dismal, we had to select 10 more from each group off the 5% or greater concentration listing, making a total of 40 enumeration districts for each of the ethnic groups.

The method used for enumeration in the field is that as outlined by Wood (1984). There were two exceptions. Firstly, the size of the gap for the lower concentration enumeration districts was always seven. The size of the gap for the greater concentration enumeration districts remained at three.

The second exception involved the actual surveying of the enumeration districts. As with the general sample, a surveyor/sampler went into the field for each of the districts selected. A complete listing of all individual dwelling units was produced for each of the enumeration districts, and the sampler would indicate the location addresses on the sheets as well as the secondary addresses for which enumerators would be allowed to substitute if contact proved impossible at the location addresses. Finally, the surveyor/sampler would deliver a letter from the council to each of the addresses in the district indicating that enumerators would be possibly calling, outlining the purpose of the enumeration, and encouraging response. In total six surveyor/samplers were used on this phase of the enumeration, each of which was carefully briefed and supervised.

Two teams of enumerators were used for the project. It was decided to match each of the relevant target groups with an enumerator from the same background due to the sensitive nature of the enumeration, particularly for a study of crime and policing in which details such as name, age, and gender were being requested.

For the Asian enumeration, a team of nine enumerators were utilised in the field. Each of the enumerators was at least bi-lingual, and the entire range of Asian languages, including Chinese was represented on the team. The difficulty on this phase of enumeration was twofold. Firstly, because the majority of the households were white, the enumerators found themselves subject to much racial abuse. Secondly, because of the time of the year, and due to the most productive period for fieldwork being the early evenings, enumerators found themselves uncomfortable, alone in the dark, in multi-racial areas in the inner city. In part these two difficulties were met with a modification to the method. In some cases we would send two enumerators to work together, one white, one Asian and where possible, one male and one female. In this way when a call was made at an address, if the respondent was white, the white enumerator would ask the questions and if the respondent was black the Asian enumerator would ask the questions. While this method cut down on racial abuse, it did not seem to improve the response rate.

For the Afro-Caribbean enumeration a total of six Afro-Caribbean enumerators worked on the project with varying degrees of success. In most cases they did not see the project through to completion. The same difficulties were experienced on this phase of the project as the Asian phase with one further problem. Those households at which target group respondents were identified displayed a high frequency of suspicion and a high refusal rate was observed. Some of the enumerators found that they were questioned so strongly as to their motives, that they withdrew from the project. These enumerators were replaced by white ones who did no better in terms of response rates.

The difficulties experienced on the enumeration phase of the project will be the subject of a further paper. These difficulties persisted despite the fact that all of the enumerators were well briefed, well supervised, and equipped with identity cards complete with photographs.

Table A.10 provides a breakdown of the results of the enumeration by the number of enumeration districts for each of the relevant ethnic groups:

Table A.10   Results of Enumeration

	Afro-Caribbean	Asian	Total
Total addresses covered	5610	4373	9983
Number of E.D.'s	40	40	80
Refusals to co-operate	87	69	156
Refusals by relevant members	206	13	219
Households identified for sampling	168	134	302
Individuals identified for sampling	294	336	630

It can be seen from Table A.10 that there was a substantial rate of refusal overall, particularly for the Afro-Caribbean sample. Given the recent difficulties with crime and policing in London, it is not surprising, to say the least, that such a poor response rate should be exhibited by this community. In all cases complete anonymity was guaranteed and the enumerators insisted on being assured of this before going into the field. Nevertheless, a high level of suspicion was observed, and it is this suspicion which we suspect detracted from the response rates for this particular phase of the research.

Table A.11 provides a breakdown of the enumeration results by age, race, and gender:

Table A.11   Enumeration Results by Gender, Race and Age

Age	Afro-Caribbean		Asian	
	Males	Females	Males	Females
16–24	53	65	60	44
25–44	46	47	103	56
45 plus	46	37	42	31
TOTAL 1	145	149	205	131
TOTAL 2	294		336	

From Table A.11 the sampling pool for the actual generation of the ethnic minority booster sample is observed. Of interest is that although the concentration of Asians is much lower than that of Afro-Caribbeans, we generated a larger possible sample of the former due to the differential in response rates.

One reason for this differential is that we had much more success in having the project endorsed by the Asian Community Groups than we did by the Afro-Caribbean Groups.

Ethnic Minority Booster Sample

The samples for each of the relevant groups was drawn from the enumeration sheets generated by the enumeration phase and summarised in Table A.11. Sampling had to progress from the youngest group to the oldest group in order than an over-representation of younger people could be established on this phase of the project as well. The sampler would select the target values from the 16-24 age group for each group. The remaining sheets were then placed in with the sheets from the 25-44 age group for each sample. The target sample was then drawn from each of the two sub-sets to generate the 16-44 age group samples. Finally, all of the left over sheets were then placed together for each group to establish the sampling pool for the 16 plus category. Due to the rather small numbers being generated by the enumeration phase, this sampling strategy seemed the most appropriate despite the fact that the younger people had a disproportionate probability of selection.

The target of 400 interviews completed was that originally proposed. It also seemed appropriate that because of the relatively small numbers, a maximum of two interviewers would be allowed for any given household. This is a similar decision to that of Wood (1984) in his work for the Policy Studies Institute.

It was decided that for purposes of encouraging a high response on the one hand, and in order to compensate for any language problems on the

Table A.12   Ethnic Minority Booster Sample – Issued Sample by Age, Race and Gender

Age	Afro-Caribbean		Asian		TOTAL	
	Male	Female	Male	Female	Male	Female
16–24	30	30	30	30	60	60
16–24	30	30	30	30	60	60
16 plus	40	40	40	40	80	80
TOTAL 1	100	100	100	100	200	200
TOTAL 2	200		200		400	

other, interviewers would be matched with respondents on the basis of gender, ethnicity, and language where possible. Most of the Asian and Afro-Caribbean women were interviewed by matched interviewers as were the Asian men. It was difficult, however, to maintain a suitable interviewing team of Afro-Caribbean men. As a result some of these interviews were conducted by White males or Asian males.

The team of Asian interviewers was nine and was the identical team as the enumeration phase, whereas this continuity was not maintained for the Afro-Caribbean team. All interviewers were properly briefed along the lines of those working on the general sample, although for these groups, the briefings were separate, and the content was different than for the general sample.

The results of the fieldwork for the Ethnic Minority Booster Sample are presented in Table A.13:

Table A.13   Analysis of Response – Ethnic Minority Booster Sample

Issued Sample	Afro-Caribbean		Asian		TOTAL	
	No	%	No	%	No	%
	200	100	200	100	400	100
LESS:						
– moved	10	5	4	2	14	4
– not known	23	12	9	5	32	8
TOTAL	33	17	13	7	46	12
Eligible for Survey	167	100	187	100	354	100
LESS:						
– No contact with person after 4-plus calls	18	11	7	4	25	7
– Refusal by other person	12	7	6	3	18	5
– Refusal by person	31	19	16	9	47	13
– No interpreter for language spoken	–	–	8	4	8	2
– Other	1	*	–	–	1	*
Total Not Interviewed	62	37	37	20	99	28
Total Interviewed	105	63	150	80	255	72

The higher response rate observed in the Asian sample is probably due to a number of reasons. Firstly, the Asian people were more co-operative on the enumeration phase and it would seem that this co-operation extended to the actual data collection phase. Secondly, due to the continuity of the enumeration and data collection phase in respect to fieldworkers, we expect that an effect on the response rates was achieved. During the enumeration phase, enumerators had the opportunity to develop a good rapport with the potential respondents, and these would then be more co-operative at the data-collection phase. These developments could not be maintained for the Afro-Caribbean sample which is probably why the response rate is much lower.

By way of comparison, Wood (1984) found response rates of 68% and 69% for Afro-Caribbean and Asian samples respectively. It would seem that matching and continuity produced a much higher rate of response in the Asian sample, indicating that preliminary legwork with community groups combined with this methodological strategy may improve response rates for this group of people.

The final sample generated by the two phases of enumeration and data collection is broken down by age, race, and gender in Table A.14:

Table A.14   Ethnic Minority Booster Sample: Fieldwork Results

| | Black Sample | | Asian Sample | | | | TOTAL | |
| | | | | | Asian | Other Non-White | | |
	Male	Female	Male	Female	Male	Female	Male	Female
16–24	25	28	31	27	0	2	56	57
25–44	14	15	30	19	2	1	46	35
45 plus	11	12	21	14	2	1	34	27
TOTAL 1	50	55	82	60	4	4	136	119
TOTAL 2	105		142		8		225	
			(150)					

It can be seen from Table A.14 that the sample proportions of the age and gender groups are at a slight variance with those obtained from the general sample. It would seem that this outcome was unavoidable given the low productivity achieved at the enumeration phase.

Also worth noting from Table A.14 is that eight respondents from the Asian sample ended up being classified as other Non-White after the interviewers had a more ample opportunity to evaluate their ethnic characteristics. It is also worth noting that a comparison of these results to those of Table A.7 indicates that all of the careful planning and execution of the Afro-Caribbean Booster Sample was probably not worth the time or the effort. The general sample actually picked up more cases from this group than did the Booster Sample with much less work or expense. Nevertheless the special sample did boost the proportions of visible minorities sufficiently to achieve sub-samples which could be worked with for purposes of analysis.

Finally, Table A.15 and A.16 indicate the sampling points from which the final sample was drawn for the Afro-Caribbean and Asian samples respectively.

Table A.15   Sampling Points – Afro-Caribbean Booster Sample

Barnsbury:	AA25	Junction:	AM03
Bunhill:	–		AM14
Canonbury			AM29
East:	AC28	Mildmay:	AN01
Canonbury			AN19
West:	–		AN36
Clerkenwell:	–		AN45
Gillespie:	AF04	Quadrant:	AP09
	AF18	St. George's:	AQ38
	AF21	St. Mary's:	–
Highbury:	AG36	St. Peter's:	–
Highview:	AH08	Sussex:	AT01
	AH09		AT09
	AH19		AT10
Hillmarton:	AJ04		AT16
	AJ25		AT19
Hillrise:	AK18		AT21
	AK20	Thornhill:	–
	AK25	Tollington:	AW03
Holloway:	AL03		AW15
	AL09		AW23
	AL23		AW27
			AW36

Table A.16 Sampling Points – Asian Booster Sample

Barnsbury:	AA09	Junction:	AM12
	AA21		AM14
Bunhill:	–		AM30
Canonbury		Mildmay:	–
East:	–	Quadrant:	AP15
Canonbury		St. George's:	AQ14
West:	AD09		AQ24
Clerkenwell:	AE26		AQ26
Gillespie:	AF04		AQ31
	AF14	St. Mary's:	AR05
	AF15	St. Peter's:	AS10
Highbury:	AG13	Sussex:	AT01
	AG37		AT02
Highview:	AH12		AT19
Hillmarton:	AJ01		AT21
	AJ21	Thornhill:	AU02
Hillrise:	AK26		AU06
	AK27		AU22
Holloway:	AL03	Tollington:	AW03
	AL13		AW15
	AL14		AW18
			AW27
			AW35

Field Supervision

Due to the complexity of the research design and the delicate nature of the research topic it was decided that a strict programme of field supervision was not only desirable but vital. The division of labour on the entire fieldwork was such that independent checks could be carried out for each phase of the fieldwork.

The fieldwork supervision strategy consisted of four specific components:

1. Briefing sessions.
2. Supervised fieldwork
3. Personal callbacks for debriefing of respondents
4. Statistical control

Briefing Sessions

All interviewers and enumerators were required to attend a series of three briefings designed to improve their productivity in the field. Seminars were presented on topics such as interviewing technique, strategy, and tactic. These included discussions of non-verbal communication used in the interview situation, and how this might be used to develop rapport very quickly with respondents.

Interviewers were briefed on the nature of the project, the issues involved, the content of both the questionnaires, and the potential points of trouble and how they might be avoided. They were also instructed on delicate areas such as assault which may be domestic, sexual assault, and under what circumstances the indirect method of questioning (outlined in Chapter 3) may be utilised to the best advantage.

Since a number of the questions involved open-ended responses, the interviewers were instructed on how to probe and what kind of information was being looked for.

Finally, all of the interviewers engaged in mock interviews for both questionnaires, under the supervision of the principal in order that any difficulties might be identified and corrected.

Supervised Interviews

All interviewers were instructed not to carry out more than three, or less than two interviews before contacting the field supervisor for purposes of arranging a supervised interview. In this manner, interviewers would have the opportunity to feel comfortable with the interview schedule, but if they were engaging in a style which was non-productive, this could be identified and corrected early, before too many interviews had been completed. After the interview, the field supervisor would comment on what points the interviewer excelled and to point out some useful tips on how to improve their style. In this manner, we not only had the opportunity to view the range of interviewing styles on the project, but also the opportunity to try and develop a greater degree of uniformity.

In total, 63 interviews were supervised or 3% of the total sample.

Personal Recalls

Personal recalls were made on a number of completed interviews for two purposes. Firstly, this would act as a check that the interview had been completed properly. The other reason was to provide the opportunity for the respondents to be de-briefed. Sometimes they may have relived a frightening experience during the interview, or sometimes they were not entirely clear about the purpose of the project. Also, it was felt that the public would end up being much more supportive if they were given the opportunity to give their impressions about the project generally, their participation specifically, and their reactions to some of the questions asked. Overall, there was frequently the feeling that the respondent was happy to have participated and found it quite interesting.

In total, 253 callbacks were made or 12.9%. This meant that in total 316 completed interviews or 15.9% were subject to supervision or recall.

Statistical Control
Each interviewer was given a number which was coded according to the
sex of the interviewer and the sample within which they worked. The interviewer number was included as a variable in the study in order that any
statistically significant differences between interviewers might be identified, if indeed they existed, on any of the responses to any of the variables. This control has not been analysed for the first report but will be
reported in the final report.

Weighting
The sampling design dictated that weighting be carried out in a number of
stages in order to correct for the disproportions generated by the booster
samples for age and ethnicity. Also, it was discovered that due to the
slight deviation of the male-female ratios of the overall combined sample,
there was a slight bias in favour of women.

Before any weighting of the data files could be carried out, it was necessary to estimate the true population parameters for the variation in ethnicity. As previously discussed, the 1981 census only provides very crude
measures for this variable, and estimates of population parameters based
upon census information are bound to be incorrect and probably conservative. There are almost certainly more visible minorities in the Islington
population than census estimates provide.

Initially, it was decided that estimates of the ethnic proportions would
be made by a combination of estimates from both the general sample and
the booster sample. However, because the enumeration results were less
than anticipated, it was decided that the combination of measures would
certainly bias the proportions downwards. For this reason, it was finally
decided to assume a representative sample had been generated by the
general sampling design so that an estimate could be made from this
measure. It happened that the Policy Studies Institute had carried out a
study of *Ethnic Minorities In Public Housing In Islington*, which was submitted during the month of September 1985 to the Council. It was decided that estimates derived from the general sample of The Islington
Crime Survey could be compared to those estimates arrived at in the PSI
study.

For purposes of the Islington Crime Survey, data was recorded to produce the following four measures of ethnicity:
1. White
2. Afro-Caribbean
3. Asian
4. Other Non-White

For purposes of this framework, Mediterranean borns who did not get
classified as either Afro-Caribbean or Asian were considered as other
Non-Whites. While it was true that we were interested in visible min-

orities, our main concern was for Asian and Afro-Caribbean people. For this reason, we weighted down the original 5.8% of Other Non-Whites to 2.0% of the final sample. While this may have the disadvantage of slightly over-representing white persons at the expense of the residual category, we felt that this procedure would be better than to overweight people from the special samples.

Age also presented a difficulty in that we over-sampled younger people. For purposes of correcting for this over-representation, we used the census proportions as observed in 1981.

A final weight which was calculated and applied to the sample had to correct for household size on those calculations for which we conceptualised the household as the unit of analysis. The following is the deriviation of weights:

Weight 0
This weight corrects for the gender imbalance. Since females were slightly over-represented, we applied a weight of .92 to female respondents and a weight of 1 to male respondents.

Weight 1
This weight was calculated on the basis of age. Since we had decided to over-sample younger people, we applied a weight of 1 to those people in the 16-24 age category. In this way all other cases would be weighted upwards leaving us with the logical sample containing the actual number of these people interviewed. If the age of the respondent was 25-44 we applied a weight of 1.33, and for all the older respondents the weight of 2.54 was applied. Since each of the older cases was counted two and one half times in the final calculations given in this report, we feel that the over-sampling of young people does not bias the results.

Weight 2
This weight was to correct for imbalances due to the ethnic booster sample. Since visible minorities are a greater proportion in the sample than they are in the population, we would have to weigh the white respondents upwards. Again it was decided to leave the smallest proportion group at a weight of 1 and weigh everything else upwards, except Other Non-Whites. In this case, therefore, we applied a weight of 1 to all Asian cases as well as the residual category, in effect weighing the latter downwards. Afro-Caribbean cases were weighted at 2.3 and all white cases were weighted at 3.8.

Weight 3
This weight is the product of weight 1 and 2 and, therefore, is the combined weight for the effects of all over-sampling in the survey.

Weight 4
This weight was used to correct for the number of persons per household for all calculations in which the household is used as the unit of analysis. The weight applied would be equal to one divided by the number of total persons in the household. The formula used for the calculation of this weight was:

1/1+e where 'e' is equal to the number of other adults living in the household.

Weight 5
This weight was the product of weight 4 and weight 3. In this way, weight 5 represents the corrections for over-sampling when households are the units of analysis.

Weight 6
This weight is the product of weight 0 and weight 3. Since weight 3 is the correction for over-sampling when units of analysis are the individual, and since weight 0 corrects for the slight imbalance of females, weight 6 is the final weight used on all calculations where the unit of analysis is the individual.

Weight 7
The final weight calculated is the product of weight 5 and weight 0, or household size corrected for the slight female imbalance. Weight 7 is the weight used, therefore, for all calculations involving the household as the unit of analysis.

Since these preliminary weights were calculated for purposes of this report, they may be altered slightly for the final report. For example, if so desired, we can alter the weights upwards for Mediterranean borns difficult to classify.

Furthermore, since no tests of statistical significance were carried out in the calculations reported herein, it did not seem necessary to scale down the final weights to the original sample size. In the final report, however, we will scale down to original sample size for multi-variate analyses in which significance tests are affected by sample size.

Table A.17 provides the breakdown of the final sample corrected for age and gender which can be compared directly to the census.

Table A.17   Comparison of Final Sample to 1981 Census on Age and Gender for Weighted and Unweighted Data

	1981 Census		Unweighted Sample		Weighted Sample	
	No	%	No	%	No	%
MALES	60962	47.5	909	46.0	4472	47.6
16–24	12659	9.9	273	13.8	820	8.7
25–44	22261	17.4	373	18.9	1513	16.1
45 plus	26042	20.3	263	13.3	2139	22.8
FEMALES	67282	52.5	1065	54.0	4915	52.4
16–24	12998	10.1	341	17.3	952	10.1
25–44	22355	17.4	442	22.4	1715	18.3
45 plus	31929	24.9	282	14.3	2247	23.9
ALL PEOPLE 16 plus	128244	100	1974	100	9386	100
16–24	25657	20.0	614	31.1	1772	18.9
25–44	44616	34.8	815	41.3	3227	34.4
45 plus	57971	45.2	545	27.6	4386	46.7

From Table A.17 it can be seen that there are no substantive differences between the sample and the 1981 census. Elderly males are slightly over-represented at the expense of the younger males but this difference is not substantive and if anything places a slight conservative bias into the sample. The slight imbalance is due to the combined effects of all weighting.

Table A.18 provides the figures for the non-weighted and weighted samples by ethnicity:

Table A.18   Comparison of Unweighted and Weighted Samples by Race

Race	Unweighted Sample		Weighted Sample	
	Number	%	Number	%
White	1400	71	8119	86
Afro-Caribbean	265	13	828	9
Asian	203	10	282	3
Other	109	6	158	2
Total	1977	100	9387	100

Both Tables A.17 and A.18 show the samples after being weighted by weight 6. It was felt that the simplest procedure would be to conceptualise all of the visible minorities generated by both samples as one sample for the calculation of weights. Since we do not have any figures for comparing the age and sex breakdowns by race, we have not included this table here. By way of comparison, however, the PSI study (1985) cited earlier does show similar proportions by race that our final weighted sample demonstrates.

In conclusion, the weights applied make the sample representative. Because of the weight applied to correct for ethnic booster sampling techniques, other Non-Whites difficult to classify have been weighted downwards. In this manner, any differences observed in the results by ethnicity may be safely argued as being conservative estimates.

Sampling and Measurement Error

Sampling errors have been calculated for the five major categories of crime followed-up on the survey only. It was felt that for the preliminary report the complex standard errors would suffice. For this reason, simple random sample standard errors have not been estimated, nor have the design effects upon the complex standard errors. Since the mean is the best predictor in any event for the type of presentation and analysis of data contained in this report, the complex standard error should suffice. It should be pointed out, however, that one consequence of the complex sampling design and the clusters which it has produced is a loss of accuracy. Said differently, clustering has produced a wider margin of error. This fact should be considered when interpreting the results of chapter three.

Measurement Error

Regardless of the type of measure or the type of measurement instrument there is always a degree of error. For this survey, the measurement errors of most concern are those associated with the measurement of the frequency of the various crime classifications.

Since the survey asked respondents about the one year immediately prior to the date of the interview, it is not always possible to ensure that the crimes reported fell within this period. Furthermore, there may be crimes which did happen but which were not disclosed on the survey. Sometimes respondents lie, sometimes respondents forget, and sometimes respondents' memories are incorrect. Very little can be done about lying except to provide the most congenial atmosphere for the disclosure of crimes about which the respondent feels uncomfortable disclosing. The procedure outlined in chapter three by which an indirect method of questioning was used for female respondents on assault and sexual assault is one example of how this was accomplished for this survey. The latter two difficulties can be overcome to some extent by the procedure of bounding. While the British Crime Survey decided to use a bounding procedure which used Christmas as a point of recollection for the respondent, we felt that to do so would create more error in that the period of our fieldwork was, from the earliest, three months after Christmas, and from the latest eight months after Christmas. The major reason for the

British Crime Survey to follow this bounding procedure is twofold. Firstly, Christmas is one event which respondents do not have any difficulty remembering. Secondly, this procedure makes for an easy comparison to police statistics since the survey covers a calendar year the same as do the police statistics.

We felt that by instructing our interviewers carefully in bounding we would be able to improve upon the measurement errors of the British Crime Survey, however, at the expense of making direct comparisons to annual police statistics more difficult. Interviewers were instructed on how to ask the respondent to recall last year at the same time, and particularly to recall an event. Once this was accomplished, the respondent was asked about criminal events which may have occurred from that event until the present time of the interview. We felt that by using this bounding procedure, and the period of time of the immediately preceeding year there would be less chance of memory fading, and less chance of either forward or backward telescoping. This procedure, however, means that the period of time covered by the survey is out of synch with the police records. We have probably heightened the accuracy of measurement at the expense of reducing the validity of direct comparison to police statistics.

A number of factors were considered in making this decision. Firstly, it was clear that a number of crimes reported on the survey may have been reported to other jurisdictions in the MPD. Also, there may have been a number of crimes recorded by N District which did not involve residents of Islington. Secondly, we could not begin fieldwork until March which meant that a minimum of three extra months of memory fading would be incorporated into the survey. Thirdly, we considered that it is very unlikely that there are great shifts in actual crime levels, reporting behaviours of victims, or recording behaviours of police over the period of one year.

For these reasons, therefore, we assumed a stable rate of crime, reporting, and recording over the period covered by the survey. This meant that there would be some crimes on the police statistics which were carried out in a period preceeding that covered by the survey. Conversely, there would be crimes picked up by the survey which extended beyond the reporting period for the police statistics. By assuming stable rates on all levels over the period covered by the survey, the differences should equal out.

The second problem arising from the bounding procedure, which represents another cost of increased measurement accuracy, is that the duration of the fieldwork dictates that the survey actually covers a period greater than one year in total. Because the bulk of the interviewing took place in a period of two months, this problem is at a minimum, although there is no doubt that a number of crimes measured by the survey probably represents about a 13 month period in actuality. This problem is reduced somewhat, however, when one considers that the unit of analysis for these variables was the household. In essence the rate of personal crimes is bound to be a conservative estimate due to the third party questions so that this more than compensates for the difficulty on personal crimes at least.

In any event these difficulties should be kept in mind when interpreting the results presented in chapter three on comparisons to police statistics. When the final report is prepared, these difficulties may be overcome to some extent and a much more accurate comparison to the police statistics can be made if N District makes available their month by month breakdown of recorded crimes for the period covered by the survey.

Another source of measurement error arises from using the household as the unit of analysis. Sometimes the respondent is displaying a characteristic which is individual and comparisons between households are based on this characteristic. Information provided in the breakdown of crime rates by personal characteristics should be interpreted as households with a respondent displaying that characteristic. For variables such as household income, type of tenure and race, this is not a consideration. However, for breakdowns such as gender, age, employment status and scale scores it is a consideration. It was felt that for the 37% single occupant dwellings this factor is not a consideration. However, for the rest of the households in the Borough in which there is more than one occupant it is a factor. For purposes of this report, we feel that any errors of this nature will equal out in the long run so that the differences reflected are real. For example, if a female respondent living alone answers the question on burglary, we are safe in comparing her response to a male living alone. When more than one occupant is in the household, the probability of selecting a male is approximately equal to that of selecting a female, so that over the long run these will cancel out and any gender differences observed should be reliable estimates. This difficulty only applies to chapter three, and should be taken into consideration when interpreting the results. Again, this difficulty can be overcome in the final report if individuals are used for units of analysis at the request of the Council.

Scaling

For purposes of the preliminary report, it was decided that much of the data might be efficiently summarised by scaling a number of independent measures into composite measures. A total of five scales were tabulated and inter-item reliability scores were tabulated for each. Researchers generally agree that an alpha coefficient of greater than .7 indicates that a scale is reliable. Below is a list of the scales compiled for the report, how each was tabulated, and the alpha scores for each:

Scale A – Satisfaction with the Neighbourhood
This scale is the total of phase one questionnaire items 4.a to 4.l. Only valid scores were considered so that missing values or 'don't knows' were not included in the sum. In order for a case to be valid there had to be at least nine valid responses. Each scale score was the sum of the valid scores divided by the number of valid responses, leading to a possible range of values from one representing high satisfaction to three representing low satisfaction. Individual scores were then assigned a value for the possible range which was evenly divided into the three ordinal measures of low, medium and high. The alpha value for scale A was .73.

Scale B – Fear of Crime
Scale B is the mean value for phase one questionnaire items 5.a to 5.h. The procedure here is slightly different than scale A in that some of the items refer to women only. For women the case required at least six of the eight items were valid scores in order for the case to be considered valid. For men, at least three of the five items required valid scores before the case would be valid. The final range of between one and four was evenly divided to produce a value of high, medium, or low for each case. The alpha value for this scale was .91.

Scale C – Perception of Risk of Crime in the New Year
Scale C is the mean score for all valid responses on phase one questionnaire items 62.a to 62.f. Again some items were for women only. At least five of the seven items had to have a valid score before a female case was considered valid. For men, three of the five items required a valid score before the case was considered valid. The final possible range of values from 1 to 4 was evenly divided, thereby assigning a value of low, medium, or high to each valid case. The alpha value for this scale was computed to be .82.

Scale D – Avoidance Behaviour
This scale is the mean value for questionnaire items 8.i to 8.vi. In order for a case to be considered valid at least four of the six items were required to have valid responses. The possible range of one to four was produced by dividing the sum of the valid items by the number of valid items. The range was equally divided in order to produce the values of low, medium and high for each valid case. The alpha value for this scale was .87.

Scale E – Perceived Relative Frequency of Crime
This scale is the mean of the valid responses for phase one questionnaire items 11.a to 11.g. At least five of the seven items had to have valid responses for the case to be considered as valid. The final range of one to three was evenly divided to produce the scores of high, medium and low for each valid case. The alpha value for this scale was calculated at .88.

Due to the high alpha values for the scales they were used for break-downs of other variables and were considered to be reliable measures. Because most of the comparisons on a number of other variables in relation to these scales reported in the main body of this report turned out to be in the predicted directions, we feel confident that not only are the scales reliable measures, but they are also valid.

Questionnaires, coding and data files

The two questionnaires were constructed in such a manner as to allow for the generation of a complex data structure consisting of nested records. This was necessary because not all cases would be eligible for follow-up questionnaires, and some cases would be eligible for more than one follow-up interview. When cases were subject to follow-up interviews, the same case number was assigned to the follow-up interview. Relevant information was asked of the respondent and recorded on the phase two questionnaire. This procedure would not only allow the cases to be matched, but various record type indicators allowed for the segregation of each of the follow-up interviews. Furthermore, since sometimes the respondent on the phase two questionnaire would not be the original respondent, this information was also recorded in order that proper partitioning of the data could be achieved.

Essentially the questions were mostly closed-ended and pre-coded in order to allow for efficient data entry. Coders were instructed and briefed on how to edit the questionnaires for data preparation which also included the coding of all open-ended questions. Except for the enumeration district indicator and Ward indicator, which were both alpha-numeric values, all other values were numeric and recorded as integers.

Two data structures were produced from the questionnaires, one for each. After a careful cleaning of the data, the two files can be merged in order to produce one or a number of subfiles with either, all, or some of the cases.

Both data files were cleaned, and system files were produced. A number of constructed variables such as the scale scores and weights are now variables in the study and each case has a value for each of these cases.

Due to the elaborate coding scheme necessary to separate the broad categories of crime from the phase one questionnaire to the narrower measures on phase two questionnaire, it was not always possible to calculate the standard errors, since more than one variable was used to determine the classification of an offence. For this reason, those variables are reported in chapter three as percentages of the broader categories. When the final report is completed, these values will be included.

There are now two major data files, two major system files and a number of smaller system files on system containing a variety of combinations of variables and cases. Each of these can be weighted according to any combination of weights as described in the weight section of this appendix.

In total the phase I system file contains 1977 uncoupled cases and a total of 404 variables. By comparison the phase II system file contains 897 cases and 207 variables.

A Final Note on Interpretation of Findings

Sometimes the elaborate breakdowns of data produce cells in which such a small number of cases are partitioned that generalisation is risky. These have been highlighted on tables where they apply.

Because of the preliminary nature of this report the conclusions drawn by the authors are not final. Nevertheless we feel confident that within the qualifications of the methodological limitations pointed out in the above discussion, the data are as accurate as they can possibly be within the resources allocated to the project.

Bibliography

Bittner, E., 1974, 'Florence Nightingale in the Pursuit of Willie Sutton: A Theory of the Police' in H. Jacob (ed), *The Potential For Reform of Criminal Justice* (Beverley Hills: Sage)

Blom-Cooper, L. and Drabble, R., 1982, 'Police Perception of Crime', *British Journal of Criminology*, pp.184-7

Bottomley, K. and Coleman, C., 1981, *Understanding Crime Rates* (Aldershot: Gower)

Brogden, M. and Wright, M., 1979, 'Reflections on the Social Work Strikes', *New Society*, 53

Chambers, G. and Millar, A., 1983, *Investigating Sexual Assault* (Edinburgh: HMSO)

Chambers, G. and Tombs, J. (eds), 1984, *The British Crime Survey: Scotland* (Edinburgh: HMSO)

Christian, L., 1983, *Policing by Coercion* (London: GLC)

CIPFA, 1985, *Police Statistics 1984-85 Actuals* (London: CIPFA)

Clark, R., 1970, *Crime in America* (London: Cassell)

Clarke, R. and Hough, M., 1984, *Crime and Police Effectiveness* (London: HMSO)

Comrie, M. and Kings, E. 1975, *Study of Urban Workloads* (London: Home Office Police Research Services Unit)

Ekblom, P. and Heal, K., 1982, *The Police Response to Calls from the Public* (London: Research and Planning Unit Paper 9, Home Office)

Evans, R., 1973, *Developing Policies for Public Security and Criminal Justice* (Ottawa: Economic Council of Canada)

Farrington, D. and Dowds, E., 1985, 'Disentangling Criminal Behaviour and Police Reaction' in Farrington, D. and Gunn, J. (eds), *Reaction to Crime* (Chichester: Wiley)

Friedrichs, D.O., 1983, 'Victimology: A Consideration of a Radical Critique', *Crime and Delinquency*, 29 (April) pp.283-94

Hagan, J., 1977, *The Disreputable Pleasures: Crime and Deviance in Canada* (Toronto: McGraw-Hill Ryerson)

Hall, R., 1985, *Ask Any Woman* (Bristol: Falling Wall Press)

Hall, S. *et al.*, 1978, *Policing the Crisis* (London: Macmillan)

Hanmer, J. and Saunders, S., 1984, *Well-Founded Fears* (London: Hutchingson)

Hillyard, P., 1981, 'From Belfast to Britain', *Politics and Power*, no. 4 (London: RKP) pp. 83-97

H.O.R.U., 1984, *Research Programme, 1984-1985* (London: HMSO)

Hough, M., 1980, *Uniformed Police Work and Management Technology* (London: Home Office, Research Unit Paper 1)

Hough, M. and Mayhew, P., 1983, *The British Crime Survey* (London: HMSO)

Hough, M. and Mayhew, P., 1985, *Taking Account of Crime* (London: HMSO)

Jones, S., 1983, 'Community Policing in Devon and Cornwall' in T. Bennet (ed), *The Future of Policing* (Cambridge: Institute of Criminology, Cropwood Conference No. 15)

Joyce, M., 1985, *Spending on Law and Order* (London: NIESR)

Kinsey, R., 1984, *First Report of the Merseyside Crime Survey* (Liverpool: Merseyside County Council)

Kinsey, R., 1985, *Final Report of the Merseyside Crime and Police Surveys* (Liverpool: Merseyside County Council)

Kinsey, R., Lea, J. and Young, J., 1986, *Losing the Fight Against Crime* (Oxford: Blackwell)

Lea, J., 1986, *A Study of Neighbourhood Watch in the London Borough of Islington* (Middlesex Polytechnic: Centre for Criminology)

Lea, J. and Young, J., 1984, *What's to be Done about Law and Order* (Harmondsworth: Penguin)

Levine, J., 1976, 'The Potential for Crime Overreporting in Criminal Victimization Surveys', *Criminology*, 14 (November) pp. 307-30

MacLean, B.D., 1986, *The Political Economy of Crime: Readings for a Critical Criminology* (Toronto: McClelland and Stewart)

McCabe, S. and Sutcliffe F., 1978, *Defining Crime* (Oxford: Blackwell)

Marshall, T., 1985, *Alternatives to Criminal Courts* (Aldershot: Gower)

Matthews, R. and Young, J. (eds), 1986, *Confronting Crime* (London: Sage)

Maxwell, M., 1984, *Fear of Crime in England and Wales* (London: HMSO)

Metropolitan Police, 1985, *The Principles of Policing and Guidance for Professional Behaviour* (London: Public Information Dept., Metropolitan Police)

Morris, P. and Heal, K., 1981, *Crime Control and the Police* (London: HMSO)

Newman, K., 1984, *Report of the Commissioner of Police for the Metropolis, 1983* (London: HMSO)

Newman, K., 1985, *Report of the Commissioner of Police for the Metropolis, 1984* (London: HMSO)

Phipps, A., 1981, 'What about the Victim?' *The Abolitionist* 9, pp. 21-3

Phipps, A., 1986a, 'Radical Criminology and Criminal Victimization' in R. Matthews and J. Young, *op cit.*

Phipps, A., 1986b, 'Crime and Victimization in a Political Perspective', PhD Thesis (CNAA) (London: Middlesex Polytechnic)

Palmer, J., 1973, *Thrillers* (London: Edward Arnold)

Pearson, G., 1984, *Hooligan* (London: Macmillan)

Provincial Secretariat for Justice, 1983, *Justice for Victims of Crimes* (Toronto)

Punch, M., 1979, 'The Secret Social Service' in S. Holdaway (ed), *The British Police* (London: Edward Arnold)

Punch, M. and Naylor, T., 1973, 'The Police: A Social Service', *New Society*, 17 May

Radford, J. and Laffy, O., 1983, *Violence Against Women: Women Speak Out* (Wandsworth Police Monitoring Group)

Reiner, R., 1985, *The Politics of the Police* (Brighton: Wheatsheaf)

Russel, D., 1982, *Rape in Marriage* (NY: Macmillan)

Smith, D., 1983a, *Police and People in London: A Survey of Londoners*, Vol 1 (London: PSI)

Smith, D., 1983b, *Police and People in London: A Survey of Police Officers*, Vol 3 (London: PSI)

Smith, D. and Gray, J., 1983, *The Police in Action*, Vol 4 (London: PSI)

Southgate, P. and Ekblom, P., 1984, *Contacts Between Police and Public* (London: HMSO)

Sparks, R., 1981, 'Surveys of Victimisation' in Tonry, M. and Morris, N. (eds), *Crime and Justice*, Vol 3 (Chicago: Chicago University Press)

Sparks, R., Genn, H. and Dodd, D., 1977, *Surveying Victims* (London: Wiley)

Stanko, B., 1983, 'Hidden Fears' *The Guardian*, 5 Sept.

Wilson, J.Q., 1968, *Varieties of Police Behaviour* (Cambridge, Mass: Harvard University Press)

Wilson, J.Q., 1985, *Thinking About Crime* (Rev. Ed) (NY: Vintage Books)

Wood, D., 1983, *The British Crime Survey: Technical Report* (London: SCPR)

Wood, D., 1982, *A Survey of Londoners' Relations With The Police: Technical Report* (London: SCPR)

Young, J., 1981, 'A Critique of Left Functionalism in Mass Media Theory'; in S. Cohen and J. Young (eds), *The Manufacture of News*, (Rev. Ed) (London: Constable)

Young, J., 1986a, 'The Failure of Criminology: The Need for a Radical Realism' in R. Matthews and J. Young, *op cit.*

Young, J., 1986b, *Realist Criminology* (Aldershot: Gower)